UNDERSTANDING CHILDREN AND YOUNG PEOPLE

Development from 5–18 years

Jennie Lindon

Hodder Arnold
A MEMBER OF THE HODDER HEADLINE GROUP

DEDICATION

To Tanith and Drew – fellow-adults now – thank you for everything.

The author and publishers would like to thank the following for the use of photographs in this volume:
p.12 © Photofusion Picture Library/Alamy; p.93 © Dick Makin/Alamy; p.206 © Photofusion Picture Library/Alamy; p.220 © John Powell Photographer/Alamy; p.253 © Profimedia International s.r.o./Alamy; p.312 © Julie Fisher/zefa/Corbis.

Orders: please contact Bookpoint Ltd, 130 Milton Park, Abingdon, Oxon OX14 4SB. Telephone: (44) 01235 827720. Fax: (44) 01235 400454. Lines are open from 9.00–5.00, Monday to Saturday, with a 24 hour message answering service. You can also order through our website www.hoddereducation.co.uk.

British Library Cataloguing in Publication Data
A catalogue record for this title is available from the British Library

ISBN: 978 0 340 93910 9

First published 2007
Impression number   10 9 8 7 6 5 4 3 2 1
Year   2012 2011 2010 2009 2008 2007

Hodder Headline's policy is to use papers that are natural, renewable and recyclable products and made from wood grown in sustainable forrests. The logging and manufacturing processes are expected to conform to environmental regulations of the country of origin.

Cover photo © Purestock.

Typeset by Phoenix Photosetting, Chatham, Kent.
Printed in Great Britain for Hodder Arnold, an imprint of Hodder Education and a member of the Hodder Headline Group, an Hachette Livre UK Company, 338 Euston Road, London NW1 3BH by Martins the Printers, Berwick-upon-Tweed.

CONTENTS

CONTENTS

ACKNOWLEDGEMENTS

I appreciate many conversations I have had over the years with fellow adults, in their professional and personal roles. The fellow professionals have worked in early-years settings offering after-school and holiday facilities, in a range of playwork services, in schools and in residential and foster care services. I also welcome the insights I have gained from many conversations – individual and in small groups – with children and young people.

I wish especially to thank the following people and organisations:

- For their welcome within group discussions and for allowing me to take photos – Jane Whitehurst, her team and the children at Crabtree Infants School, and also Jackie Nunns and Brid Muldoon of Kids City, with the staff and children of the Bonneville and Sunnyhill playschemes. Thanks also to the Randolph Beresford Early Years Centre.

- Gideon Henderson, Chloe Maber and the young people from the Young Carers Project, at the Princess Royal Trust Hammersmith and Fulham Carers Centre, for their input about life as an adolescent and young carer.

- Thanks also to the many clubs and playschemes that I have visited or spoken with over recent years, especially Battersea Park Adventure Playground, Jacqui Dickinson and Cool Kids at St Josephs (Cleethorpes, Lincolnshire), Jonathan Harvey and KidsComeFirst (Colchester, Essex), Jackie Clasby and the Balham Family Centre (London) and the team at the Poplar Play Centre in east London.

- Thanks also to groups from Burntwood Secondary School, Chestnut Grove Secondary School, Ravenstone Primary School, The Angmering School and Wallington County Grammar School. They were all generous with their views in discussion groups during the mid-1990s. What they said to me still resonates with the concerns of children and young people ten years later.

- Thank you to the many young people in their 20s who shared their views looking back over their adolescence. These contacts were mainly from my family network, so special thanks to Drew Lindon, Tanith Lindon, George Belfield, Lowell Belfield, Joe Halloran and Gonzalo Garcia.

I have benefited from guidance via telephone and email from advisors at many of the organisations that I have referenced. My thanks extend to the unnamed individuals who create informative websites. I wish to thank the following people and organisations for their direct help and leads: The Play Research Network (led by Issy Cole-Hamilton), Jane Turner (Deputy Director of the Science Learning Centre East of England), Paul Bonel (Director of the Playwork Unit, SkillsActive) and Tim Gill

ACKNOWLEDGEMENTS

(consultant and writer, Rethinking Childhood). Thanks for specific help from Drew Lindon (sections on counselling in further education, mental health services and internet safety), Steph Taylor (career guidance and the work of Connexions), Ruben Kuyper and Roger Sutcliffe (Philosophy for Children).

I took all the photographs, with the exception of the ones on pages 12, 93, 206, 220, 253 and 312. Many thanks to Lance Lindon for his fine work in editing my digital images.

I take the usual responsibility for this book. If you disagree with my perspective, I hope that will stimulate reflection and discussion. The information on resources was correct at the time of writing (2006), but organisations move and websites are changed. Readers have the responsibility to follow up information on which they plan to change practice or give advice, for instance on health. If I have made actual errors, then please contact Hodder Arnold and we will correct mistakes as soon as possible.

1 Children and young people in society

Children and young people grow up within a time period and place(s). The social context of development makes a difference to the details of individual experience for children and young people. Prevailing views within a society, and variations between particular social and cultural groups, shape the experience of growing up for boys and girls, young women and young men. This chapter considers some key issues around what growing up means in practice and what is expected of children and young people by familiar adults in their lives.

> **The main sections of this chapter are:**
>
> ✷ **Making sense of childhood and adolescence.**
>
> ✷ **Growing up into adulthood.**

MAKING SENSE OF CHILDHOOD AND ADOLESCENCE

Those of us now in adulthood have all once been children and then adolescents; that statement is not open to any argument. You have to be a child before you enter the years of adolescence. You have to pass through that period, however it is defined, to reach the point where you, and most other people, judge that you are definitely within the adult years. But the process, details and timing of growing up, and being grown up, vary considerably. There is variation between social and cultural groups and life conditions around the world. There has been variation within those same groups and countries in the historical past. This book concentrates on growing up within the UK for the current younger generation: what happens, or can happen, within development for children and adolescents.

Use of words

In any book about childhood and adolescence, an author has to make some decisions about words and phrases. These are my choices.

- **Parent**: anyone who takes the main family responsibility for children and acts in a parental role, whether or not that person is a birth parent. Please assume the word always includes any other family carers.
- **Practitioner**: anyone whose work brings them into face-to-face contact with children and young people on a regular basis. I have been specific about the profession whenever the information is relevant.

- **Pupil** or **student**: it feels appropriate to me to call children in primary school 'pupils' and reserve the word 'students' for adolescents in secondary and further education.

Opinions vary on how to refer to the blurred age boundaries on the way to adulthood. I have made the following decisions.

- **Early childhood**: the period from birth to 5 years. The upper age is the boundary for statutory education in three nations of the UK, but Northern Ireland currently requires education from 4 years of age.
- **Middle childhood**: the period from 5–12 years. The upper age limit is the boundary of what is known as the teenage years, because of the numbering system, starting with 'thirteen'. Some 'children' of 11 or 12 years are well into the changes of puberty.
- **Adolescence**: the period from 13–19 years, the same age range as the teenage years. In some services all **adolescents** are called **young people** and I have used the terms interchangeably.
- **Young adulthood**: the age range from the final years of adolescence to the mid-20s.

Potential developments

Development for children and adolescents is full of possibilities – what can happen, what might happen – and then experience shapes the details. There are few, if any, events for children and adolescents for which you can say that this development will unfold in *this* way and with *this* timing. The aims of this book are to:

- offer a balanced description of the kinds of changes that are likely within development from the end of early childhood to the brink of young adulthood;
- place that description within the social context for children and young people – what is going on around their development, how childhood and young adulthood is shaped in UK society of the early 21st century;
- and explore the implications for adults who work with children and young people in different roles and services.

Realistic adult expectations

Of course children and young people grow up in a time and place, with part of their identity shaped through social and cultural influences. I am well aware that some academic theories for childhood and adolescence are hostile to what is dismissed as the concept of the 'universal child'. Of course, it would be ridiculous to claim an unvarying pattern of development across all types of social boundaries. However, it is equally pointless, and unhelpful to the wide range of professionals involved with children and young people, to step aside from discussing realistic expectations across the age range.

I believe it is possible to respect individuality as well as identify communal strands within a psychologically and physically healthy childhood and adolescence. Then practitioners in regular, sometimes daily contact, with children and young people can be enabled to develop realistic expectations. There are indeed problems with the word 'normal', but it is possible to shift in words, and understanding, to a sense of 'normal range', 'normal variation' or 'what usually/often happens'.

There are also potential problems in how development is viewed. Children and young people do not develop within neat boxes limited to specific aspects of development. They are poorly supported when key adults ignore the holistic nature of all development. However, there are immense difficulties in writing about development if authors back away from recognising the different strands of development. I have chosen to organise this book into broad areas and to highlight the holistic nature of development within that context.

Explanations of development

Theoretical approaches to describe, explain and in some cases predict development have, in their turn, been dependent on time and place. Academic theorists and researchers are people too. They are affected by prevailing views in their own intellectual community – what is currently a mainstream view, what is regarded as on the fringe yet still a stimulating challenge and what is unacceptable, at least within a given intellectual sub-culture. In every decade, theory and related research is affected by professional values but also by funding, dominant social values and current political priorities.

For many decades, mainstream psychology was uninterested in the social and cultural context of childhood. It is certainly much easier to undertake research about child development when you conveniently ignore the random noise of ordinary daily life. However, developments over the end of the 20th and beginning of the 21st centuries have established the necessity to see children and adolescents within their social and cultural context. Equally importantly some theoretical approaches have acknowledged how children and young people are active in their own development and not passive recipients of what life brings to them. However, children and young people do not have direct control over the social and financial circumstances in which they spend the years before adulthood.

Theory and research about development is rarely now held within tight, exclusive boundaries. Ideas about child and adolescent development have been enriched by a greater willingness to cross academic subject boundaries. Over the last quarter of the 20th century, theorists increasingly attempted to reflect more accurately the genuine complexity of life for children and adolescents. The increasing interest from psychology in social factors met with a new interest within sociology about the more individual dynamics. The development of a sociology of childhood by researchers like Berry Mayall (2002) has contributed to understanding how individual experiences of childhood and adolescence are shaped by social factors, such as the dominance of school in family life.

The approach of social constructivism has become very influential in childhood studies. There is considerable value in this approach but it is not the only possible theoretical position. There is still considerable interest in a stage theory approach to explaining development, although with more flexibility than some earlier versions. Some proponents of social constructivism are hostile to the approach of social behaviourism and sometimes misunderstand key concepts. Behaviourism has developed far beyond the early, simplistic notions and a thoughtful approach can enhance making sense of behaviour – that of adults as well as children and young people.

Stark questions about childhood and adolescence regarding 'is it nature or nurture?' do not make sense any more – if they ever did. All theorists or researchers, except possibly a few at the extreme fringes, accept that there is a continuing interaction between the core of what makes this child or adolescent a unique individual and experiences that are delivered and shaped by external conditions. However, different theoretical stances emphasise a different balance of the 'inside–outside' factors that affect childhood and adolescence.

There has been a resurgence of interest in the biological basis to behaviour and patterns of development. Few biological theorists want to discount the influence of nurture on children, nor the impact of their immediate physical environment. They wish to redress a perceived imbalance that has sidelined acknowledgement of instructions laid down in the genetic material; patterns of maturation triggered by aspects of body chemistry; and basic drives that are probably shared by all individuals of the human species. An emphasis on what is probably going on inside our bodies should be of interest to anyone involved with children and young people. Key areas include the importance of early attachment, continued research into the function and chemistry of the human brain and also the biological programme of puberty.

It is useful, and important, for practitioners to be aware of broad strands, so this section does not attempt to cover named theorists or specific theories of development. If you wish to explore these in more detail, please see Lindon (2005).

WHAT DOES IT MEAN?

- **Nature**: all the influences on development, including an individual's genetic inheritance, distinguished from the impact of experience.
- **Biological programming**: the basic materials with which human babies are born, including how their brains operate and their body chemistry.
- **Nurture**: all the influences other than genetics and basic biological programming. From infancy onwards, the details of brain development are influenced by experience.
- **Environment**: the physical features of the location(s) in which children and young people grow up.
- **Experience**: what happens to children, young people and adults – through direct action of their own, the impact of the behaviour of other people and how broad social conditions affect them through family and community.
- **Theory**: a framework incorporating a set of ideas or principles that is used to guide description (in this case of development), planning and interpretation of research or prediction – and sometimes all of these.
- **Stage theory**: a particular approach to theory-building for development in which it is proposed that all children and adolescents pass through the same, distinct broad stages on the route to adulthood.

Vulnerability and resilience over childhood

From the 1980s there was growing interest in understanding the reasons why very similar negative social circumstances did not affect all children in the same way. Researchers like Norman Garmezy and Michael Rutter (see Haggerty et al., 1994) explored the significance of strong family support for children in the face of realistically tough social conditions. Studies confirm that often the best way to support children in areas of serious social disadvantage is to enable parents and other family carers to provide an emotionally secure home life. There is no support for an approach that de-skills parents and allows the view to grow that some unspecified 'they' should take over all parental responsibilities through service provision. Children need families and they need strong and safe parenting.

It is very difficult in research terms to unpick factors about individual children from social aspects. However, there still seems to be an impact arising from the individuality of children and adolescents. A supportive family increases the chances that children and adolescents emerge with skills and, equally important, an outlook that enables them to operate safely in society. However, strong family support is not always enough and some children go awry despite having been raised within families who seem to have very favourable social circumstances.

There seems to be a complex pattern of cause-and-effect that combines protective and vulnerability factors within individuals, such as 'easy' or 'difficult' temperament (see page 29), higher potential intelligence or specific areas of competence, genetic predispositions to illness or some risk behaviours like alcoholism. For instance:

- A child who is potentially vulnerable may cope within a positive family life and social conditions. A child who is potentially resilient may make the very best of unpromising circumstances, perhaps by seizing opportunities within or outside the family. Vulnerable children in realistically tough social conditions, including a fragmented family life, have the least optimistic outcomes.
- There is always an interplay between individual children or adolescents and their environment. Even young children strive to make sense of their experiences, including their family life. So from the youngest age, children's actions and reactions exert an impact on what follows and how they are viewed by family members and any other adults who are directly involved with them.

Patterns of cause-and-effect are rarely simple, one-off or linear. They are better seen as possible routes, branching systems or cycles – of a virtuous or vicious nature. For instance, a baby who is hard to settle and cries a great deal may soon be seen as a burden by parents, especially if they have limited support. It becomes harder to respond positively, even when the older baby or toddler is in a friendly mood. Normal young testing behaviour is seen as further evidence that this is not a 'nice' child and the boy or girl learns that more attention is gained by being 'naughty'. Other examples could be the combination of circumstances that follow from children who are pressed too young into formal reading (see page 169) or young people whose capacity to cope is overwhelmed by continued sources of stress (see page 89).

WHAT DOES IT MEAN?

■ **Resilience**: an outlook for children and young people characterised by the willingness to confront challenges, with a sense of confidence that it is possible to deal with setbacks. Resilience is built from a foundation of emotional security that key, familiar adults will help.

What is happening 'inside'?

The development of the human brain up to adulthood goes in spurts; it is not a smooth, continuous process. The years of childhood and adolescence are characterised by significant bursts of activity that shift brain development into a qualitatively new phase. What is happening inside the brain of children and adolescents can be observed through external changes in how they behave, talk and deal with their familiar world. Between the spurts there are periods of relative stability, in terms of changes to brain functioning. However, these are not stagnant times when nothing is happening. Useful experiences and a motivating environment enable children and adolescents to build knowledge, practise skills and consolidate thinking power.

Brain development from middle childhood

Early childhood is a crucial time for laying down neural networks for emotional security, an enthusiasm for language and secure physical skills. However, the human brain is far from mature by 4–5 years of age.

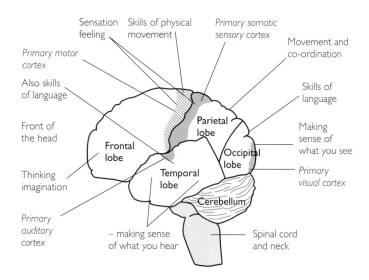

Areas of the human brain and the abilities that they mainly control

7

- At around 4 years of age a spurt in brain development is associated with a new level of fluency in spoken language: what children say and understand and how they use their skills.

- Over the period of 6–8 years of age you should be able to see striking improvements in children's fine motor skills and their ability to co-ordinate what they see with how they use their hands and feet.

- Under-10s can be busy thinkers, but between the ages of 10 and 12 the frontal lobes of the cerebral cortex take a leap in maturity. The results can be seen as these older children become more adept at planning ahead, working logically and organising their memory skills.

- From early to mid-adolescence, 13–15 years old, there is a sustained burst of energy in the areas of the brain that deal with spatial perception and how physical skills function. A qualitatively different neural network is also emerging that enables greater capacity to think abstractly and to reflect on that thinking. Adolescents are increasingly able, with suitable experiences, to mentally step back from their own process of thinking.

- Over the years of adolescence the human brain is working hard to bring together the parts that deal primarily with emotions and those that are more concerned with the skills of thinking. Bursts of brain activity, which bring more integration between feeling and reasoning, seem to be one explanation for sudden mood swings and apparently irrational choices shown to some extent by many adolescents.

- Development of the human brain is not fully complete within adolescence. The refining of the frontal lobes of the cerebral cortex in the brain continues from around 17 years of age until about the mid-20s. This part of the brain, which controls the ability to use logical thinking and build that skill into planning ahead, is not usually fully mature until early adulthood.

Impact of experience

Brains mature through the years of childhood because the connections between neurons are strengthened. An experience of any kind leaves a chemical signal in that neural pathway. When the signal reaches a threshold level, that linkage becomes a permanent part of the individual brain. Human brain development does not work simply by addition. A regular process of pruning ensures that the adult brain is not cluttered up with every single experience from childhood and its traces in the neural networks.

On a basic principle of 'use it or probably lose it', the human brain has bursts when it deletes scarcely used neural connections. The flipside of this spring cleaning is that well-used neural connections are strengthened.

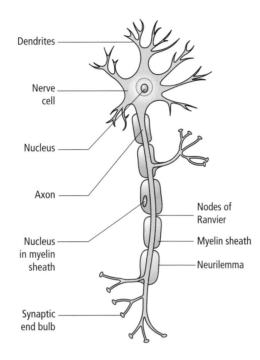

A mature human brain cell

The human brain works on what experience has told the cells is important. So the neural pathways that become stabilised can confirm patterns that, with a broader perspective, have potentially positive and negative consequences for this child or adolescent. Young brains become attuned to what experience has told them is 'normal' and this baseline might be that daily life is emotionally safe, conversation is enjoyable and it is worth the effort to try something new. On the other hand, some children may have become so adept at filtering out the background noise of television and raised voices that they do not easily attend to conversational approaches. Other children, by the age of 5, are already sure that daily life is risky and adults cannot be trusted. They are fine-tuned to a high level of wariness, which is not an emotional state that helps general attention and the more complex thinking that is otherwise a real possibility in older childhood.

Messages within the brain
Eventually each individual axon is covered in myelin, a substance that insulates the cells so that they send messages more effectively and swiftly. The process of myelination starts from before birth, works steadily to a

biological programme through the different parts of the brain and is not fully complete until early adulthood. Myelin works to ensure that messages travel effectively and swiftly within and between the areas of the brain that control different functions. Myelination is more rapid within the first two years of life, but the process is far from complete by the end of early childhood.

- The parts of the brain that control motor movements are not fully myelinated until about 6 years of age. This development explains why the over-6s can be even more impressive physically than the most confident under 5–6 year old.

- The reticular formation is the part of the brain responsible for keeping your attention properly focused on what you are currently doing. It also helps you to distinguish between important and unimportant information, for the task currently in hand. The myelination of this area starts in infancy but it then continues in spurts throughout childhood and adolescence and is not fully complete until about the mid-20s. So attention spans do get longer, but there is a qualitative difference as well: concentration comes more within the individual's control, along with more sophisticated ways to process information.

- Important neurons link the reticular formation to the frontal lobes of the brain. This area is progressively myelinated from 6 to 7 years of age, enabling the more selective attention of middle childhood. Younger children really struggle to focus their thinking power on the important elements of a problem or situation. They can easily get lost in the detail, without helpful and patient adults.

- Our brain works hard to bring together information from the senses, physical movements and the intellectual functions of making sense of it all. The linkages are myelinated to an extent by the age of 5–6 years, but over middle childhood, the sheaths covering the axons become almost completely mature. This development, which cannot be hurried, seems to contribute to the greater ability of older children to recall and bring together different sources of information.

Human brains have two hemispheres that specialise in rather different functions. However, they also work together and are linked by a bundle of nerves called the corpus callosum. This bridge starts to develop at around 4 years of age and is not fully mature through myelination until about 12 years. Younger children's brains are clearly working well for their age, but it takes time for children to be able to bring different functions together. Part of the maturation of the brain is also that the different tasks of each hemisphere become more specialised and located in the right or left side. This process of lateralisation enables skills like spatial perception to be more finely tuned. Across early and middle childhood this ability area is firmly located, for most people, in the right hemisphere. Complex spatial perception – the kind you need to read a map and then relate the information to the real world, is not strongly lateralised until about 8 years of age.

GROWING UP INTO ADULTHOOD

Children and young people are affected by the prevailing social views about children and adolescents. Psychological theories filter through to general attitudes. For example, the view that adolescence is inevitably an awful time for families seems to underpin the titles of many advice books and magazine features, with liberal use of the word 'survive'. The rather dusty psychological view that this age period was nothing but 'storm and stress' has been overtaken by a more realistic approach that it is a time of transition with some challenges and necessary adjustment in relationships. However, the grunting, miserable teenager is as much a stereotype as 'the terrible twos'.

TAKE ANOTHER PERSPECTIVE

In September 2006, a large group of professionals, involved with children in different ways, sent an open letter to *The Telegraph* newspaper. The import of the letter was concern that pressures on children and young people were making their lives more stressful and less happy than should be the case in childhood. The particular issues raised included commercial and academic pressures, restricted opportunities for active, non-electronic play and a lack of awareness of children's emotional well-being.

Sue Palmer, who was central to the drafting of the letter, provides a link to the full text of the letter on her website www.suepalmer.co.uk. Read it and consider – what do you think?

What is happening 'outside'?

Once you recognise that childhood and adolescence happen within a time and place, it has to be appropriate to ask whether the key experiences of children and adolescents nowadays differ in any significant ways from the childhood of generations within the current adult population. The approach of this book is that the current younger generation is not essentially much different from previous younger generations. However, they face aspects of daily life that were not faced by earlier generations. These are real differences of experience between generations but it is much more difficult, and probably pointless, to try to assess whether life for children now is 'better' or 'worse'. At the very least, any writers who make the 'worse' judgement should talk with adults whose years of childhood or adolescence coincided with the Second World War.

Social hostility to young people?

'Everybody knows' complaints about an impossible and ungrateful younger generation can be found in written materials over many centuries, well back to ancient Greek civilisation. A proportion of every adult generation seems to manage the intellectual sleight of hand to talk as if they bypassed being a child or adolescent, or achieved perfection at an early age. However, there seems to be a particular enthusiasm in early 21st-century UK for sweeping negative statements about children and young people. Martin Narey, Chief Executive of Barnardo's, the national children's charity, spoke to *The Times* newspaper (10 July 2006) because he was so uneasy about the current government's attitudes towards young people. He highlighted the regular use of words like 'yob' and 'feral' to describe young people, and pointed out that no other minority in society is routinely criticised in this indiscriminate manner.

The Labour government has been keen to appear 'tough on crime and tough on the causes of crime', and one strategy has been to agree that groups of young people pose a threat because anxious adults believe that

'Hanging about' in a group is not a 'crime'

to be true. Some neighbourhoods in the UK are genuinely dangerous, but the dangers do not all arise from children and adolescents. The Respect Agenda (www.respect.gov.uk) has a broad remit, yet some of the details for England and Wales, such as ASBOs (antisocial behaviour orders) and creating dispersal zones have disproportionately affected young people. The problem arises from working definitions of antisocial behaviour which allow it to be determined by adults' discomfort and fear, even when they have neither been threatened nor attacked by the young people on their street corner.

Bernard Davies (2005) describes the serious problem that is created when ordinary social activity for the younger generation is regarded as suspicious and an entire age group is treated as a potential threat. The positive effects of peer pressure are undermined when just hanging around can be seen as evidence of criminal intent. Basically well-meaning adolescents also begin to feel antagonistic towards an adult world that appears keen to judge and criticise, without solid information. It is possible to challenge this approach, while acknowledging that some children and adolescents cause immense trouble in their local neighbourhood.

Headlines and features often over-simplify social groupings and significant issues. But there is a general acceptance of stereotyping younger age groups into extremes for news: they are either extraordinary wonder-children and little heroes, or a generation of ill-mannered, potentially violent thugs. Violence towards adults, especially vulnerable or very elderly people, seizes the headlines. However, male adolescents and young men continue to be the section of the population most at risk of being attacked. Consequently, this regular occurrence is not judged newsworthy without additional features, such as racist or homophobic intent. Nicola Madge (2006) quotes a MORI poll carried out in 2004 for Young People Now. They surveyed press articles over a week in the main national daily newspapers. One in three youth-related articles was about crime; the vast majority of all articles were negative in tone; 14% were entirely positive and 15% were judged to be neutral.

Many researchers, writers and practitioners are concerned to challenge the media and political image that this adult generation is the first to be given serious trouble by their children and young people. There is considerable support for an interpretation of increased adult intolerance of the normal lack of conformity and ordinary challenge from a younger generation. Alan Steer, head teacher at Seven Kings High School in Essex, was part of the team who compiled the *Learning Behaviour* report for the DfES in 2005. Alan Steer focused on the reality that children and

13

young people will behave if they are taught how to behave. His quoted view is that, 'The majority of children today are as nice as they were 20 years ago, but the adult world is extremely good at demonising young people and extremely bad at recognising its own failings' (*Children Now*, 1 March 2006, page 20).

TAKE ANOTHER PERSPECTIVE

Adolescents often have time on their hands and, in disadvantaged areas, have very few alternatives other than hanging around. They can be seen as a threat or as legitimate users of public space or services. Sighthill library in Edinburgh turned around their perception of local young people and their initiative won the 2006 CILIP/LiS Libraries Change Lives Award.

The library staff dealt with unaccompanied young people in the library, who had nowhere else to go – unemployment runs at 18 per cent in the local area. The young people were behaving inappropriately for a public space. But the preferred approach of staff had been to ban the young people, which just led to their hanging around the entrance to the library. A changeover in staff led to a re-think, with a focus on how to engage with the young people, rather than on punitive control.

New staff, some of whom were younger, set out to discover what the young people would like from the library and gradually offered different facilities. Young people who misbehaved were sent outside for 15 minutes to calm down and then come back; there was no attempt at an unworkable ban. Over time, the library team ran graffiti art courses and exhibitions, a football-based literacy programme, and a gamers' workshop where adolescents learned to develop their own games. The atmosphere in the library improved for all users and staff. Additionally, some of the young people became enthused with new interests. Some have returned to their education and gone on to college.

For further information, see the news and press release on the website of the Chartered Institute of Library and Information Professionals – www.cilip.org.uk.

Nicola Madge (2006) reported a largely positive view from children and parents about each other, in a survey of over 2,000 primary and secondary school students and interviews with just over 500 parents. However, she points to the anomaly that nine out of ten parents in the interviews said that they felt their own children showed sufficient respect for adults. Yet only one in three of the same group of parents considered this judgement was true of children in general today. Unless many children are behaving rudely outside the sight of their parents, these family adults seemed to be too ready to contribute to negative stereotypes of the younger generation.

Being a commercial target

Children and adolescents are now heavily targeted by advertising in a broad-based marketing approach that really took off during the 1980s. Eric Schlosser (2001) describes how companies aim to create brand loyalty in even very young children. The younger generation is viewed as a fully legitimate target: because they are purchasers themselves, but also because of the 'pester power' lever to nag parents to buy toys and games, clothes and snack foods.

WHAT DOES IT MEAN?

- **Marketing**: the entire process of promoting a service or product. The aim is to bring a product to the attention of potential purchasers, to create positive associations and, in the end, to get them to buy.
- **Advertising**: an activity designed to raise awareness of products and services and encourage people to make purchases. Advertisements may be placed in the written or visual media but are increasingly linked with internet websites.

The *International Journal of Advertising and Marketing to Children*, now called *Young Consumers*, brought together ideas, market research and the identification of the new target group of 9–12 or 13 year olds, who they call the 'tweens'. Technological advances now enable advertising to hitch a ride with internet websites and mobile phone technology: an approach sometimes called viral marketing (I think by those who disapprove). Messages can appear very personal to children and adolescents, who do not realise how they are being tracked and may still be naïve about the consequences of revealing their personal data (see page 294).

The difference made by technology

It is a matter of observation that children and young people now have a wide array of sophisticated technology as part of their normal, daily life.

Children still enjoy simple games

Many, not all, children have access to personal computers at home. Most, probably all, will have access at school. A previous younger generation became adept at programming the video, working the remote control and becoming familiar with a wide range of computer and hand-held games. Mobile phones have joined this list from many older children and adolescents, along with electronic toys from early childhood and sophisticated miniaturised music systems (currently MP3 technology).

Older children and young people need to become computer literate, without having leisure time or education dominated by computers. Jane Healy (1998) expressed serious, and in my opinion well-supported, concerns about an uncritical acceptance that computers are always an effective, perhaps the best, support for learning in school and elsewhere. However, this younger generation is very open to using technology alongside other forms of communication. You can find positive examples from primary and secondary school practice from the Learning and Teaching Scotland online magazine *Connected* (www.ltscotland.org.uk/icineducation/connected). Another positive example is provided by how young people worked in partnership with adults on the Aspire Pilot Project (http://schome.open.ac.uk/wikiworks/index.php/The_Aspire_Pilot) to set up the basic infrastructure enabling young adults to develop visions of the education system for the Information Age. They use the term 'schome', meaning not school and not home. (With thanks to Jacqui Cousins, who told me about this initiative.)

Sophisticated technology opens doors for easy communication, in one way, and provides access to a world-wide web of information. But technology also affects children and young people through the huge expansion of CCTV in public places, in the name of safety and crime prevention. This huge change affects all age groups who walk along high streets, into many shopping precincts and buildings or use the public transport system. However, this younger generation is observed and tracked electronically to a very high degree, starting sometimes with webcam technology in their nursery.

A further development, for England, is the creation of an electronic database containing the details of every child and young person: this is called ContactPoint. The aim is that the database will connect with a more specialist database which tracks children and their families about whom there is a social care concern. The Children Act 2004 set up the legal framework to enable such a development and it is promoted as part of safeguarding children and young people. Civil liberties organisations remain concerned about the safeguards for personal privacy and the scope for children and young people themselves to access and, if necessary, challenge their own records. There have also been concerns about whether details will be deleted when young people reach the age of 18 or whether the electronic records will slide into creating a population database.

MAKE THE CONNECTION WITH . . . LOOKED-AFTER CHILDREN

Looked-after children and young people already experience a high level of being observed and having the details of their life recorded. They have become the responsibility of their local authority and live in foster or residential care. Good professional practice has to build in proper checks and balances.

Roger Morgan is the Children's Rights Director at the Commission for Social Care Inspection. Part of his role is to consult with the looked-after population and to raise issues that children or young people say are a matter of concern for them. Look at some of the topics raised on the website, www.csci.org.uk, for instance the report of *Passing it on: views of children and young people on the government's guidelines for sharing confidential information about them.*

Safety, risk and a playful childhood

The impression from the national media is one of extremes. Statistically very unusual incidents of abduction by strangers who murder children or young people are given saturation coverage. Before it becomes clear what has happened, the pattern is one of extensive speculation and photo linkages with other children who have been murdered or are still missing. Headlines run about 'every parent's nightmare' and feature writers fill columns with 'Are our streets no longer safe for children?', giving the impression that predatory paedophiles are very common. However, this generation of children continues to be statistically most at risk of injury or murder from people they already know, including their own family members.

During quieter news periods some of the print and visual media are keen to criticise parents for making their children into 'cotton wool kids' and sedentary 'couch potatoes' who never leave the sofa and screen. Yet many adults, along with their children, have become convinced that life is considerably less safe for all the younger generation. Some children and young people in the UK live in truly dangerous neighbourhoods. These families and their children have less to say about the risk from invisible paedophiles than their daily struggles to deal with highly visible drug dealers, armed street gangs and adults seriously the worse for drugs and alcohol (see page 291). Otherwise, it is inaccurate and disruptive for development when risks are overstated, especially if the consequence is that children experience limited opportunities for lively, physical and outdoor play (see page 218).

Children, school and childcare services

There is a possibility that children and young people are viewed mainly through the lense of services that are provided for them or for their families. My aim in this book is to approach children and young people as distinct from settings they attend or services who know them. Of course children take on roles like pupil or student, and school is a significant part of life for most children and young people. They really appreciate good quality services, delivered with respect, and part of support for growing up is that young people are enabled to feel confident to track and access services that they need.

TAKE ANOTHER PERSPECTIVE

The national childcare strategy has brought children and families to the fore through expansion of childcare from the early years and through the years of statutory education. The political priorities have been largely driven by concern about raising school achievements, lifting families out of poverty through parents (especially mothers) getting into paid work and, in some initiatives, an aim to reduce later levels of juvenile criminal activity.

Richard Reeves and Mary Riddell, two contributors to a Fabian Society book exploring the 'new politics of childhood' (Diamond et al., 2004), emphasise how much adult requirements dominate the discussion and organisation of childcare. Richard Reeves argues that, 'rather than creating a family-friendly economy we are busily creating economy-friendly families' (page 55). Mary Riddell points out how much general/media discussion around children focuses on the expense of raising children, as if choosing to start a family is mainly, or exclusively, a financial decision. She argues that, 'Even the increasing, and welcome, emphasis on work/life balance and good parenting is seen through the prism of adult needs and rights' (page 67).

These provocative ideas raise the problem that standing up for the well-being of children – young and older – is frequently dismissed as an attack on parents' rights to work, especially mothers'. For all the rhetoric about a focus on children, their position can sometimes be like the smallest figures in a set of nesting dolls: hidden by all the outer layers of bigger dolls.

What do you think? Discuss these issues with your fellow students or colleagues. If you work with older adolescents, invite their views.

The majority of this younger generation has experienced some kind of early-years group setting prior to entry into primary school. There has been a steady shift in the UK to dividing childhood by the service framework, dominated by schooling. In early years this has led to fragmentation and a series of additional changes for many young children, who are required to move on between group settings perhaps only after less than a year. Berry Mayall (2002) explores the concept of the 'scholarization of childhood and family life'. She uses this concept to explore the ways in which the early years of childhood and the objectives of daily family life risk being seen through the filter of what is required by the educational process of schools. Her approach is not a criticism of teachers; it challenges assumptions that the main task of families and early-years practitioners is to prepare children for school.

TAKE ANOTHER PERSPECTIVE

The whole concept of 'pre-school' dominates discussion and choice of words around early childhood. My particular dislike is when young children are actually called 'pre-schoolers'. I have never heard or read of adolescents being called pre-adults or pre-workers. School is an important part of life and is the way that most children and young people receive their legal entitlement to an education. But early childhood should not be defined as a kind of waiting room.

The term 'pre-school' has a longer history than I had assumed. While writing this book I found the phrase 'pre-school children' in a book published in 1948 – Stuart Miall: *The World of Children* (London: The Caxton Publishing Company).

Schools can be really positive hubs for the neighbourhood. The concept of community schools has been around in the UK for decades. But developments in Scotland seem to have started the most recent interest in the idea with the initiative for 'new community schools' at the end of the 1990s. The extended schools initiative in England includes some diverse patterns for services based on what are felt to be under-used primary and secondary school sites. Mark Smith (2005) shows that the lack of agreement about what constitutes an extended school complicates any reliable evaluation. In many instances, childcare services and out-of-school time provision are being offered within the school grounds. It seems very likely that the views of children and young people will depend a great deal on whether their non-school time, but on the school site, feels to them like proper play and leisure. It is fair to ask whether many adults would want to spend significantly more hours at their place of work, either because it suited their families or in order to access enjoyable recreational activities.

When are you grown up in the UK?

There is no simple answer to this question and, in recent decades, the years of dependent childhood have in some ways been extended so that young people face inconsistencies over their level of maturity.

One example is that for the first part of the 20th century young people could leave school and start full-time work at 14 years of age. This situation continued until 1947, when the age was raised to 15. In 1972 the upper age limit for statutory education was raised to 16. During the time of writing (2007) the government has raised the possibility of extending this age to 18 years. Professionals involved with post-16 education have been outspoken about the impractical nature of the proposal, without serious attention to vocational options. It also raises the strange prospect of insisting that young people, who could legally be married and have started their own family, must continue in some kind of compulsory education (see page 28).

Some of the oldest members of the UK population left school at 14 years of age and started jobs, sometimes having to leave home for their employment, at an age when young people now are sometimes still described as 'boys' or 'girls'. Yet a great deal continues to be expected of 14 year olds in current society. They are regarded as past the age of criminal responsibility, and in secondary school life, they are expected to be able to grapple with some very complex ideas and to have the study skills to operate with reasonable independence. Despite the legal position that young people of 14 years old are in many ways still 'children', some young people carry a great deal of domestic responsibility: firstly for themselves, but also for their siblings and, in some families, for their ill or disabled parents.

The point is not that we should hold young people as 'children'. Older children and adolescents have impressive capabilities that flourish with a welcoming atmosphere and supportive adults. The message is that children and young people receive some very mixed messages, because the adult world is confused. Most social groups and cultures have some way of acknowledging, and celebrating, the transition from being a child to joining the adult world. However, there is no single event that creates a rite of passage for all young people. Some of the major world faiths have specific rituals that celebrate recognition of a spiritual maturity (see page 36). Secular traditions include the 18th birthday party, which steadily replaced the 21st birthday after the voting age was reduced from 21 to 18 in 1969.

A young person is just about fully an adult in the eyes of the law at 18 years of age. But both the legal system and general social expectations give a confusing set of messages for when children are capable of taking on adult responsibilities. For example, in most parts of the UK:

- At 7 years old children can open and draw money from some savings accounts but cannot use that money to buy a pet until they are 12.
- 10 year olds are regarded as fully responsible for their own criminal actions and 12 year olds sign their own passport, but children cannot take on part-time paid work until they are 13.
- 16 year olds can get married or join the armed services, but only with

parental consent. It is not until the age of 18 that all these choices can be made independently of parents' views.

- 16 year olds can now enter or live in a brothel, which has been prohibited since they passed their 4th birthday. This legal oddity, along with others such as 5 being the legal age for drinking alcohol in private, is left from the Children and Young Persons Act 1933, some of which has not been repealed by subsequent legislation.

- 17 year olds can hold a licence to drive a car, small goods vehicle or tractor on the road but still cannot legally view some films at the local cinema.

- 18 year olds have most of the legal rights and responsibilities of the adult world, including the right to vote in local and national elections. But they still have to wait until the age of 21 to be able to adopt a child, supervise a learner driver or become an MP.

Primary legislation is introduced and then finely tuned for a wide range of reasons. New laws do not necessarily repeal old legislation. So the legal framework across the UK does not give consistent messages over when individuals are no longer children, nor is every law applicable in each nation of the UK. England and Wales share the same legislative structure, although the Welsh Assembly has increasingly opted for its own interpretation of social and educational legislation. Scotland and Northern Ireland have the right to introduce their own laws. Children and young people do not spend their leisure time reading legal materials to establish the boundaries to being genuinely grown up. Nor, of course, do young people, any more than adults, necessarily follow the letter of the law when they are aware of the facts. However, the legal anomalies are a reflection of the general social uncertainty over when young people should be trusted to act as fully mature citizens.

Families matter: parenting matters

Family life is very diverse for children and adolescents in the UK. It is all too easy to get enmeshed in discussion about different kinds of family structure and whether some patterns are better than others. Barn et al. (2006) highlight the many concerns that families have in common, as well as different perspectives arising from social and ethnic group background. A positive focus on the well-being of children and adolescents needs practitioners to focus on the basic objective of raising the next generation in partnership with families.

The following points emerge from a wide range of sources of information. I have expressed them in my own words and they are underpinned by the key values to which I commit. Please consider the issues, and perhaps use them as discussion points with colleagues or fellow students:

* Children need to be raised, they need parenting, and the best way to do that is within family life. Adolescents continue to need the security of family life, even and especially when they kick against the perceived restrictions.

* Families, parents in particular, have a primary and continuing responsibility to care for, cherish, champion and guide their sons and daughters. Children and adolescents need their parents to be precisely that; they rarely, if ever, want parents who deny their role and claim to be 'really a big sister' or 'just like a friend'.

* Children and adolescents can survive without this safe context, but they pay a high price for effectively raising themselves or having to find support and identity from peers who are similarly adrift (see page 313).

* The exact details of the family structure matter much less than what the family adults actually do day-by-day. Being a lone parent – mother or father – can be hard work and lone parenting is statistically linked with greater financial stress. But two-parent families have not cornered the market for being the 'best' kind of parent. The few studies of children raised in lesbian or gay households suggest that children's outcomes are within the same range as children raised by heterosexual couples.

* Children and adolescents need time, attention and a conviction that their family adults keep them in mind even when they are apart. It is not possible for parents to put children and adolescents on hold indefinitely in order to deal with what are judged to be higher priorities, whether these are a demanding career, busy social life or addictions.

* When parents cannot, or will not, parent their own children, a safe childhood requires that someone else fills that gap in a predictable way. The outlook is poor for children who become the responsibility of the local authority (looked-after children) when they experience further disruption and changes of primary carer. The Quality Protects programme in England includes the concept of 'corporate parenting'. But in practice this idea only works when actual people – foster carers and residential care home workers – form a close and enduring relationship with children and adolescents. Corporations cannot parent; children can only be parented by people.

* Fathers matter to children and adolescents. It can be difficult to focus on the importance of fathers to children without, in some cases, being accused of hostility towards women in general or specifically critical of

lone-parent families, most of whom are led by women. From the
perspective of children it is necessary to step aside from adult
divisiveness and territory building. It really matters that children have
a positive role model from the two sexes as they grow up into
adulthood. Boys need a positive model for being a grown man, ideally
from their own father.

If you want to find out more

- **4 Nations Child Policy Network.** Online resource about law and
  policy that directs you to sites relevant to England, Wales, Scotland
  and Northern Ireland. See www.childpolicy.org.uk.

- **Alderson, Priscilla** (2000) *Young children's rights.* London: Jessica
  Kingsley/Save the Children.

- **Barn, Ravinder; Ladino, Carolina** and **Rogers, Brooke** (2006)
  Parenting in multi-racial Britain. London: National Children's Bureau.
  Summary at www.jrf.org.uk/knowledge/findings/socialpolicy/0396.asp.

- **Children's Legal Centre** and **National Family and Parenting Institute**
  (2004) *Is it legal: a parent's guide to the law.* See www.nfpi.org.

- **Davies, Bernard** (2005) 'Threatening youth revisited: youth policies
  under New Labour' *The Encyclopedia of Informal Education* at www.
  infed.org/archives/bernard_davies/revisiting_threatening_youth.htm.

- **DfES** (2005) *Learning behaviour: the report of the practitioners' group
  on school behaviour and discipline.* Working group chaired by Alan
  Steer. See http://publications.teachernet.gov.uk.

- **Diamond, Patrick; Katwala, Sunder** and **Munn, Meg** (eds) (2004)
  Family fortunes: the new politics of childhood. London: Fabian Society.

- **Haggerty, Robert; Sherrod, Lonnie; Garmezy, Norman** and **Rutter,
  Michael** (eds) (1994) *Stress, risk and resilience in children and
  adolescents: process, mechanisms and interventions.* Cambridge:
  Cambridge University Press.

- **Hamilton, Carolyn; Fiddy, Alison** and **Paton, Laura** (2004) *At what
  age can I?: a guide to age-based legislation.* Colchester: Children's Legal
  Centre.

- **Healy, Jane** (1998) *Failure to connect: how computers affect our children's
  minds and what we can do about it.* New York: Touchstone.

❖ Healy, Jane (2004) *Your child's growing mind: brain development and learning from birth to adolescence. New York: Broadway Books.*

❖ Kirsch, Michele (2006) *Behaviour: the behaviour experts.* In: Children Now, 1 March 2006. See http://www.childrennow.co.uk/news/index.cfm.

❖ Lindon, Jennie (2005) *Understanding child development: linking theory and practice.* London: Hodder Arnold.

❖ Madge, Nicola (2006) *Children these days.* Bristol: Policy Press.

❖ Madge, Nicola with Burton, Sheryl; Howells, Steve and Hearn, Barbara (2000) *9–13 The forgotten years.* London: National Children's Bureau.

❖ Mayall, Berry (ed) (1994) *Children's childhoods: observed and experienced.* London: Falmer Press.

❖ Mayall, Berry (2002) *Towards a sociology of childhood: thinking from children's lives.* Buckingham: Open University Press.

❖ Maybin, Janet and Woodhead, Martin (eds) (2003) *Childhoods in context.* Milton Keynes: Open University.

❖ Moss, Peter and Petrie, Pat (2002) *From children's services to children's spaces: public policy, children and childhood.* London: Routledge Falmer.

❖ Palmer, Sue (2006) *Toxic childhood: how the modern world is damaging our children and what we can do about it.* London: Orion Publishing Group.

❖ Schaffer, H. Rudolph (1998) *Making decisions about children: psychological questions and answers.* Oxford: Blackwell Publishing.

❖ Schlosser, Eric (2001) *Fast food nation: what the all-American meal is doing to the world.* London: Penguin Press.

❖ Scottish Child Law Centre – the source for information about the law for Scotland. Tel: 0131 667 6333. See www.sclc.org.uk.

❖ Smith, Mark K. (2005) 'Extended schooling – some issues for informal and community education' *The Encyclopedia of Informal Education* at www.infed.org/schooling/extended_schooling.htm.

2 Personal identity and social networks

From middle childhood to early adulthood children and young people develop a sense of themselves as individuals, but also as people who are connected to others through a range of social networks. The same boy or girl has a role in the family as son/daughter, grandchild or sibling, yet can also be a pupil in school or a team leader in sporting activities. Children and young people develop significant friendships, which matter as much as their family relationships.

> **The main sections of this chapter are:**
>
> ⁎ **Developing as an individual.**
>
> ⁎ **Relationships and social networks.**

DEVELOPING AS AN INDIVIDUAL

Parents, and other adults closely involved with children and young people, realise that they cannot treat all individuals in exactly the same way, because no two people are ever the same. Good practice is for adults to behave in an even-handed way and to be fair, but this pattern has to be responsive to individual reactions.

Individual differences

Helen Bee and Denise Boyd (2004) discuss the range of research and theory into individual development and identity. Despite the use of different terms, there was a reasonable level of agreement that individual differences cluster in broad patterns and there is some continuity over time in what makes any individual a recognisable and familiar person within social interaction. Generally speaking, research into individual differences in early childhood uses the word 'temperament'. The term 'personality' tends to be applied from the later part of middle childhood.

The main strands that emerge for temperament are that children vary in the following ways:

▓ Some children are more active than their peers as part of their normal pattern. Regardless of direct experience, some children seem more inclined to be passive and less active.

▓ Children vary in their response to new people and situations. Some children typically move towards less familiar people and take a positive approach to unknown situations. Such children may be seen by others as open, amiable, and willing to have a go.

- In contrast, some children react with much more wariness, sometimes anxiety, when they are faced with anything unfamiliar. They may be very cautious about unknown situations and be seen as shy in a social context or very sensitive.

- From a young age, some children seem to have a low tolerance of problems or frustrations. They react more swiftly than their peers with irritation or anger and may be experienced as difficult by adults; as children who over-react and fret a great deal.

- Children's ability to concentrate and stay on task is partly a matter of development over early childhood. But even over those earliest years, some children show more ability to stay focused on a task appropriate to their age and interests and to persist even with a difficult activity.

None of this research and theory implies that children and young people are on a fixed track into adulthood. The work is an attempt to make sense of persistent differences that can be observed between individuals within daily life. Older children, adolescents and adults are then described along five broad dimensions, summarised below, by Helen Bee and Denise Boyd:

- **Extraversion**: how much individuals choose to actively engage with other people and a social world, as opposed to acting to avoid social interaction.

- **Agreeableness**: the extent to which interactions with other people are emotionally warm rather than prickly or antagonistic.

- **Conscientiousness**: how far and how easily individuals are able to take a long-term perspective, and control and direct their impulses.

- **Emotional stability or instability**: the extent to which someone sees their world as a source of worry and threat.

- **Openness and intellect**: not intelligence as the word is usually meant, but how far someone is original in their thoughts, and is imaginative or insightful.

TAKE ANOTHER PERSPECTIVE

Psychological research and human experience suggest that the core of what makes a child or young person a recognisable individual does not really change. Parents are sometimes convinced their adolescent has had a personality transplant, but the ups and downs seem to be more about changes in body chemistry (page 247), a significant burst of brain development (page 10) and the social adjustments towards young adulthood.

The temperament of early childhood, or the personality of older children and adolescents, acts as a filter for events and affects how experiences are interpreted. Take, for example, the pattern for children in families who move every few years, like service families. Children who are temperamentally favourable towards new experiences might find that the moves bring interest and stimulation. They might still regret the loss of friends, but feel far less disrupted than a sibling who by temperament is uneasy about losing familiar people and places.

▨ Can you think of other examples of how temperament, or personality, could operate in interaction with life events?

A practical problem is that, although some studies have been carried out in non-Western cultures, much of the research has been undertaken in the USA and Europe. There is some degree of continuity across cultures. The approach can allow for the impact of broad cultural values on attitudes about more and less favourable personal characteristics. In every social or ethnic group adults have their own individuality, so there is always scope for match, or mis-match, between children and adults.

Adults have their own personality, which will be a more comfortable fit with some children and young people than others. Vicious or virtuous circles can be established – in family, school or club life. For instance, children who are experienced as 'difficult' or 'hard to understand' by an adult are sometimes treated with less leniency or patience. The child or young person responds in a negative way. Their behaviour is seen as further evidence that they cannot be given any leeway and are poor company in contrast with a child whose personal style is a better match to that of the adult.

WHAT DOES IT MEAN?

- **Temperament**: a basic pattern of personal tendencies, assumed to be inborn, that shapes how babies and young children react to social interaction and events.
- **Personality**: a pattern established by late childhood or early adolescence that determines how individuals react to events and interact with other people.
- **Personal identity**: an individual sense of 'who I am' for children and young people, drawing on a range of possible social and cultural sources.
- **Identity crisis**: a period of personal disruption in which a young person, or adult, seriously questions the sources of identity that have so far answered the question of 'Who am I?'.

A sense of personal identity

Over childhood, girls and boys steadily develop their view of themselves. Their sense of 'who I am' extends from basic personal descriptions such as age or the colour of their hair. Over middle childhood they become more able to describe themselves in terms of what they like or dislike and what they feel they are or are not 'good at'. By 8 or 9 years of age, sometimes younger, children may describe their abilities through comparisons with other children: that they are 'better at maths' than their friend or 'not as good at football'. Not surprisingly, this kind of comparison seems to be especially noticeable within school life. Older children tend to allow for more possibility of change, perhaps that they are getting 'better' at maths, or that they 'used to dislike' something but now they have changed their mind. Children's judgements are shaped by what family and friends have let them know is important in life.

Many children show that it feels important to place themselves in terms of their family, perhaps that they are the eldest or the only girl in the family. Some children and adolescents have committed to a religious faith, almost certainly that of their family, and they are likely to include that aspect of themselves in any personal description. Children and adolescents may describe themselves in terms of the school they attend, other significant group membership, like being on the swimming team or a keen Sea Scout. They may also include some mention of ethnic group or cultural background, depending on whether that aspect seems important to them.

Research into children's and adolescents' concept of themselves has suggested that by mid-adolescence the self-descriptions are progressively less about physical appearance and more about beliefs, values and feelings. However, much of the research quoted was undertaken in the 1980s and 90s and the conclusions may not allow for the increased focus for many adolescents, and older children, on looks and clothes. Anecdotal evidence would suggest that boys as well as girls can be very sensitive to their appearance and how they measure up against ideals of attractiveness and fashion-conscious outfits.

An identity crisis?

Psychological theory about personal identity has proposed that some kind of struggle over 'who am I?' is common for adolescents. However, a period of identity crisis does not seem to be an inevitable part of normal adolescence. Many adolescents do not spend the time and emotional energy on pure identity issues that is implied by such theories. Reflection over identity, when it happens, seems to happen in later adolescence, as part of the social and personal experience of higher education. The notion of an identity crisis for adolescents also presumes that there is a clear time span and choice of options as adolescents move into adulthood. For a proportion of adolescents, there are few options: their identity is determined by family and/or social circumstances. Of course, some children and adolescents face significant family events (see page 97) that force a rethink of their place within a familiar social network. But this kind of reflection is as much about practical action and coping as a more conceptual sense of personal identity.

TAKE ANOTHER PERSPECTIVE

Dorothy Rowe (1996) describes how adults have a 'structure of meaning' around their sense of self, which has developed through earlier experiences. When individuals are very dependent on the social details of that structure, then the collapse of key elements, like a marriage or job, can be devastating. Adults may feel they have lost themselves as an individual with a clear and positive identity: that they are 'nobody' without this partner or that career. Some adults, on the other hand, are still distressed by the significant life change, yet feel they are intact as an individual.

Family experience is influential in whether children and adolescents feel accepted and loved for the person that they are, and will continue to be, whatever happens. Over childhood and adolescence, some individuals are already building a firm belief that their personal identity depends on passing the exam into the school their parents have chosen or being very popular among their peers.

Sex and gender

Children will be clear whether they are a boy or a girl and that this source of identity is fixed. They will have realised that their future self is also decided: girls will grow into women and boys into men. The details about what this process means will be a bit blurry. But, unlike their younger selves, over-5s are very unlikely to think it is possible to change track on biological sex identity.

WHAT DOES IT MEAN?

- **Sex and sex differences**: these refer to the biological differences created by the genes when babies are conceived; the differences between boys and girls, men and women
- **Gender**: this describes the psychological identity of being female or male, and the awareness of what sex differences mean within the social context.

31

Children within middle childhood have already developed a sense of what being a boy or girl means. They have a view on the social role of gender expectations. The details may vary, but children can have a clear idea of how girls and boys are supposed to dress. Like the adults, children may allow girls more leeway, for instance, girls can wear skirts or trousers but boys are not supposed to wear something that is or looks like a girl's skirt or dress. In choice of fiction books it seems that often boys can be put off a book if it has a female main character, yet girls do not seem to react in the same way to stories built around a male central character.

LOOK, LISTEN, NOTE, LEARN

Similar views may be well established about what kind of games and toys are more for one sex than another and which can, at least for the moment, be played and enjoyed by either sex. Awareness of being a girl or boy is linked in middle childhood with a greater tendency to play with your own sex, but this pattern is by no means an absolute.

■ **Observe any primary school playground, after-school club or playscheme, or look at what is happening in local parks or other public spaces: girls and boys do still sometimes play together out of choice, although a wide range of freely chosen games are single sex.**

Older children's views of what it means to be a girl or a boy will be heavily influenced by expectations they have learned that are built around gender. For adolescents this aspect of their identity becomes entwined with coming to terms with their own sexuality and sexual orientation. Attractiveness also becomes an issue, and this area is discussed on page 258.

Disability and health

For some children their sense of identity will be closely entwined with beliefs about what they are 'good at', whether that focus is academic work, sporting activity or perhaps talent within the creative arts. It seems likely that health is a given for identity, so long as children and young people are reasonably well. However, some children within the 5–11 age span will be aware that in a permanent way their life is different from that of their peers. Children with a physical disability or chronic ill health can understand that this condition will not go away; it is not like 'being ill' and getting better. Some children through middle childhood have to deal with issues around how far cerebral palsy or cystic fibrosis defines the person they are and/or the details of how their life needs to be organised. A great deal will depend on children's family and other support and how children and adolescents are enabled to learn ways to talk about their condition, as part of their identity.

Adolescents often experience another level of coming to terms with their disability or chronic ill health. It is not unusual that adolescents, who are capable of managing their own condition, become lax about following procedures that are essential for their continued well-being, even their life (see page 258). What seems to happen is that young people become frustrated with not being a 'normal teenager'. They may feel self-conscious about being open about 'normal life' for them, especially with a new friendship circle. Adolescents sometimes become careless about checking their health or stop wearing their medical identity bracelet.

Ethnic group identity

All children and adolescents belong to an ethnic group, or sometimes more than one because they have dual heritage through their parents. Cultural background and ethnicity are integral to the personal identity of all children. But this aspect can have more direct meaning at a younger age when children live in a diverse area. Unless children can see people who look and dress differently from them and their family, there is no reason to distinguish a source of identity that seems to be shared by 'everyone'. Practitioners who work in diverse, urban areas can easily forget that many areas of the UK have limited, obvious ethnic group and cultural diversity. In cities that are overall very diverse, some children may live in communities that are largely settled by one ethnic group.

WHAT DOES IT MEAN?

- **Ethnic group**: a grouping of people who have a shared heritage of customs, language and possibly faith. Every child has an ethnic group identity.
- **Cultural background**: the patterns of behaviour and associated beliefs (not necessarily of faith) that are shared by the individuals within a given group.

There are many good reasons (explored in Lindon, 2006) to extend all children's understanding beyond their immediate area. But it takes time before children understand what contributes to their own sense of ethnic group identity, as well as how their peers may differ from them. Much depends on children's own families and some parents are active in promoting a sense of pride in the family identity. The terms 'culture' and 'cultural identity' are often used now when previously 'nationality' might have been the chosen word. However, culture will not always link with a specific nationality, for instance children whose source of identity is from a family background that is Traveller, Roma or Gypsy.

LOOK, LISTEN, NOTE, LEARN

Family and neighbourhood experiences through childhood build a perspective for children, and later young people, of what is 'normal for people like me'. There is, however, a great deal of variety within groups as well as between groups, defined by ethnic group and/or culture. It is difficult to decide on accurate definitions because the terms 'ethnic group' and 'cultural background' are used in different ways, which sometimes overlap completely.

▨ Take the definitions that I have offered and consider your own source of personal identity from each of those perspectives.

▨ Share your thoughts with colleagues or fellow students in a group discussion.

Whatever the nature of their local neighbourhood, older children and adolescents will become far more aware of ethnic group diversity. They learn, through the media as well as their expanding general knowledge, and an awareness of their own ethnic group identity develops, however they choose to describe it in words. Children and young people do not necessarily view their social world in line with adult perspectives or preferences. For instance:

▨ It is not inevitable that adolescents and young adults feel uncomfortably between two cultures, when their family pattern of faith and cultural background differs from that which is presented as mainstream traditions in the UK. Some adolescents feel torn between their own wishes and the priorities of their family, but some appear to manage a blend that works for them.

▨ A proportion of children and young people have more than one source of ethnic group identity, or faith, because their parents differ on these aspects. It is important to listen to the views of older children and young people, who are sometimes very clear that they want to be proud of both sources of their mixed heritage and resent being told by adults that they have to choose a single identity.

▨ All children need positive sources for their sense of personal identity. It is crucial that practitioners avoid assumptions that children from the majority ethnic group – most likely children of white UK background

– will develop a positive sense of identity with no particular support. Children and adolescents from disadvantaged backgrounds, providing very limited sources of pride, can be tempted to build a positive sense of themselves by targeting minority ethnic groups. Indeed, they may learn this precise pattern from what is common in their family or neighbourhood.

- All children and adolescents need a positive pride in their sources of identity from ethnic group, family culture or faith. It is unacceptable that any group, whatever its precise background, builds a strong sense of self for children and adolescents through rejection of another group and negative stereotyping.

Faith and identity

Children's personal identity may be supported by a sense of belonging to a community and of being of value to those around them. Being part of a religious or philosophical community can provide children with a sense of connectedness: of 'who we are' and so to 'who I am'. Children's sense of personal identity can be supported by family commitment and shared celebrations that bring the family together. Some of these events have evolved into a blend of religious and cultural aspects. Christmas and Easter are examples of celebrations when families join in the secular festival without commitment to the underlying faith of Christianity.

WHAT DOES IT MEAN?

- **Faith** or **religion**: a set of beliefs and practices built around one or more deities or individuals with paranormal powers.
- **Sects**: the sub-divisions that have formed within most world faiths after disagreements over detail of belief or religious practice.
- **Religious intolerance**: hostility expressed by members of one faith towards a different faith or between those who hold a faith and people who do not follow any religious faith.
- **Sectarianism**: intolerance expressed towards members of another denomination of the same religious faith. **Anti-sectarianism** is the active attempt to challenge bigotry arising from this type of religious intolerance.

All world faiths have applications to daily life: what should be done and what should not be done. Children learn what their family faith means for them in terms of daily life, such as decisions about diet or style of dress. Adolescents may find that the code of conduct becomes more prominent after the age when they are judged to be spiritually mature.

Children tend to accept ideas and codes of behaviour as normal and right until such time as experience makes them question. They may begin to wonder about alternatives when and if their daily life in the local community or through school shows them that not all families operate in the same way. However, that sense of contrast is less likely to happen if residential and schooling patterns are such that children do not mix much with families of a different background. The integrated schools movement in Northern Ireland was set up to counter the religious segregation created by a schools system in which children attended faith schools that were either Protestant or Catholic – different sects of the Christian faith.

Spiritual maturity

Religious practice within a faith often has traditional ways to involve children and bring them officially into the faith. There may be naming ceremonies and the commitment of personal guardians for a child, sometimes at a very young age. Older children may be given specific instruction before being accepted into the faith as a young person who can now make a personal commitment.

Ceremonies and rites of passage mark symbolically that a boy or girl is now judged to be spiritually mature and can fully join in religious practices. Examples include the Bar Mitzvah ceremony for 13-year-old boys in Judaism and sometimes Bat Mitzvah for girls, at 12 years. However, some Jewish sects hold ceremonies up to 18 years of age. Sikh boys and girls are formally introduced to the code of conduct for their faith at puberty, or an age when they are judged to be ready. There are no formal ceremonies as part of Islam, but girls are presumed to be spiritually mature at about 9 years of age and boys no later than 14 years. Christian sects vary as to when they judge that individuals have the maturity to commit to the faith. For example, confirmation into the faith is offered to children, who were christened as babies, at around 8 years of age in the Catholic sect, and around 13–14 years in the Protestant sect. Some Christian sects do not christen babies and prefer to baptise adults who choose to commit to the faith. In some faiths there is a different pattern of involvement for males and females: separate areas for worship or restrictions during menstruation.

Identity from family

Children and adolescents really need a secure family life (see page 23) and parents who are committed to their well-being. Studies like that of Ravinder Barn and colleagues (2006) highlight the variety in parenting practice and family life within any given ethnic group, as well as the common issues between families, whatever their background. It is possible to say that families, especially parents, are a powerful influence on how children develop without claiming that parents are responsible for every detail of how their sons and daughters learn and change.

Judith Rich Harris (1998) challenged what she called 'the nurture assumption' in developmental psychology that, after genetic influences, the most powerful influence on child development is parents' behaviour and choices over how to raise their children. Harris points to the strong influence of peers on how children behave – a stance with which many psychologists would agree. She also gives a timely reminder that what children learn within their family does not necessarily generalise to other situations. Children and young people regularly behave differently in response to what they have learned as the ground rules and priorities in non-family settings.

Children, and young people, really do seem to learn from their peers in a different way from how they learn from adults. A well-rounded approach has to allow for sources of learning that are not controlled by the grown-ups. Tim Gill (personal communication) raises the useful question of whether there are some areas of learning that children gain better from their peers than from adults. (See also the section about peer support programmes, page 161.) However, Judith Harris's criticism of what is allegedly proposed by child psychology rests on a narrow view of psychological theory, without any reference to the more social models. She also appears to be reacting to the more extreme approaches in the US in which some adult writers are keen to blame their parents for every problem they now experience.

The importance of siblings

Judy Dunn, who has a long-term research interest in sibling relationships, confirms that the only certainty about this aspect of family life is that sibling relationships matter a great deal to children and young people. She points out 'the distinctive emotional power of the relationship ... from infancy onwards ... that emotional intensity, and the intimacy of the relationship, the familiarity of the children with each other, and the significance of *sharing parents* mean that the relationship has considerable potential for affecting children's well-being' (2000, page 244, original italics). Judy Dunn estimates that about 80 per cent of children in the UK and USA have siblings. This figure leaves a significant minority who remain as an 'only child' in a family – either because their parents wish to remain with a single child or because plans to have more children have not been successful.

General discussions about family life often propose 'everybody knows' type statements about birth order and sibling relationships. From her own research and in reviewing other studies, Judy Dunn concludes that there are no certainties about the details of a sibling relationship and outcomes into adulthood. It is very difficult to unravel patterns of cause and effect in real family life where one person's behaviour affects another's reactions and cycles are established. However, some broad themes include the following:

- Siblings get to know each other very well and it seems that they learn a great deal about emotions from each other. Siblings become adept at how to interpret feelings from actions, how to support but also how to tease and annoy someone you know inside out. Siblings exert an influence on each other's behaviour – for good or ill. Parents definitely matter, but it is crucial not to under-estimate the contribution of children to family dynamics.

- Parents have to cope with the temperament of their children and it is rarely, if ever, possible for them to treat siblings exactly the same. Children generally require fairness and an absence of favouritism. They are very sensitive to differential treatment in the family: that a sibling seems to get more attention, is more admired for achievements or is punished less often. Some situations may be relatively short-term, for instance the readjustments that are triggered by the arrival of a new baby. Persistent differential treatment leaves a mark on children's sense of self. But it is hard to predict the final outcome of feeling more or less favoured.

LOOK, LISTEN, NOTE, LEARN

Birth order does not exert a predictable and measurable effect as observed by research, but children often believe it matters and can place themselves as an individual within the age ordering of siblings. I have listened to several discussion groups of children who have been very articulate about the daily reality of being the eldest child, the youngest or the middle. Interestingly, they all believed that their position in the family was the least favourable.

- What have you heard from children's spontaneous conversations? One impact of stepfamilies is that an existing birth order and pattern of siblings can be changed. Birth order for children can also be more about role than actual age order. For instance, the child who becomes the most responsible, the 'eldest' in a sibling group, is not necessarily the oldest in years, just as the 'baby' of the family is not always the youngest.

- What variations have you noticed in terms of how children behave and their actual place in the family? Are you aware of these issues as they affected your own childhood and adolescence?

■ Sibling relationships are rarely static. Some siblings, of any mix of sexes, have warm relations from the earliest years. Some go through tough times, often it seems over adolescence when one or other is judged to be impossible to live with, but relations mellow after time. On the other hand, some siblings exist in a state of continued hostility that scarcely ever lifts and continues into adulthood.

Children and adolescents often define themselves at least partly by their family links. Alison Pike and colleagues (2006) found that even 4 and 5 year olds were able to give a coherent description of family life and their narratives were consistent with those of their parents, despite their being asked different kinds of questions. This research team drew from interviews and video-taped observations of family life to conclude that structural factors like children's age/birth order or sex did not relate in any consistent way to relationships between siblings. What did matter was the emotional climate of family life, such as whether parents got along well together and whether the home felt organised. However, this research established that the sibling relationship had an impact on children's adjustment above and beyond the effect of the parenting the children received.

Children have clear, sometimes very strong, views about family life and researchers have increasingly tried to reflect children's perspectives rather than hold to an objective outsider perspective. Rosalind Edwards and her colleagues (2005) echo the views of other teams, and my own observations, that children are insightful commentators on sibling relationships. It is only possible to understand the importance of this aspect of their lives by listening to the views of children and adolescents themselves.

Siblings often provide some kind of support for each other, usually but not always from elder to younger. Such caretaking arrangements can be informal and regarded as acceptable by both siblings. More time-consuming responsibilities are sometimes regarded as a burden by the older child, especially if their social life is curtailed by having to take care of one or more younger siblings. However, in some families, children and young people simply regard this pattern as the normal sharing of family responsibilities.

RELATIONSHIPS AND SOCIAL NETWORKS

The social network of older children expands beyond the family and they are able to manage different kinds of relationships, some of which are closer than others. Young children need positive early experiences in which they form affectionate, and in the case of their family, enduring, personal relationships. Without these they have no basis for later distinguishing between people with whom they have a truly close relationship and people to whom they relate in a less personal and more episodic nature.

Close relationships with non-family adults

Over middle childhood children learn to cope with the situation that their close relationships with adults outside the family, although important, are diluted, because that adult's attention is shared between many other children. But many children in primary school still show they wish to feel close to school staff, whether their class teacher, specialist teaching assistants or playground support staff. Many of these relationships are very important to children. During my visit to Crabtree Infants School I was happy to observe how the children were delighted to greet the cook when she emerged from the kitchen. They gathered round her and chatted as she moved across with them to start the process of organising the hall for lunch. There was no doubt that the children regarded the cook as a very important member of the school team. Children may attend breakfast or after-school clubs and some boys and girls may feel very close to a playworker. Adolescents too can form a strong link with a youth worker in out-of-school or leisure facilities.

Relationships are often strengthened through play

Not all children attend school, nor do they have to gain their education in that way. The legal situation across the UK is that education is compulsory but attending school is not. Some families home educate over the entire span of childhood. Some children start in school and are withdrawn to be educated at home. Some children are home educated over the primary years and then as adolescents join a school within the secondary period. There are a wide range of reasons why parents opt for home education, including large class sizes and children being 'lost', unresolved learning or bullying issues, failure to enrol at a preferred school, or disagreement with the curriculum or testing.

Education Otherwise is an organisation that supports families who wish to educate their children at home – www.education-otherwise.org. The name arose from the wording in the Education Act 1944, which was continued in the Education Act 1996 applying to England and Wales. In paragraph 7, chapter 56 there is the legal requirement that, 'the parent of every child of compulsory school age shall cause him to receive sufficient full-time education suitable a) to his age, ability and aptitude and b) to any special educational needs he may have either by regular attendance at school or otherwise.' The Education (Scotland) Act 1980 has similar wording.

The importance of friendships

A consistent message from children and adolescents is that friends really matter: they are a source of support as well as a strand in personal identity. Having friends is crucial and being without friends, even temporarily, is serious because it is awful to be lonely. Children and young people regularly comment that significant transitions like moving into junior or secondary school are much better if you have friends who move with you. Problems and arguments with friends are distressing. Even 7–8 year olds are able to say, after the event, that it was maybe not that important and they made up afterwards, but it was still very upsetting at the time.

By 5–6 years of age the majority of children will be active in choosing their own friends, from the circle that is available. Some children extend their social life from school into having friends to play at their home or for tea. Some children socialise with peers at school but for various family reasons the friendship does not extend beyond those boundaries. Some children wish for friends but circumstances make friendship difficult, such as having a quiet and cautious temperament or the practical problem of joining a school after everyone else has made friends. Disabilities that affect social understanding, such as autism or Asperger's syndrome, can mean that a child or young person struggles with the skills that start and maintain friendships. They may also have limited interest in an interaction that seems to have no real point to them.

Friends become increasingly central to a young person's life. Adolescents spend proportionately more time together because many of them are allowed more independence by their families. By mid-adolescence, young males and females may well be mixing socially again, although a great deal will depend on their family's attitudes to freedom of social life for their daughters. Friendships can be sustained for many years; some young people are still close friends with individuals they met in early primary school, even in nursery. Some friendships do not last, perhaps because boys and girls drift apart in the more segregated play that evolves over middle childhood. Families may move away from the neighbourhood and contact is lost. Also, the transitions created by the schooling system may divide friends if they do not move on together to the same next stage.

Looked-after children and young people can suffer serious disruption to their friendships as well as to other significant aspects to their daily life. Good practice is to reduce the number of changes for looked-after children, and great efforts are often made to ensure that children and young people continue to attend the same school. The objective on paper is often to avoid disruption to education. But residential and foster carers are very aware that children and young people need regular contact with their close friends. After too many changes, children give up trying to make local friends in yet another locality.

Loyalty and identity

Children tend to come together as friends over shared interests and games. Shared attitudes and priorities become more important through early adolescence, as well as enjoyment of the same activities in their leisure time. Family remains important for children and young people, even when relationships become fraught over disagreements, some of which arise because parents are doubtful or actively disapprove of the friends chosen by their son or daughter.

Tensions in the local community are almost certain to be brought into primary or secondary school both on the site itself and on school transport. Children and young people develop friendships over any kind of divide. But some are pressured, especially in secondary school, to make a choice in line with their ethnic group or faith and to abandon friends who do not share this identity. Gerard Lemos (2005) describes how local tensions are reflected in adolescents' views of groups they dislike. A significant minority of 11–21 year olds from a range of ethnic groups expressed negative views of a range of other groups, not always present locally. However, most of the adolescents and young adults in each of the case studies did not join in the rejection.

Friendship groups in adolescence are often created around and supported by visible markers of belonging: dress, use of specialist words and phrases in a group language, preferences over music and leisure activities, along with choices over the kind of behaviour that is likely to bring parental disapproval, such as drinking or drugs. Distinct groupings will almost certainly have a name label, like Goths or Computer Nerds, that young people may use for themselves or may be the label applied by adolescents external to this group.

LOOK, LISTEN, NOTE, LEARN

Children can be very supportive of their friends, so adults in school or after-school clubs need to appreciate that loyalty to peers can overrule adult requests for openness, for instance about who was responsible for damage or what happened during an incident.

Supportive commitment between friends in late childhood and adolescence can be especially strong. I have known directly of significant support between peers for troubles such as family breakdown, eating disorders and different kinds of self-harm. Good friends sometimes need to grasp when some kind of external, adult help is needed – when problems have gone beyond what peers can manage.

- What experiences can you recall from your own childhood or adolescence when significant support was given to you, or a peer, from the friendship circle?

Girls and women seem, on balance, to talk more about issues and invite confidences, but boys and men also offer support, sometimes more through shared activity than talking.

- What broad differences have you noticed between the sexes? In a mixed student or colleague group, use that opportunity to listen to the experiences of the opposite sex.

Male and female adolescents face significant dilemmas about speaking up when they believe a good friend is putting themselves in danger, yet they expect a friend to keep confidences. Peer support of the informal kind can be strong and peer pressure is not always negative: some friends support, even persuade, their peers to do the right or wise thing. However, friends within adolescence sometimes become enmeshed in supporting a friend against their family, providing an alibi for where they were supposed to be and otherwise bending the truth in the name of friendship.

The flip side to the support of friendship is the high level of social disruption for older children and adolescents when a serious disagreement escalates into demands from individual members of the friendship group to take sides. Close friends and groups splinter over issues such as the acceptance or not of a new member to the friendship circle, unresolved disagreements over important issues of dress or choice of music, or divided loyalties arising from the behaviour of a friend, which is acceptable to some but not all within the group.

At some point in adolescence, young people start to form close relationships based on going out with one particular young person. Some adolescents are allowed to develop these couple relationships with a high level of freedom. Some young people, often more likely females, are restricted to some extent, possibly completely, by their families, who consider it their responsibility and right to control the development of an adult relationship that could lead to marriage. Some young people are in the process of realising that they are sexually attracted to their own sex (see page 258).

Faith and friendships

It is probably accurate to say that all faiths attempt to create strong internal support for their religious community. However, for some groups, perhaps only some sects within a given world faith, that internal strength is also boosted by minimal contact, even active rejection, of anyone not of this faith or this particular sect of the faith. Children find then that their friendship patterns are shaped by whether a family is a part of the same faith or sect. Even in mixed schools, in terms of faith, some children may be actively discouraged from exchanging play or other invitations with children who do not belong to the same faith or sect.

Greg Smith (2005) reported that cross-faith friendships for 9–11 year olds were more common within the school day than in the hours outside school and that community tensions could be reflected in the playground. Paul Connolly et al. (2002) described how children in Northern Ireland learned the cultural symbols and events linked with the Catholic or Protestant denomination (or sect) of the Christian faith. In a study of 3–6 year olds he described how there was a significant increase in the proportion of children who identified clearly with one religious community over the other at the older end of the age range. There was also an increase in sectarian comments made by children. The 5–6 year olds were older, of course, but the most relevant change seemed to be that the vast majority of them had by then spent at least one year in a primary school that was affiliated to one denomination. Only about 4 per cent of children in Northern Ireland attend integrated schools.

Some adolescents are expected to find girl/boyfriends and then serious partners from within the faith or sect. The general impression is that across different faiths and sects more latitude is given to young men prior to marriage than to young women, although males are just as likely to be expected to fall into line for a marriage partner. Cross-faith partnerships and marriages occur, and many thrive. However, like any couple bringing together disparate family traditions, cross-faith/sect unions are vulnerable to pressures, especially when one or both families are hostile to the couple and uncompromising over the faith, or version of the faith, in which any children are to be raised. The stress on this kind of mixed union is reflected in the situation in Northern Ireland, where children of cross-sect marriages are over-represented in the population of looked-after children.

Friendships supported through play

Children are ready to describe the importance of play and playful activities to their daily life. Part of the gradual shift is whether older children or adolescents use the word 'play' to describe their leisure-time social

Children are very clear that play matters a lot to them

activities. Play works as a social experience for children – a chance to be with friends and to cement the friendship through shared activities, to which children choose to return on a regular basis. Children often have long-running pretend play themes, which last for days, even weeks. They enjoy a wide range of physical games in their own leisure time but also in a school playground that allows time, space and basic play resources.

A great deal of the research into the play of children of school age has been undertaken in school playgrounds. Partly the playground is an easy location for observing play, but also it seems that children have steadily lost easy access to open play spaces with less obvious boundaries. Research reviews like that of Beth Fowler and Chris Taylor (2006) have brought together the evidence for the importance of play for children and young adolescents. Organisations like the Children's Play Council point out that local, publicly accessible play provision is not a high priority for local authorities; their obligations to provide childcare are much stronger. Adrian Voce, Director of the CPC, wrote in *Playtoday* (Spring 2006, issue 52) that, 'For every acre of land in England dedicated to public playgrounds, over 80 acres is given over to golf. On average, there is 2.3 sq m of public play space for each child under 12. That's about the size of a kitchen table' (page 4).

Children can really enjoy their play opportunities within school time but their experience is limited when they do not go out much into public spaces and open-ended play provision. There are undoubtedly some developments in some areas, including experiments with home zones – streets and neighbourhoods where traffic is severely limited (for more information, see www.homezones.org.uk) – and some improvements in parks with the introduction of Park Rangers, often with the aim of making children and families feel safe. Without a sense of security, families will not allow their older children to go out with friends, and generally adults have become highly concerned with risk (see page 220). The Home Office's own Citizenship Survey (DfES/Home Office, 2005) estimated that as many as 25 per cent of 8–10 year olds had never played out without an adult. Play England, a 5-year project led by the Children's Play Council from 2006, aims to promote strategies for free play, encourage more public play spaces and support play providers.

In the UK there is considerably more out-of-school provision for children than for adolescents. Most after-school clubs cover only the primary school years. Adolescents often welcome some kind of out-of-school and holiday provision, although they understandably want it to look different from that provided for under 11s. The service probably lies within the boundaries between an after-school club or holiday playscheme – where childcare is an avowed aim of the service – and the youth club model. Adolescents tend to want a place to hang out (where adults are there as a resource but not in the childcare role); activities with real choice; quiet space for homework for term-time facilities; and relaxed food and drink. Successful schemes are sometimes built around a physical activity that is definitely wanted by local adolescents, like somewhere to skateboard without being shouted at by tetchy grown-ups.

Play within school time and spaces

Anthony Pellegrini and Peter Blatchford (2002) point out that school teams often want to promote social skills, yet often overlook the great potential for adults to support this learning within the school playground. When breaktime is undervalued, then this valuable time is reduced literally. They report that in England the lunchtime break had been reduced from 1990 to 1995/6 by an average of 38 per cent in junior and secondary schools and by 26 per cent in primary schools. Afternoon breaks had been eliminated altogether in 27 per cent of junior, 12 per cent of infant and 14 per cent of secondary schools. Adult reasons for taking away what was valued by children included perceived behaviour problems in breaktimes and a view that additional classroom time meant children would cover more of the full curriculum. The school teams did not value breaktimes so lost the opportunity to share skills of problem-solving over any playground issues. They also overlooked the interaction between physical activity breaks and mental alertness: sitting for longer in a classroom does not mean children will inevitably learn more during that time.

A PLAYLINK action research report (1999) confirmed anecdotal as well as other research findings that the adults in school life frequently view breaktime as precisely that: a 'break' for children from the structure of classroom learning, rather than a positive contribution to their day and important to the children. The time is also a break/rest for teaching staff, since much playground supervision is the responsibility of non-teacher-trained staff. The report authors wrote, 'Conceptually, schools conceive of breaktime as the period when their primary purpose – formal education – is temporarily suspended . . . (then) play will be marginalised and seen through the distorting prism of "behaviour management" and the need for games-based activities' (page 4). This deficit model of breaktime easily spreads to a lower status for the support staff who supervise the playground area.

Children play in many school playgrounds, even those spaces that are not very friendly. Research studies of what children actually do – rather than what often hard-pressed playground staff believe is happening – have

LOOK, LISTEN, NOTE, LEARN

Of course some schools, with or without external support, have addressed the issues around the school playground. The change could best be describing as transforming breaktime into playtime. Look around your own neighbourhood and find schools that have undertaken a playground make-over or are still in the process of change. If they are happy for you to visit, find out about the timescale for the changes and the ways in which children were consulted.

The children in Crabtree Infants School were keen to tell me about what they enjoyed in their breaktimes. The ideas poured out: the willow structure, the curvy benches, the tennis, skipping ropes, water, playing chase and being allowed to run up and down the slopes, the construction bricks and everything that was available each day under the wooden canopy. This school team had improved and equipped the outdoor area over several years and one team member took special responsibility for this outdoor learning.

In autumn 2006 the government announced a financial package for schools as part of the *Learning outside the Classroom Manifesto.* Look at the Manifesto on www.dfes.gov.uk/pns/DisplayPN.cgi?pn_id= 2006_0175.

confirmed again and again that primary-school aged children play sustained games: pretend, chase, physical games with props like skipping ropes, rhyming and clapping games (sometimes with rather rude words). Children appreciate suitable play resources, enough time and supportive (not nagging) adults. In unhappy playgrounds, the very people who complain that 'children don't know how to play any more!' are usually busy disrupting and banning existing play. Adults worry and have a duty of care, but they need to take the opportunity of problem-solving with children where there are issues around shared space or genuine dangers. In every study and informal observation there has been more play going on than most teachers or supervisors believe to be the case. For a summary of some of the research see Lindon (2001).

The children from the Kids City holiday playschemes, with whom I talked in 2006, were clear what they enjoyed in the playscheme and in their school playground in term time. They liked being outside and were enthusiastic about physical games; they wanted to be energetic. The boys and girls mentioned all kinds of ball games, including football, cricket and basketball. They liked doing sports, PE and swimming at school. I watched them be very active with wheeled vehicles, playing chase, skipping, practising again and again with hula hoops, climbing and clambering. Most of these activities were with other children, sometimes one or two and sometimes larger groups and often with the involvement of the playworkers.

Wendy Titman's observations (1992 and 1994) were part of genuine consultations with children about possible improvements to their playground spaces. Features of the school grounds are important and can easily be lost to children, because adults do not check out their significance. Even 'improvements' to the playground can have negative consequences, if these remove an important feature. For example, a drain cover may be an important stopping place, or a set of steps may be part of a physical or dancing routine.

Marc Armitage (2001) describes how over the 1970s and 80s the prevailing design of school grounds became more square or rectangular. Consequently the available play space for children had fewer nooks and crannies, which feature as important aspects to many of the games played in school playgrounds. In his research, Marc Armitage has found that space and shape of available spaces interacts with children's choices over particular kinds of games. There tend to be more minor accidents in single large spaces. There are fewer accidents when a series of naturally occurring smaller spaces enables children to locate particular kinds of play in those spaces. Otherwise children have to organise all their different playful activities within the same larger space, without any boundaries. Armitage found a continuity of play in schools that had been functional over several generations. Parents and grandparents of the current pupils could recall using the identical playground feature as a necessary part of a game that was still being played by children now.

Inclusion and play

Schools and play settings are required to offer a proper welcome to children whose disability or chronic health condition could mean they are excluded. Inclusion is often not about special equipment. Practitioners need to deal as much with invisible barriers of attitudes and assumptions as with the actual physical struggles of disabled or chronically ill children. Theresa Casey (2005) is clear about the need to demystify what is meant by 'inclusive play'; that it has much in common with general good practice for any children's play. Disabled children benefit when adults pay attention to the actual interests of individual children, provide a range of play resources and talk with children (in different ways) to find out their experiences and perspectives.

Theresa Casey's report (2004) of the Play Inclusive (P.Inc) Action Research Project at The Yard in Edinburgh shows how physical

boundaries create a sense of place and of safety. Helpful adults are then
necessary to:

- provide an opening for a child to join in, when the child will not
  manage without support;
- provide a role for a child, for instance by joining in pretend play
  together;
- model the play so a child can see and hear what is expected in this
  kind of play;
- pair up with the child for play, when a playful and knowledgeable
  companion is needed;
- make complexities of any game more explicit and sufficiently clear so
  that a child can keep up; and
- provide a way for a child to leave a game/ease out when they are ready.

In a mixed-ability group of children a great deal of play can unfold when
games do not depend too much, if at all, on being able to talk and
explain. Children with limitations to their skills of communication can
watch and copy. So long as their disability does not significantly reduce
their ability to understand, children can be effectively included in the
same way as children who are fluent in another language manage to
follow and be active in play.

Children who cope within the autistic spectrum can be genuinely
mystified by the patterns and rules of play. Their peers confidently move
in and out of pretend and weave complex fantasy games that can
persevere over days. These boundaries are perplexing to children on even
the milder end of the autistic spectrum. The puzzlement, and sometimes
distress, of these children can highlight the developmental leap of their
peers. You may not be fully aware of the assumptions behind children's
play until you need to understand the rules, because you want to support
a child who is otherwise unable to join in.

Children on the autistic spectrum usually have to be taught the social
skills and responses that their peers have picked up through observation,
direct imitation and trial-and-error. Sensitive adult support can make the
difference, especially when combined with the abilities of informed peers.
Older children are able, and often willing, to operate as 'buddy peers' to
ease the entry of a child who does not find play an easy task. Simple
explanations and suggestions about a supportive role can work well. The
feelings of all the children need to be considered: a child with a disability
has to want to be involved. Also, peers should not be asked to moderate
their play to the point where they are unable to play what they want –
the result will only be resentment of the less able child.

MAKE THE CONNECTION WITH ... LEARNING SOCIAL SKILLS

Some children benefit from discreet help with social skills important for play and forming friendships. A practical example is provided in the Mental Health Foundation report (2001) entitled *I want to be your friend but I don't know how.*

Arbours Lower School, Northampton is an infants school, for children aged 4–7 years who come from 31 different housing estates. The project's aims were that the staff team of the school should understand better the needs of depressed and isolated children, as well as helping children to learn practical social skills. The main work was led by a specially recruited support assistant who ran lunchtime activity groups, mainly around sport or music. Children were nominated by their teacher because they were observed to be girls and boys who were friendless, isolated and were sometimes displaying behaviour that actively annoyed other children.

A small group of no more than five or six children worked with the staff member in 20-minute sessions built around small games equipment and a music resource box. Activities were planned to ensure that children used language and actions that could improve their social skills in general. The specialist assistant was also able to support some of the children at playtime, and a small amount of the special work was undertaken with the children within the classroom, to give the message to teachers that the project work was an integral part of the school day.

Friendships and technology

The current younger generation has wide possibilities for using technology as part of building and maintaining friendships. They use mobile phones as well as conventional landlines. Ways of keeping in touch include voice and texting as well as contact by email. The other form of technological contact is through internet communication such as chatrooms.

During the 1990s, the technology supporting internet chatrooms became available to adolescents who are now the young adults within the overall population. In the intervening decade, technological innovation has given rise to social networking sites and these sections of the internet are not only used by under-18s. The sites are an indication of how the World Wide Web has evolved. Websites were initially places to find information or make a purchase. However, there are now substantial numbers of websites that enable users to make social contact online.

At the time of writing (2006), MySpace is said to be the most popular site on the web, with about 90 million users, according to 'The World of Virtual Friendship', *The Week*, 19 August 2006, although a report in *Computing Which?* in September 2006 (www.which.co.uk/computing) suggests the still large but lower figure of about 60 million users. MySpace is a highly sophisticated site which provides a free messaging service where site members are given their own web page in which they create their individual profile in words and images. Other site members can leave messages on the page and online exchanges follow – written but also visual when members have a webcam facility. Other sites offer an entire fantasy life online. Second Life, for instance, is a 3-dimensional virtual world, like a video game but created by the 100,000 odd 'residents' who subscribe to the site. These sites are accessed by users of all ages. It is estimated that about 25 per cent of the users of MySpace are younger than 18.

Many online contacts are generally trustworthy, with the proviso that the real-life issue of 'But I only told one other person' can multiply at a breathtaking rate with internet messages. Banning children and young people from internet contacts is about as pointless now as refusing to let them learn how to use public transport. So it is crucial that coaching them in personal safety online includes a high awareness that what is written in messages and transmitted through a webcam facility can become entirely public. A useful rule of thumb could be 'would you say or do this in the middle of the local high street?' (see also page 294).

TAKE ANOTHER PERSPECTIVE

The advantages of sites such as MySpace are that they offer a much broader base of social interaction. Supporters say that a long, online 'buddy list' boosts self-confidence. Members of any age who struggle with the early stages of social contact can break the ice and identify online friends who have enough in common before organising a face-to-face, real-world meeting.

On the other hand, potential concerns are that site members, of any age, can lose their hold on the boundaries between virtual (fantasy?) friendships and real-life interaction. People are not necessarily entirely truthful in face-to-face contacts but online communication gives considerably more scope for bending the truth through to outright lies.

◼ What do you think?

If you want to know more

- **Armitage, Marc** (2001) 'The ins and outs of school playground play' in Bishop, Julia and Curtis, Mavis (eds) *Play today in the primary school playground*. Buckingham: Open University Press.

- **Barn, Ravinder; Ladino, Carolina** and **Rogers, Brooke** (2006) *Parenting in multi-racial Britain*. London: National Children's Bureau. Summary at www.jrf.org.uk/knowledge/findings/socialpolicy/0396.asp.

- **Blatchford, Peter** and **Pellegrini, Anthony** (2000) *The child at school: interactions with peers and teachers*. London: Hodder Arnold.

- **Brown, David** (1994) 'Play, the playground and the culture of childhood' in Moyles, Janet (ed.) *The excellence of play*. Open University Press.

- **Children's Play Council** (2002) *Making the case for play: building policies and strategies for school-aged children*. London: National Children's Bureau. See www.ncb.org.uk/cpc/.

- **Casey, Theresa** (2005) *Inclusive play: practical strategies for working with children ages 3–8*. London: Paul Chapman Publishing.

- **Casey, Theresa** with **Harper, Ivan** and **MacIntyre, Susan** (2004) *Play inclusive handbook: A practical guide to supporting inclusive play for children of primary school age*. Edinburgh: Scotland Yard Adventure (Tel: 0131 476 4506).

- **Connolly, Paul; Smith, Alan** and **Kelly, Berni** (2002) *Too young to notice? The cultural and political awareness of 3-6 year olds in Northern Ireland*. Belfast: Community Relations Resource Centre.

- **Dunn, Judy** (1993) *Young children's close relationships: beyond attachment*. London: Sage.

- **Dunn, Judy** (2000) 'State of the art: siblings', *The Psychologist* 13(5), pages 244–8. Available for download from www.bps.org.uk/publications/thepsychologist/search-the-psychologist-online.cfm.

- **Edwards, Rosalind; Hadfield, Lucy** and **Mauthner, Melanie** (2005) *Children's understanding of their sibling relationships*. London: National Children's Bureau. Summary at www.jrf.org.uk/knowledge/findings/socialpolicy/0245.asp.

- **Fowler, Beth** and **Taylor, Chris** (2006) *The benefits of play and playwork: best evidence-based research demonstrating the impact and benefits of play and playwork*. London: SkillsActive. See www.skillsactive.com.

✤ **Free Play Network** offer a rich source of photos and articles on www.freeplaynetwork.org.uk/playlink/exhibition/index.html.

✤ **Harris, Judith Rich** (1998) *The nurture assumption: why children turn out the way they do.* London: Bloomsbury.

✤ **Home Office** (2005) *The Citizenship Survey.* www.homeoffice.gov.uk/ rds/citizensurvey.html.

✤ **Lemos, Gerard** (2005) *Challenging and changing racist attitudes and behaviour in young people.* York: Joseph Rowntree Foundation. Report also on www.jrf.org.uk/knowledge/findings/socialpolicy/0135.asp.

✤ **Lindon, Jennie** (2001) *Understanding children's play.* Cheltenham: Nelson Thornes.

✤ **Lindon, Jennie** (2006) *Equality in early childhood: linking theory and practice.* London: Hodder Arnold.

✤ **Madge, Nicola** (2001) *Understanding difference: the meaning of ethnicity for young lives.* London: National Children's Bureau.

✤ **Pellegrini, Anthony** and **Blatchford, Peter** (2002) 'Time for a break' *The Psychologist.* Volume 15 no 2. www.bps.org.uk/publications/ thepsychologist/search-the-psychologist-online.cfm.

✤ **Pike, Alison**; **Coldwell, Joanne** and **Dunn, Judy** (2006) *Family relationships in middle childhood.* London: National Children's Bureau. Summary on www.jrf.org.uk/knowledge/findings/socialpolicy/ 0436.asp.

✤ **PLAYLINK** (1999) *Play at school,* www.playlink.org.uk.

✤ **Rowe, Dorothy** (1996) *The successful self: freeing our hidden inner strengths.* London: Harper Collins.

✤ **Save the Children** (2004a) *Think of me, think of you: An anti-discrimination resource for young people by young people.* Available for download from www.savethechildren.org.uk/scuk/jsp/resources.

✤ **Save the Children** (2004b) *Count me in.* Belfast: Save the Children.

✤ **Smith, Greg** (2005) *Children's perspectives on believing and belonging.* Joseph Rowntree Foundation/National Children's Bureau. Summary at www.jrf.org.uk/knowledge/findings/socialpolicy/0375.asp.

✤ **The Mental Health Foundation** (2001) *I want to be your friend but I don't know how.* See www.mentalhealth.org.uk.

❖ **Titman, Wendy** (1992) *Play, playtime and playgrounds*. Winchester: Learning Through Landscapes/WWF UK.

❖ **Titman, Wendy** (1994) *Special places; special people: the hidden curriculum of school grounds*. Winchester: Learning Through Landscapes/WWF UK.

❖ **Woolley, Helen** with **Armitage, Marc; Bishop, Julia; Curtis, Mavis** and **Ginsborg, Jane** (2006) *Inclusion of disabled children in primary school playgrounds*. London: National Children's Bureau. Summary at www.jrf.org.uk/knowledge/findings/socialpolicy/0016.asp.

3 Emotional development and well-being

Children and young people develop an emotional life during childhood and adolescence. They become aware of their own feelings but are also more aware of the emotional life of other people they know well. They learn, within their own social and cultural group, whether some emotions are more acceptable than others and how they should express or suppress strong feelings. At the same time, their brains are still maturing in ways that bring together emotions with more logical reasoning and judgement. Supportive adults need to be aware of their own emotions as well as realising that even very resilient children and young people can be overwhelmed by continued pressure or worry.

> **The main sections of this chapter are:**
>
> ★ **Making sense of feelings.**
>
> ★ **Emotional well-being.**
>
> ★ **Spiritual development.**

MAKING SENSE OF FEELINGS

Emotional development through childhood and adolescence has several main strands, including:

- how children recognise that they have an emotional, as well as an intellectual and physical, life;
- how children learn how to recognise their own feelings and name them: developing an emotional vocabulary and the ability to talk about feelings;
- how children become more aware of why feelings arise and learn choices regarding how their own emotions are expressed; and
- how children understand that other people – of their own age and older – have feelings too and that it is possible to acknowledge those emotions.

There is a great deal of potential in terms of what children can manage, even at the youngest end of middle childhood, but there are few, if any certainties. Experience will tell children whether their familiar adults want to acknowledge feelings and what are the acceptable choices for expression. Some 5 and 6 year olds have already started on the road to emotional literacy and elements of pro-social behaviour (see page 124), but this development depends on their experience so far.

WHAT DOES IT MEAN?

- **Emotional literacy**: the ability to express your own feelings and to recognise and understand the emotions of other people.
- **Empathy**: sensitivity to the feelings of other people and the ability to tune in to their emotions – the sense of 'feeling with . . .' and not pity or 'feeling sorry for . . .'. The implied meaning is also that children, young people and adults who show empathy will use their awareness to support others and not to undermine them on the basis of emotional insights.
- **Emotional vocabulary**: words that describe different emotions and phrases that can be used to express or invite an expression of feelings.

Understanding and expressing feelings

Children of 5, 6 and 7 years old can already have firm foundations for emotional literacy, so long as familiar adults have shared an emotional vocabulary that steadily helps children to recognise and name their feelings. Within middle childhood, some children are confident to say out loud, 'I feel cross', 'I'm so happy about . . .' or 'I was so worried about . . .'. They have started to build an emotional vocabulary and continue to add to it over the years. They may use words to express a fairly wide range of emotions: being happy, sad, excited, worried, scared, puzzled, fed up or angry.

However, all children will not inevitably talk in this way; it depends on their experience in their own family, their out-of-home early years' provision and then school. Children learn a vocabulary for emotions because they have heard familiar adults use the words, to apply to the feelings of this child, to their peers and to adults themselves. In this way, young children can head into middle childhood with the abilities to put feelings into words.

- Some children have learned from their family, and/or time within some kind of early years provision, that it is preferable to 'use your words' to express feelings like anger or frustration. They have accepted the moral value that, no matter how cross you feel, it is not acceptable to let the feeling out through your fists or other kinds of physical imposition on other people.

- Early experience may have taught them that adults who are responsible for children should also care about their feelings, so they feel confident that it is right and proper for them to tell a non-family adult, for instance in school or after-school club, what they feel today – whether that is happy or sad.

- So children who want to share their excitement about a family outing expect that their class teacher will understand and share that excitement. Older children feel their playworker at club will respond with empathy when the child asks, 'Can I tell you something sad?' and is at ease to continue with, 'Grandad is really, really ill and Mum keeps crying.'

Are some feelings not welcome?

In a supportive atmosphere, for instance in a primary school that values emotional literacy, children will continue to use and extend their skills. If their school, club or other familiar setting does not value emotional expression, then children will most likely learn to inhibit that expression. Children who have not been helped to express feelings in words or other safe ways still experience a range of feelings, some of them very strong, but the emotions emerge through their behaviour, sometimes in ways that bring more trouble to the children rather than adult help. Children have also begun to learn that there are social expectations within their immediate group regarding how even children should deal with and express feelings. Older children and young people may be very aware that their important adults disapprove of some emotions. Maybe nobody is supposed to appear ungrateful or jealous, or perhaps girls are permitted to appear more 'sensitive' than boys.

If children have experienced a great deal of dismissal of their emotions by adults, then they may have learned not to say or show any feelings. Children of 5, 6 or 7 years old can have already developed a tough exterior because they have been told not to whinge or that they are behaving like a cry-baby – a criticism more likely to be levelled at boys than girls. Children still feel hurt, perhaps by unkind words or physical rough handling from peers. But, as Jackie Nunns described to me (in a conversation I had with her about an unpublished playground support project), children work hard not to show that emotion. Jackie Nunns and her colleagues worked with a small group of boys, who had been identified as the main source of playground troubles in their primary school. These children had learned to laugh whenever they were hurt. Part of the support for changing their behaviour was to encourage the boys in a more accurate expression of their feelings, but in an assertive way that did not feel weak. It became acceptable for them to respond firmly with 'That hurt. Don't do that!'.

MAKE THE CONNECTION WITH ...
ADULTS' OWN FEELINGS

Adults, in their turn, have been shaped by their own childhood within their social and cultural background. Some adults appear very insensitive or uninterested in children's feelings. You may hear people who dismiss any possibility that children have strong feelings about an experience – remarks like 'children don't care about . . .' or 'they don't notice'.

Sometimes it seems that adults cannot face their own feelings provoked by the distress of children or young people. It is easier to side-step the emotion by trying to jolly children or young people out of sadness, offering something to do, underpinned by clichés like 'Least said soonest mended'.

■ A problem with a friend is better met with, 'I know you liked Maria – that makes it more hurtful that she . . .', rather than 'Never mind, come and help me with the snacks.' The latter comment has a place but only after an acknowledgement of the child's feelings and without the 'never mind'.

■ Young adolescents who are distraught at the loss of their first important girl/boyfriend are not impressed by adult reactions of, 'Never mind, it's just puppy love. You'll have forgotten all about her/him by next week.' (Even if young people have effectively moved on by next week, they do not want know-it-all adults to make the prediction.)

Adult reactions that ignore feelings are disrespectful and confusing for children. The adult appears not to have noticed strong feelings that have been clearly expressed. Older children and young people usually appreciate that a trusted adult cannot step in and easily make everything alright. They want to be taken seriously, have friendly attention and fellow-feeling.

■ What do you think? If you are honest with yourself, have there been times when you chose not to acknowledge the feelings of a child or adolescent? Can you recall similar incidents from your own youth – how did you feel?

The feelings of other people

Some children still in the early part of middle childhood are aware of the feelings of other people, especially familiar children and adults. They have learned to attend to the body language as well as the words of people whom they know well. Many children have learned to recognise the

Children learn to be gentle and considerate

feelings of their peers, perhaps joining in the excitement of a friend when they succeed in getting to the top of a large climb. Children may express empathy with friends who face distress or disappointment. If they are puzzled by someone else's demeanour, they ask, 'What's the matter?' or some other phrase heard from familiar adults. Under 7–8 year olds may comment from alert observation, asking a familiar adult, 'Are you alright? You look a bit miserable'. They might say, with discomfort, 'You've got your fierce face', or request help, for example 'My friend is so unhappy and I don't know what to do'.

Emotional development depends a great deal on children's experiences and this section continues to explore different aspects of this area. However, children and young people who cope with autistic spectrum disorder or Asperger's syndrome, will always struggle with decoding their own and others' emotions. Children and young people with a less severe version of the condition sometimes gain an intellectual grasp of what emotion appears to mean to other people. They may choose to behave in ways that make life easier in social situations but are still perplexed about feelings and the social clues that provide this knowledge.

How adults express feelings

Children and young adolescents can be puzzled about the emotions felt by adults. Partly it seems to be a separate step to recognise that grown-

MAKE THE CONNECTION WITH ...
MENTAL HEALTH

Children and young adolescents can be especially puzzled when the emotional expression of familiar adults is affected by coping with mental health problems (see page 302). Some families live with the effects of severe depression or anxiety disorder on a parent or older sibling. Children face difficulties when some feelings shown by their parent do not relate to events that make sense to children. It is possible, especially if the family has limited or no support, that children try to explain their parent's reactions through what they, the children, have done or not done. Some children and young people become the carers of their parent (see page 274). They then understand considerably more about the adult's mental health condition through carrying that responsibility in the family.

ups have feelings too, especially when they seem to be in control most of the time. But also adults may be less than honest about their feelings, perhaps saying, 'Yes, I'm fine' when their body language tells a child the precise opposite. Children and adolescents also learn that adults vary and some may respond with, 'Don't be cheeky!' to what the child or young person feels is a friendly enquiry of, 'Is something up with you?'.

Children and young people can be adept at reading verbal and non-verbal clues from familiar people. However, adult emotions sometimes emerge in confusing ways. A classic example for family and non-family caring adults is that fear about what could have happened to a child or young person comes out as anger. Adults may react with apparent anger to a child who has nearly walked into the road, or an adolescent who has seriously outstayed the agreed return time in the evening. Adolescents sometimes work out that fear and relief is behind their parent's anger, but they would be spared a detective job if adults were more able to recognise and be honest about their own feelings.

Children and adolescents do not want to feel overwhelmed, or embarrassed, by adult emotions. There are good reasons to protect them from high levels of anxiety, yet there has to be a balance. Children are not helped when adults are less than open about their feelings, for instance in family crisis or bereavement (see page 106). Children and adolescents still observe the non-verbal signs of their parents' emotions and are left confused and concerned about the causes.

TAKE ANOTHER PERSPECTIVE

Children and adolescents can seem oblivious to the feelings of grown-ups and perhaps some level of misunderstanding is inevitable.

I realise, that in my own adolescence, I simply did not factor in that adults might experience emotions like embarrassment or serious unease. I think now that a couple of teachers probably felt intimidated by me and my friends as we became confident and very outspoken sixth formers, but it never crossed my mind at the time; I labelled their behaviour as irritation or impatience.

Children are sometimes confused by grown-up emotions and motivation. I recall a teatime conversation with my then 9-year-old daughter and her friend. That day they had noticed one of their teachers in tears, with a colleague. They were taken aback by the obvious signs of distress because this teacher was regarded as one of the fierce ones, no soft side at all. I commented that teachers were people and they sometimes got upset just like anyone else. The girls looked surprised at this idea but then speculated that perhaps Miss had boyfriend troubles. I added another idea that controlling a large class was wearing and even those teachers who got cross with the children were sometimes still upset afterwards. This suggestion was greeted with disbelief by both girls.

■ What do you think? Recall events of your own childhood or adolescence and look again now with adult knowledge. Can you recognise feelings of familiar adults – what range of emotions? Are there some emotional circumstances that perhaps do not make sense to children?

EMOTIONAL WELL-BEING

Another approach to emotional development is through the concept of overall emotional well-being. The underlying aim for helpful practitioners is to support children and young people, through adult awareness of what are the likely emotions. Well-being involves a sense of emotional awareness and balance; it is not a case of being happy all the time. Well-being brings children and young people the confidence that they can deal with their feelings and consider options when faced with a tough situation.

Brain development and emotions

The research into how young brains develop has shown that strong emotional states provoke chemical changes in the brain. Experiences of early childhood have already set up expectations and patterns as children enter middle childhood. Children are not fixed forever, but all kinds of early experience have created neural connections in the brain. Important maturational changes continue throughout childhood. Over the years of adolescence, the human brain works hard to bring together the different areas of the brain that deal with intellectual and emotional tasks.

Children whose early years have been emotionally harsh develop elevated, above-average levels of the chemical cortisol in their brain. Cortisol is a steroid hormone necessary within the balance of the biochemistry of the brain. It is released when individuals feel under threat or are highly stressed and helps you to focus on the present risk. However, it is not healthy for anyone to be in a regular state of readiness to deal with anticipated threat and unpleasant uncertainty. In this state it is not possible to reflect and learn from people or other resources; children are too busy making sure that nothing and nobody is about to hurt them.

Some older children are already at a disadvantage because their early childhood has left them hard-wired for trouble. In the classroom or playground such boys and girls can be swift to interpret the actions of others as a potential threat. Practitioners cannot wipe away the impact of previous experiences, but patient support can create some new experiences and different neural connections.

Possible sex differences

Some writers suggest that some male–female differences related to emotional development may be linked with brain chemistry. Simon Baron-Cohen (2003) considers that the male brain is more attuned, on average, to logic and systems, and female brains are more attuned to the complexity of empathy and communication. He also makes the connection that more males than females live with autism and Asperger's syndrome. He suggests that such conditions, where individuals are perplexed by emotions and subtle social cues, are possibly an example of 'the extreme male brain'.

Louann Brizendine (2006) comes in from the side of 'the female brain'. She argues that the most usual brain chemistry for the female brain, due to its hormones, creates a situation in which girls and women are, on balance, more attuned to emotional communication than their male peers. The potential advantage, especially if this tendency is respected, is that emotional awareness is part of a rounded package in an adult team. The downside is that females, on average, may well be more stressed by emotional disharmony and conflict than males.

It is important to note that neither of these scientists claim that one pattern is better than the other. They both argue that it is time to consider broad sex patterns, even though average differences mean that of course it is not possible to say 'all girls ...' any more than 'all young men ...'. Both authors express a sense of trepidation that their messages may be misunderstood – concerns justified by some negative reactions to each book.

MAKE THE CONNECTION WITH ... SOCIAL PROBLEM-SOLVING

Happy social interaction depends on some level of emotional regulation (see below) and children learning that it is considerate to moderate how you express feelings, however genuinely felt, if someone else will be hurt by blunt statements.

However, such consideration raises social dilemmas around honesty, which children and young people become increasingly able to discuss. For instance:

- One friend is comforting another because someone has made rude remarks about her mum. The child says, 'But my mum's not fat, is she?' The good friend is stuck for words because the mother is seriously overweight.
- Does a concerned brother tell his sister that her boyfriend boasts about still going out with other girls?

Have similar dilemmas been brought up by children or young people with whom you work?

Children and young people often appreciate the opportunity to talk through social dilemmas to which there is not a simple answer. Trusted adults may sometimes be asked directly, 'What should I do?' Sometimes tough choices are aired in snack-time conversation in an after-school club or youth club. Helpful approaches from adults explore the different strands of a dilemma and offer a problem-solving approach that weighs up priorities (see page 142).

Emotional regulation

Nancy Eisenberg (1992) has described the importance of children's ability to control their own emotional expression, although the meaning of 'control' is not that children learn to deny or suppress feelings. Emotional regulation evolves from children's awareness of feelings and making active choices about how and to what extent the feeling is expressed. Eisenberg suggests that this kind of emotional impulse control is an important part of adult guidance through the years of childhood. Examples could be the following:

- Children who have not learned to address their own strong emotions may well unleash anger or feelings of revenge, with no concept of limitation, and wreak havoc in a school playground or the peace of an after-school club.
- But also children will feel increasingly at odds with the adult world if they have no way to express sadness or frustration other than desperate bouts of crying. Other children also look askance at persistently tearful peers.
- Young people who have no concept that they should limit the expression of what they feel or want, can pose a risk to their peers and anyone else who crosses their path. There is an unjust readiness in the media to demonise the younger generation as a whole (page 12). However, a proportion of children and young people have not learned pro-social boundaries.

Feelings and behaviour

Some adults muddy the waters between a child's feelings and honesty about their own, adult emotions. For example, some practitioners (and parents) are keen to play the guilt card, most probably because that was the pattern of their own childhood. Adult discomfort then emerges as, 'Don't you think that was a rude thing to do when . . .?' The focus is then on the child or young person, who 'should have known better'. If adults genuinely want to promote emotional literacy, then they have to express the more honest, 'I felt embarrassed in front of everyone when you . . .' or, 'I feel that you were discourteous to . . . and I would like you to find a more considerate way to . . .'.

MAKE THE CONNECTION WITH . . . WHO IS FEELING WHAT?

Adults fail to set a good example of emotional regulation and literacy if they make children responsible for the adult's feelings of discomfort. For example:

- Some practitioners are worried about boisterous play, often from boys. But it is not acceptable to take the line, as I have heard sometimes, that, 'those boys make me feel intimidated'. The implication is that the children are to blame for engaging in 'rough' and 'inappropriate' play and the solution is simply that the games have to be stopped. Practitioners have to face their own emotions: they do the feeling – children do not 'make' them feel any emotion. The grown-ups in this kind of problematic interaction need to distinguish their emotions from children's behaviour and then look at what may need to be done (see also page 138).

■ Sometimes practitioners are uneasy about their ability to meet the needs of disabled children or a child with an unfamiliar, serious condition. It is possible that a child is kept on the sidelines of lively play on the grounds that she or he is afraid of being pushed – when in fact the person most worried is the adult. Practitioners need to be honest with themselves if they are anxious, and should not resolve their feelings by 'passing them on' to the child. See also page 49 about inclusive play.

Unacknowledged adult feelings, of any kind, must not become a block to children's experiences. If adults are serious about supporting the emotional development of children and young people, then they have to be prepared to distinguish their own feelings, and consequent action, as part of the situation with children.

Another practical reason for adults to be aware of their own feelings is that sometimes those emotions are a useful perspective on behaviour from children and young people that is experienced as troublesome. Children's feelings are authentic, and they may have difficulty in holding them back. However, adults can guide them towards different forms of expression. The ideas of Alfred Adler, developed by Rudolf Dreikurs and Vicky Soltz (1995), have influenced an approach through the apparent goals for children's behaviour. For instance:

▨ Children and young people who are desperate to feel more powerful in their world sometimes provoke the feelings of a power battle with their parents or teachers. So adult feelings around, 'She is not going to win on [a particular issue]' or, 'He needn't think he's going to get away with ...' can be a vital clue to the emotions driving the child or young person's behaviour. In a roundabout way they have been successful, because they have engaged an adult in a win–lose scenario.

▨ In a similar way, children and young people who feel helpless and incompetent may give up trying and take refuge in the image of hopeless inadequacy. They can trigger feelings of hopelessness in adults who struggle to help, feelings that can move onto adults wishing to give up in their turn.

Adult awareness can provide a perspective on the problem, so that the focus can become finding other ways for a child to feel powerful and in control of their own world. Adults need to find ways to acknowledge with a child or young person how far they have sunk into the conviction that they are unskilled in important aspects of their life. This approach, and other concepts from the work of Adler and Dreikurs, underpins the Systematic Training for Effective Parenting (STEP) programme developed by Don Dinkmeyer (sen. and jun.) and Gary McKay (Dinkmeyer, McKay and Dinkmeyer, 1997).

WHAT DOES IT MEAN?

- **Impulse control**: the ability to hold back on inclinations or expression of feelings.
- **Emotional regulation**: the ability to direct or re-direct the expression of feelings and choices made about expression.

Feeling self-conscious

Dealing with their own feelings can be complicated when children feel self-conscious. An uncomfortable level of self-awareness can emerge for some quite young children and is not helped by labelling children as 'shy'. It seems more accurate to describe them as boys or girls who take their time, are slow to warm up or who need to trust someone or the situation before they are forthcoming about their views or wishes. Each of these possible patterns is more complex than could be covered by the word 'shy'. Such labels also tend to undermine the confidence, of children as well as adults, that a child or young person could, with help, stretch their skills for social situations.

In adolescence, many boys and girls experience a significant increase in self-consciousness, and emotional expression can become muddled in some circumstances. Young males seem to have an especially hard time, because of the expectations laid upon them (see page 70). However, young females can also struggle with the way feelings emerge. Both sexes can feel attracted to someone and yet find themselves being rude, trying too hard to be funny or in other ways side-stepping any message that they really like the other person. Personal unease can be fuelled by the physical changes of puberty (see page 247) and feeling awkward within a body that seems to be growing, at least over some years, in a thoroughly un-coordinated fashion. Most young people of both sexes experience serious doubts about their attractiveness and in later years regret not knowing that most of their peers, even the most popular, were nothing like as self-confident as they appeared to be.

Emotional development for males and females

Dan Kindlon and Michael Thompson (1999) suggest that expression of emotions is generally discouraged for boys, or possibly more that a narrow range of emotions is permitted within a stereotypical image of masculine toughness. Adults often seem to assume that girls will be more attuned to feelings and are more ready to offer explanations linked with emotions. So boys can be denied early experiences that support an emotional vocabulary and reflection.

Kindlon and Thompson call the process of steering boys away from acknowledging their inner world, the 'emotional *mis*education' of young males, claiming that this social learning puts them potentially at a disadvantage. They sum up the problem with a visual image: 'Even the youngest boy learns quickly that he must hide his feelings and silence his fears. A boy is left to manage conflict, adversity and change in his life with a limited emotional repertoire. If your toolbox contains only a hammer, it's not a problem as long as all your equipment is running right or repairs call only for a pounding. But as tasks grow more complex, the hammer's limitations become clear' (1999, page 4).

Dan Kindlon and Michael Thompson allow that some basic differences may be laid down for males in their biological make-up; they are not claiming that females and males are the same. However, they argue that any biological sex differences are accentuated by a social culture in the western world that is more supportive of emotional health and development for girls than their male peers. Adrienne Katz (1999) reported on a large-scale survey of male adolescents and described some similar themes. Overall, these main points are relevant to any practitioners, and are supported by insights from counselling services for young people:

- Young males have feelings, but peer pressure and 'masculinity myths' can limit emotional development and close down options for communication. Young men face the dilemma of how to feel and look strong without bringing criticism for being 'aggressive'.
- Young males can be uneasy about talking of problems and feelings out loud. Communication is not just about finding the words; there is a concern about becoming vulnerable and looking soft.
- Additionally, as college and university counselling services sometimes find, females often feel better for talking about feelings and see the process of communication as a way to work towards some kind of solution. In contrast, some, but not all, males tend to be more orientated to talking about what to do and finding a solution. In their different ways both sexes welcome bouncing ideas off a friend or

counsellor. (There is no way of knowing how much of this tendency can be attributed to social learning and how much is biology or brain chemistry. It is just a matter of observation.)

- However, some male social groups are very supportive and some male friends do talk with each other in confidence, but the atmosphere needs to work. Positive male role models, preferably boys' own fathers, seem to be a key factor in showing that talking is alright and an acceptably 'male' way can be found.

- It is important that a single pattern is not imposed; young males do not have to behave more like females and just telling young males to talk about their feelings or problems is often pointless. The block in some social groups seems to be a strong homophobic undercurrent that talking about feelings or reaching out emotionally to other males is 'gay' and therefore to be avoided at all costs.

- What seems to help is some specific guidance, from trusted, non-punitive adults, probably also males, on how to handle strong emotions like anger or a fierce sense of injustice. Shared practical activities often build a sense of trust and provide an emotionally safe place for confidences (see 'make the connection with . . .' on page 71). Once children and young people feel safe, then the one-step-removed approach of role play and drama may help.

- Sometimes young people need vital information that gives them some sense of control over a problem, since even very streetwise young people (female as well as male) can have significant gaps in their general knowledge.

If boys and young men cannot get through the entrenched taboo about talking to someone, then distress, anger and unrecognised strong feelings will still be churning inside them. Some antisocial and high-risk behaviour seems to result, directly or indirectly, from this impasse (see also page 72). Adrienne Katz's *Leading Lads* report comments on campaigns that urge young men to seek help, perhaps by calling a helpline. Such campaigns are unlikely to be effective unless they focus on perceived manly characteristics for the choice to seek help. Drawing from young men's responses to the survey, Katz suggests important messages that the action to seek help takes courage, is about taking charge of your life, will be confidential and also that seeking support is a masculine choice, wanting to spare those closest to you.

Feeling angry; feeling sad
The emotion of anger can be addressed from the early years – as a feeling that everyone has from time to time, but one that can be regulated in how it is expressed. The general rule for early years and later

MAKE THE CONNECTION WITH . . . TRUST AND EMOTIONAL SAFETY

A late 1990s project is described in the Mental Health Foundation *Bright Futures* report (1999, page 36):

In the West London borough of Hammersmith and Fulham, special funding was used to employ two specialist youth leaders who worked in partnership with schools. They set up individual personal development programmes in and out of school for African-Caribbean young males, largely in response to their high exclusion rates from school.

The programmes offered a combination of leadership training, outdoor pursuits, a range of basic life skills including first aid and job training. The initiative was successful and stemmed the flow of permanent exclusions from this group. But an additional impact was that the youth-work approach of the two male leaders created an atmosphere in which some of the young men felt able to talk about problems that were affecting their daily life. The school staff did not know about these serious issues.

childhood needs to be that everyone gets cross from time to time – what matters is how the crossness comes out and that it does not hurt other people. A key pro-social message is that it is not alright in school, club or a childminder's home for children to feel better by making other people feel worse.

For some children and young people – adults too – the emotion of anger has scarcely been integrated with thinking and the process of resolving problems and frustrations.

- A constructive approach is to help children and young people to recognise their feelings as anger simmers. But it is also valuable to realise that any emotion stretches across a continuum. Feelings that children or young people label as 'anger' may actually stretch through irritated, annoyed and angry before reaching furious. This sense of a continuum, rather than an either-or, can be helpful for children and young people who struggle with other emotions, such as getting very distressed and tearful about any upset at all.

- Positive adult approaches to anger avoid a punitive response that trades anger for more of the same. A vital strand is that adults listen and show that they genuinely want to understand what is going on inside a child's or young person's head.

■ No sensible approach lets even very tough circumstances be an excuse for children or young people to hurt others or carry on with destruction, stealing or other antisocial behaviour patterns. But the whole focus is on enabling a child or young person to change how they deal with pressures and that means finding a way for them to express what has and is still happening in their life.

Nick Luxmoore (2006) describes his work with adolescents who show high levels of anger, sometimes at the physical as well as the verbal level. These young people are angry about many incidents, some that appear far more serious than others to an outsider. Young men, and some young women as well, have great difficulty in getting those feelings out in ways that do not bring more trouble onto them, from their family or school. A turmoil of inner disappointment, resentment, confusion and also rage can emerge as apparently different emotions. Adolescents who shout, disrupt, destroy and attack may be confidently labelled by onlookers as 'angry'. But Nick Luxmoore, like other writers in this area, points out that anger is sometimes the only emotional outlook that makes sense to a young person. Deep hurt and anxiety about family breakdown lie behind some furious outbursts. However, anger and resentment can also exit via failing to meet study requirements, stealing and even turning the anger inwards through self-harm. Some very angry adolescents are reacting – not necessarily consciously – to a continuing situation that adults in the family, school or elsewhere do not take much notice of them until and unless they go emotionally over the top.

TAKE ANOTHER PERSPECTIVE

Nick Luxmoore (2006) describes the different patterns that he has observed between male and female adolescents – the impact of social learning.

■ He suggests that young males long to feel part of a social group, to belong. They would like to feel they have emotions in common with male peers, yet feel that admitting this wish would put them at risk of accusations of being gay. (Despite broad social changes over sexual orientation, this fear is still a reality within the younger generation.)

■ On the other hand, young females feel at risk if they do not belong, if they disagree with key ideas or ways of behaving in their group. Nick Luxmoore observes that the social learning for girls is much more that it is alright to be sad, but not to be angry.

▓ He describes how young women may cry but that these are tears of rage. In his therapeutic work he aims to help them to separate sadness, crying and anger – even to the point of having a crying chair and an angry chair. He encourages troubled adolescents to distinguish their feelings by physically moving between the two chairs.

Nick Luxmoore works as a therapist and the help he offers to troubled adolescents can last several months. He describes his specialist work, but I think what is says offers useful food for thought for anyone involved with children and young people. What do you think?

Brian Marris and Tina Rae (2006) describe ways of supporting 9–12 year olds whose behaviour has resulted in exclusion from mainstream school. The aim is to coach children in the Pupil Referral Units, many of whom are boys, to explore their personal triggers – what sets them off towards anger. Talking, but also structured games and the format of Daniel's Letters (from a fictional boy in a similar unit) are all used to enable children to understand themselves better. They are supported to be able to notice their own warning signs, and, very importantly, to have a strategy or two for what they will do instead of physical or verbal attack. It may be that a child is ready with a sharp reply rather than an angry shout, or that they need to find the strong body language that enables them to walk away without feeling 'weak'.

The school curriculum

There has been growing concern that schools should pay attention to the emotional health and well-being of children and young people, not exclusively their academic achievements. Some schools have always had a strong pastoral system, arising from a sense of responsibility to their pupils/students as well as a practical understanding that emotional safety supports academic success. However, respect for children's emotional well-being as much as their ability to deliver on educational outcomes is a significant shift for some schools. Of course, emotional and mental health is not only the responsibility of schools. Family life matters a great deal, as does family support and community initiatives that create safe, welcoming neighbourhoods for local residents across the age span.

Effective developments in primary and secondary schools have evolved from approaches integrated into the personal and social strand of the curriculum, from the Healthy Schools Initiative (England), a move to

Children need to feel emotionally secure in school and out of school provision

integrate citizenship into the educational process, to local initiatives to counteract the impact of early disadvantage on children's behaviour and school achievement. These common strands have emerged as crucial for any approach to make a difference for children and young people.

- Commitment has to be through a whole-school approach. The whole staff team needs to know what is going on and why, to be committed to it and not undermine initiatives as side issues to the 'real' task of schooling.

- Class teachers need to feel part of special projects, to be informed and have some input into which children are invited to join. Any project workers need to be treated as part of the school team, especially if they are not from a teaching background.

- Everyone needs to appreciate that it may be some time before a payoff is seen in children's attitudes or behaviour. The approach tends to backfire if it is seen as a quick fix – something that is done by a lesson in the classroom and then ignored – or as a separate initiative about 'children with behaviour problems'.

- Special projects may be aimed at dealing with children and adolescents who show particular signs of emotional and behavioural difficulties, but these initiatives need to be integrated into the whole-school approach for the well-being of all pupils or students.

▓ Any special groups need to be set up and run in ways that are non-stigmatising for the children or young people who attend. Some projects depend for their success on a broad range of children and young people being keen to participate.

▓ It is also wise to avoid creating a situation in which it appears to pupils as a whole that the 'badly behaved' boys and girls are given special opportunities. The logical next step is then to produce the behaviour that appears to be the entrance ticket for the special group.

MAKE THE CONNECTION WITH . . . ADULT EMOTIONAL LITERACY

A great deal of children's emotional and social learning develops within the context of relationships. The closest and longest-lasting relationship for most children and young people is with their own family. However, positive experiences in school can make a difference. There are now many books, topic outlines, games and ideas for circle-time activities that aim to support the emotional development of children and emotional literacy.

Some resources are better than others, but it is striking that adult users of the resource are rarely invited to reflect on how they show their own feelings. I have encountered materials on helping children to recognise and express their own emotions, with no mention whatsoever of the adult as a walking visual aid for modelling emotional literacy. Certainly it is a very one-sided initiative when children, or young people, are exhorted to 'think about how other people feel', if the adult right in front of them shows no evidence of being interested or able to show empathy in their turn.

■ Look closely at any materials that you use. Is there scope to reflect on adult feelings and the issue of being a positive role model to children and adolescents?

I have encountered some thoughtful, unpublished local initiatives, but SEAL (Social and Emotional Aspects of Learning) is an accessible example. A key point about this educational resource is that it revisits issues around self-awareness and managing feelings over the years of primary school. The SEAL resource pack was sent out in 2005 to all English primary schools, but the materials are available on the internet. There is a range of booklets, some visuals and a set of posters, with interesting ideas like the Feelings Detective and Be Assertive. See www.standards.dfes.gov.uk/primary/publications/banda/seal.

SPIRITUAL DEVELOPMENT

It is a matter of opinion where to place spiritual development within descriptions of development during childhood and adolescence. I have placed some discussion here with emotional development, because it seems to me that feelings lead thinking in this area. There is another section within children's personal and social development and some definitions of terms (see page 35).

What is meant by spiritual development?

It is important first of all to address the uncertainty and uneasiness that arise with the word 'spiritual'. There is a lack of consensus for definitions across books about child and adolescent development and some writers simply avoid the area altogether. This section offers my approach to the question, 'What does it mean?'. Please use the points as a way to explore your own views and to support discussion between fellow students or colleagues.

Some writers about child development merge moral with spiritual development. This choice seems to evolve from a stance that spirituality does not, and should not, have anything to do with religious belief. This perspective then excludes faith from any discussion around development. I find this position unacceptable, because faith is an important part of life for some children and young people.

In contrast, some adults – practitioners and writers – feel convinced that spirituality has no real meaning unless it is grounded in personal religious faith, because 'spiritual' means 'religious'. Hence children's spiritual development means their ability to understand, and possibly also accept, religious belief and practice. Such a stance inevitably becomes fraught because the next question has to be, 'Which world faith?'.

Another viewpoint also equates the word 'spiritual' with 'religious', but those expressing the view do not commit actively to any faith. Practitioners, and possibly some writers, who feel this way are wary of acknowledging children's spiritual development because they do not wish to promote, or appear to favour, specific religious beliefs.

My working definition of spirituality (more in Lindon, 1999) is that it is an awareness of and connectedness to that part of human experience that does not have to answer to rational analysis. The spiritual dimension can therefore encompass the following:

- An inner life of feelings in which the emotional dimension can simply be experienced in response to events: the emotions of enchantment, appreciation and delight. Practitioners of all backgrounds need to consider how to encourage the opportunity for awe and wonder for children and adolescents and how to avoid blocking that development.

- A sense of the infinite, of being a small speck on a huge time flow or part of multiple universes, stretching out into the astronomical heavens or into the micro-universes of our own world. This sense can feel liberating or daunting, and is the source of some of the 'What's it all about?' really big questions that exercise some adolescents.

- A sense of powers and forces beyond human experience or control. For some children, young people and adults, this aspect has a religious meaning. This aspect emerges in terms of the origin of such forces and a conviction of faith: beliefs that lie outside the rational boundaries of evidence and proof. Such religious conviction can fuel peace and well-being, but is not essential for these feelings.

- One source of support for personal identity in some families (see page 35). Some children, young people and adults identify themselves through a sense of belonging to a specific faith or philosophical stance.

So, I choose to include religious convictions and faith within a discussion of spiritual development. The importance of faith for some children, young people and their families should be fully acknowledged. However, 'religious' is not the same as 'spiritual' for everyone. Moral development can join spiritual development through the bridge of values and the 'why' behind some beliefs about right and wrong. However, moral development is not dependent on faith for everyone.

Pleasure in the natural world

A sense of delight can be noticed as children, and adolescents too, are fascinated by events within the natural world. Excitement and interest arise through plenty of direct, often hands-on, experiences of the outdoors and changes in the natural world. But children also need adults who share in the reactions of 'Look, look!' and express their own interest in the butterflies or thrill at the rainbow.

However, a growing proportion of the younger generation do not have access to the outdoors in an unstructured, reasonably natural state. Richard Louv (2005) has raised concerns in the USA about a generation of children who spend limited, if any, time in a natural outdoor environment. Louv focuses on what children and young people probably lose when their play and leisure is mainly indoors and removed from first-hand experience of nature. He also points out a development of pre-packaging nature and an outdoors experience in the name of 'education' or 'family fun'.

Mary Pipher (1996) reflected on her counselling practice and concluded that therapy was too narrowly focused on the children and young people themselves, as if their problems were of their own making or arose only from parents' behaviour. Pipher describes how attention needs to be focused on how much of urban family life in the USA revolves around malls and consumerism. As well as specific help for children and young people, Pipher began to advise parents simply to get into the natural world with their sons and daughters.

LOOK, LISTEN, NOTE, LEARN

Richard Louv and Mary Pipher both live and work in the USA. I think their concerns are just as applicable to the UK, including the imbalance towards walking mainly for shopping, and that too many children experience the outdoors only through a 'theme park' approach. I have nothing against theme parks or shopping as such and continue to enjoy both experiences, but it is a question of balance – a bit like a nutritious diet.

■ **What do you think?**

Similar concerns have been brought to the forefront in the UK through lively outdoor and forest school movements. Practitioners involved in these initiatives want childhood to include plenty of active, physical play and for children to have adventures in the natural world. But there is an equally important strand of real experiences for children and young people, and a concern about the long-term effects of disconnection from the natural world. A wide range of developments aims to connect children and young people with all the interests and skills that revolve around time spent outdoors and the possibilities of even a small 'wild' environment.

■ These experiences are not organised exclusively for city children. Children and young people in small towns close to the countryside do not necessarily have regular access to the outdoors other than their own garden.

■ Some adolescents go through a period when it is not socially acceptable to express delight or appear to be highly interested in anything. The natural world may be dismissed as the preserve of little children and 'boring' adults who go on country walks. However, I have encountered very successful initiatives from school and holiday playschemes, not necessarily around organised residential trips.

■ Additionally I have listened to practitioners responsible for looked-after children and young people. Some individuals and teams have made the effort, increasingly having to deal with obstructive views of risk management (see page 220). Even some very disaffected young people have genuinely enjoyed rambles and scrambles, night walks and walk-and-search outings.

Adults are responsible for communicating basic safety messages without ruining an experience. The forest school movement, and other outdoor initiatives, work to ensure that children and young people learn appropriate skills of self-reliance and safety knowledge. This coaching approach co-exists with the fact that getting grubby is part of most outdoor experiences and a balance has to be created between acceptable risk and memorable explorations for children and young people.

TAKE ANOTHER PERSPECTIVE

Adults need to be ready to deal with a wide array of reactions, which initially may be buried under a layer of apparent disdain. I have been given these examples:

■ Young people who were deeply uneasy about going into a wood (daytime) and who expressed their anxiety with complaints and being cranky.

■ Despite living relatively close to open public space, some older children had never been travelled the short distance across the city to the large park. They were fearful about being completely out of their familiar neighbourhood.

■ Children who lacked the energy to climb even a short hill came across as un-cooperative, rather than as concerned because they were out of breath and wobbly.

■ Young adolescents had had so little experience of walking on anything other than a pavement that they were distressed by the physical experience of walking on very uneven ground.

Given the high sense of pressure in many schools now, it is also non-negotiable that children and adolescents have the time to stand and stare at something of interest. Intriguing experiences sometimes just need to be enjoyed, without a swift adult intervention by directive questioning or providing information. A great deal depends on adults who behave as positive role models. You need to look as if you are enjoying your time in the outdoors and set a good example as someone who is interested to stand and stare. There is no need to rush into providing further information and explanation. Children and young people will soon ask their questions and you can be guided by what they want to add to their knowledge today. A genuinely inquiring mind is exactly what is needed in early science and children are capable of asking some searching questions.

Spiritual ideas, knowledge and understanding

Children's understanding of faith and religious beliefs and values seems to evolve potentially in much the same way as any area of learning. However, books on child and adolescent development scarcely mention religion in terms of how children in families with a religious faith come to understand and commit to the beliefs and practices. If it is discussed at all, faith is usually merged with cultural background and explored through the impact on daily life.

Young children tend to believe what familiar adults, especially their parents, tell them. It seems likely that informal religious instruction within the family and the local community will work in the same way for children up to middle childhood and maybe into early adolescence. Some families choose to send their children to specific religious instruction, for instance by sending them, on a regular basis, to Qur'an class, Sunday School or special Hebrew and Torah lessons. Religious education in schools certainly assumes that children of primary school age are able to understand, and therefore be taught, about key beliefs of world faiths.

There is also an assumption, within early education as well as primary school, that information about faiths as a whole will support children to feel respect for beliefs that they, and their family, do not necessarily share. This hope is unlikely to be fulfilled unless general information is connected with real people and common ground. Certainly, there has to be significant, continued community work in neighbourhoods where there is already hostility between people on the basis of faith, or choice of sect within a faith. Otherwise, any information about the 'other side' is simply fitted into a judgmental them-and-us framework that children of 5 and 6 years old have already learned from their family and immediate community (see page 44).

Robert Coles (1991) describes the seriousness with which children and adolescents take the family faith and the need for writers, as well as practitioners, who are not practising members of any faith to recognise the central importance of beliefs in daily life for some children. A study undertaken by Greg Smith (2005) reported the views of 9–11 year olds attending primary schools in East London and a city in the North of England. Smith made sense of the children's accounts by organising the distinctions that they offered into three broad dimensions:

1 *Religious identity*: feelings of identification with a particular religious tradition. Children were willing, or were under obligation from their family, to take part in the rituals and practices.

2 *Social practice*: the structured learning and public rituals of the faith, plus any linked ceremonies or festivals.

3 *Belief and spirituality*: children's thoughts, beliefs and feelings, including their personal practices like private prayer or meditation.

By children's own accounts they varied across the spectrum from very high religious commitment to indifference. Some of the older children described a daily life that was significantly shaped by the family faith and they expressed strong commitment to the beliefs and values they had been taught. Some other children were involved, but their family faith exerted less impact on daily life. These children were less clear about the beliefs, found some of the practices rather tedious but often expressed enjoyment in festivals, especially those with presents. Some children were able to talk more within what Greg Smith describes as 'an implicit individual faith'. These 9 to 11 year olds were interested in issues of the supernatural and personal spirituality. A final group of children were uninvolved in any faith, largely uninterested and sometimes ready to mock peers who were committed.

Questioning beliefs

Children try to make sense of the ideas that are expressed to them and some children are more inquiring than others. Some 5 to 7 year olds ask tough questions about 'why nice people get hurt' or 'what happens after you die'. One way of answering is to refer to explanations based on beliefs within a given faith. Some families want to give an answer based on faith, and a similar stance will be followed in specific instruction classes to which children are sent by their family. Practitioners in school, play and youth services should reply to these important questions with honesty, but more with the sense of 'some people believe . . .' and by admitting that you do not really know for sure.

Older children and adolescents may use their thinking skills to pose more challenging questions, such as why an apparently powerful deity lets children starve to death in some parts of the world. Some adolescents reach an equally challenging question: since a large number of people with completely different belief systems are sure they have the only true faith, and everyone else is doomed, then how come 'our family/community' can be certain that we are the ones in the right? Such questions, especially if posed more than once, are often experienced as confrontational by adults who do not want, or feel unable, to discuss a rational challenge to spiritual issues. Some adults, within the family and outside, are more comfortable to explain that religious belief is less a matter of logical proof than of acceptance and faith. Some may meet the questioning challenge with unease, even anger. Older children and adolescents then grasp that questions about 'what we believe' are more acceptable to a parent, teacher or religious leader than questions to explore 'why' and 'proof'.

As with any values experienced within their childhood, adolescents will at some point decide to remain in a family faith or leave.

- Like some adults within any faith, it seems likely that adolescents steadily take the view that some parts of the religion followed by their parents are more acceptable and that they can overlook other parts.
- Some young people decide to opt out of the religious beliefs of their family. The consequences of this decision depend on the strength of the family faith and the level of exclusivity that is part of this sect. Some parents may regret the choice of their son or daughter, but maintain otherwise happy relations. However, some young people face permanent exclusion from their family.
- Alternatively, some adolescents and young adults choose to become more fervent in the religious beliefs of their family, or commit to a faith when they were raised without religious commitment in the family.
- Regardless of whether their family practises within a faith, some adolescents become intrigued by issues of spirituality and wish to explore avenues of the paranormal.

TAKE ANOTHER PERSPECTIVE

In the UK, children and young people in state schools are legally required to take part in regular, usually daily, acts of collective worship or some kind of religious observance – the exact description varies across the nations of the UK. The requirement is that the observance should be broadly Christian in nature, unless a school makes a strong case to the contrary. The pattern of this event varies between schools, and parents have the right to say they do not want their children to attend.

At the time of writing there is discussion in the government about whether to change educational legislation for England and Wales so that school students older than 16 could make their own choice to opt out of an act of worship or religious assembly.

- It is food for thought that children and young people in school are the only citizens of the UK who are required to participate in a regular act of collective worship.

- 16 year olds can exercise most adult legal rights (see page 21) but currently need their parents' involvement to be withdrawn from the act of worship in school in England and Wales. They can withdraw themselves from that part of school life in Scotland.

- Adolescents of 14 to 16 years old are judged able to make decisions about their own health (see page 262). Are they not, then, equally able to make a spiritual decision for themselves?

What do you think?

If you want to find out more

❖ **Baron-Cohen, Simon** (2003) *The essential difference: men, women and the extreme male brain*. London: Allen Lane.

❖ **Bayley, Ros** (2006) *More than happy or sad: young children and emotions*. London: Early Education.

❖ **Brizendine, Louann** (2006) *The female brain*. New York: Broadway Books.

❖ **Coles, Robert** (1991) *The spiritual life of children*. Boston: Houghton Mifflin.

❖ **Connolly, Paul**; **Smith, Alan** and **Kelly, Berni** (2002) *Too young to notice? The cultural and political awareness of 3–6 year olds in Northern Ireland*. Belfast: Community Relations Council.

❖ **Dinkmeyer, Don (sen.)**; **McKay, Gary** and **Dinkmeyer, Don (jun.)** (1997) *The parent's handbook: systematic training for effective parenting*. Circle Pines Minn: American Guidance Service.

❖ **Dowling, Marion** (2005) *Young children's personal, social and emotional development*. London: Paul Chapman Publishing.

❖ **Dreikurs, Rudolf** and **Soltz, Vicky** (1995) *Happy children: a challenge to parents*. Melbourne: Australian Council for Educational Research. (See www.adlerian.com for other publications.)

❖ **Eisenberg, Nancy** (1992) *The caring child*. Cambridge MA: Harvard University Press.

❖ **Forestry Commission** – the research agency of this organisation has reports on www.forestry.gov.uk.

❖ **Forest School Movement** – a range of articles about the UK and Scandinavia on www.forestschools.com.

❖ **Gerhardt, Sue** (2004) *Why love matters: how affection shapes a baby's brain*. London: Routledge.

❖ **Gottman, John** (1997) *The heart of parenting: how to raise an emotionally intelligent child*. London: Bloomsbury.

❖ **Katz, Adrienne** (1999) *Leading lads: 1400 lads reveal what they really think about life in Britain today*. East Molesey: Young Voice. See www.young-voice.org.

❖ **Kindlon, Dan** and **Thompson, Michael** (1999) *Raising Cain: protecting the emotional life of boys*. London: Michael Joseph.

❖ **Lindon, Jennie** (1999) *Understanding world religions in early years practice*. London: Hodder and Stoughton.

❖ **Lindon, Jennie** (2005) *Understanding child development: linking theory and practice*. London: Hodder Arnold.

❖ **Louv, Richard** (2005) *Last child in the woods: saving our children from nature-deficit disorder*. Chapel Hill: Algonquin Books.

❖ **Luxmoore, Nick** (2006) *Working with anger and young people*. London: Jessica Kingsley.

❖ **Marris, Brian** and **Rae, Tina** (2006) *Teaching anger management and problem-solving skills*. London: Lucky Duck/Paul Chapman.

❖ **McGinnis, Susan** and **Jenkins, Peter** (2006) *Good practice guidance for counselling in schools*. Rugby: British Association for Counselling and Psychotherapy. See www.bacp.co.uk.

❖ **Mental Health Foundation** (1999) *Bright futures: promoting children and young people's mental health*. London: Mental Health Foundation.

✣ **Pipher, Mary** (1996) *The shelter of each other: rebuilding our families to enrich our lives*. London: Vermilion.

✣ **Smith, Greg** (2005) *Children's perspectives on believing and belonging*. Joseph Rowntree Foundation/National Children's Bureau. Summary at www.jrf.org.uk/knowledge/findings/socialpolicy/0375.asp.

4 Change and transition

The years of childhood and adolescence are inevitably a period of change. Even children with the most stable family and social circumstances have to negotiate some changes in the detail of their daily life. Children and young people in the schooling system deal with major adjustments as they move from one stage to another. Some deal with significant changes in their family life, sometimes with warning and at other times utterly unexpectedly. Supportive adults need to be aware of the range of changes that are likely through childhood and adolescence, what the details of a transition mean to the children and young people directly involved and what actions from adults are likely to be genuinely helpful.

> **The main sections of this chapter are:**
>
> ★ **The nature of change and transition.**
>
> ★ **Personal and family life.**
>
> ★ **Transitions created by services.**

THE NATURE OF CHANGE AND TRANSITION

All children have to deal with their personal awareness of physical change in themselves during childhood and adolescence. The change through growth and physical development, as well as the significant transformation of puberty, are covered in Chapter 9. The focus of this chapter is on external changes around children and young people, which have an impact on their experience, daily life and emotional development.

Learning to cope with change

Change is inevitable over the years of childhood and adolescence. Children and young people are well served when important adults help them to deal with minor changes and unexpected setbacks. Life is neither always smooth, nor fair. It is valuable for children and young people to learn to deal with events and build their sense of competence before they are launched into fully independent adulthood. It is unwise to attempt to protect children, let alone young people, from setbacks and upheavals that are relevant to their current and future life. Adults sometimes resist letting children know, even about significant problems, on the grounds that 'it will only upset them'. On the other hand, some adults justify harsh treatment on the grounds that, 'It's a tough life and the sooner they learn, the better!' Somewhere between these two extremes there is a considered middle course that works as part of raising the next generation.

There are times when it would be overwhelming for children and young people to know the depth of an adult's anxiety or sense of loss. So it is not appropriate that children, especially, are part of every frank discussion between adults – in a family, school, play or youth setting. However, adults need to let children know, for instance, if there are serious problems in the continued funding of their after-school club. Otherwise they will wonder why the club leader looks so worried and keeps having cryptic, low-volume conversations with parents. It is also very disruptive if the first awareness for children is that the club will end this week. Older children and adolescents can feel angry that they have been kept in the dark and denied an opportunity to launch their own 'save our club' campaign.

Changes that are transitions

Sometimes a change can be foreseen, even planned, but at other times there may be hardly any prospect of anticipation. Significant changes in family life can occur without any warning, for instance the sudden death of a family member or a parent's unexpected shift into unemployment. Serious illness or accidents can strike children or adults within a family, bringing major changes and a great deal of uncertainty, especially in the period immediately after the event. However, other changes may follow a sequence, as children and young people move from one stage of their life to another. Such a sequence is often now called a transition. There is greater awareness of the responsibility of adults to smooth the path for transitions like the move into primary school and later into secondary school.

An experience in the life of a child or young person is usually called a transition when the change is not reversible; it is a permanent adjustment to what has been normal daily life up to that point. There may be observable changes in where they have to spend their time, new relationships, change in ground rules about how daily life will work or expectations for the child or young person. Transitions created by services

WHAT DOES IT MEAN?

■ **Transition**: a relatively major step, or series of steps, that result in permanently changed social circumstances for children or young people.

should approach with some warning. The changes should not simply happen to children and young people suddenly, nor be imposed on them without any consultation. Some events, like puberty or the experience of family breakdown, can look more like a transition with hindsight.

Feelings about change

Change is not always disruptive, nor it is necessarily distressing. A great deal seems to depend on the emotional literacy of the adults and their willingness to find out from children and young people how they feel, rather than assuming anything from 'all is well' to inevitable turmoil. Some feelings of confusion or uncertainty are normal when anyone is facing a change. A period of transition, such as moving on to secondary school or to sixth form college can mean a new development in personal identity for older children and young people. The prospective change may be anticipated with a mixture of emotions: excitement at the opportunity, maybe regret for what will have to be left behind, or elation at leaving a setting that did not bring much happiness, or a combination of several emotions.

Emotional distress is likely when someone's life has been turned upside down – possibly by events that could not be anticipated by anyone. However, the emotions are still not predictable – anger, sadness, grief, numbness; it could be any of these or a combination. Higher levels of distress and disruption to patterns of behaviour or development are far more likely when children and young people are not kept informed, feel out of control and cannot access emotional support. Children and young people can feel overloaded when more than one significant part of their daily life is changing over the same period, or when changes just keep piling up, with no prospect of stability.

So the experience of change matters and there can be a positive ripple effect from a well-supported transition. Even a major family change can be positive overall when children feel that they, and the adults, were able to cope, even if they all wished that this particular change had not happened.

- Children and young people can strengthen in a sense of optimism: that change is not necessarily a threat. They need to feel that it is possible to take some personal control, even if major decisions do not rest with them. Children and young people also need to feel confident that it is alright to ask for help and advice: such a request is a sign of strength and not of weakness.

- A poorly supported transition, with a sense of being at the whim of decisions made by others, can distress and/or harden children and young people into beliefs about 'Why bother?', 'Nobody cares', 'You

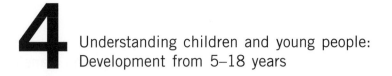
have to pick up the pieces on your own and so why cooperate at all when the next big change comes along?'. The experience of too many looked-after children and young people is so disruptive because they have major life changes with minimal warning or regard for their preference.

TAKE ANOTHER PERSPECTIVE

Sometimes even a major shift is welcomed by children or young people.

I recall my own parents' worry about uprooting me when we moved to another area after I had spent only two terms at secondary school. In fact my friendship group had been disrupted already and I thought my new school was a miserable, stuffy place. My family supported me well in the move and I much preferred the next secondary school. The new neighbourhood also had far more interesting activities for adolescents. However, I did not share these feelings with my parents until I was into my adult years. It took time to realise I was happier in the new situation. But also it had not struck me, as a young adolescent, that grown-ups might feel reassured to hear this kind of information.

■ Do you have memories of a similar major change within your own childhood or adolescence? How did you feel at the time or a bit later? Did you talk with your parents, or other important adults?

Offering support

When change unsettles children and adolescents, even to a relatively small extent, their feelings will emerge one way or another. Different patterns of behaviour show how they are trying to cope. All reactions are certainly not negative and some children make immense efforts not to impose, as they see it, on other people. These individuals run the risk of being judged unmoved by serious events, 'over it' or another inaccurate description of their true feelings.

There are many possibilities for how children and young people may react.

■ They may behave differently from the child or young person you have come to know well. Some children or adolescents may become quieter and withdraw. Some may show more obvious distress or a lowered ability to deal with the usual ups and downs of playground life or club banter. Depending on your relationship with a child or young person, they may need no more than a friendly and relatively private, 'Is something bothering you?' and the body language that says clearly that you are ready to listen.

- On the other hand, some individuals' struggle with emotional distress emerges as anger directed at peers or adults who 'deserve' a verbal or physical attack. You need to deal fairly with the outburst and any consequences, but also give the opening, then or soon after the incident, to explore along the lines of, 'I know you shouted at Damian because of the offside business but you were really angry. It looked to me like there's something else weighing you down. What's up?'

- Sometimes children will regress temporarily in their development and self-care abilities. It may be that a competent child seems struck by anxiety, really wants to be cosseted or is keen to say, 'I can't do that'. Children who were dry at night may start to wet the bed, and their distress at this situation can lead them to feel even more emotionally fragile.

- Some children and adolescents really want to talk – perhaps to a trusted class teacher or club playworker. Perhaps you even hear from the child about Dad being made redundant before the parent tells you.

- Depending on the family situation, some children find it harder to say goodbye to their parent(s) and they may worry about their well-being while they are apart.

- Children's concerns sometimes emerge through their play, or their unwillingness to play as usual. For some children and young people the issues emerge through their drawings or written stories and poems.

Listening and supportive conversation

Children and young people do not always want to talk about what is happening in their personal life and it is unwise to insist. Amanda Wade and Carol Smart (2002) highlight the fact that reluctance to talk is sometimes a wariness around trust and doubts about confidentiality. However, sometimes children and young people simply wish to keep parts of their life separate. They welcome school or club as a place where they enjoy a respite from the troubles of their private, family life. Children and young people, who are coping with a great deal, often welcome kindness and general consideration from familiar adults outside the immediate family circle.

If children and young people show they want to confide in a good adult listener, then a great deal of support can be offered through informal conversations that draw on attentive communication skills.

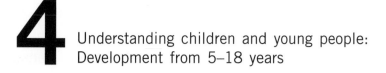

- Listen carefully to what children or young people want to tell you and how they tell you: the music of their body language as well the lyrics of their spoken words.

- Resist filling a silence quickly and opt for what is called reflective listening. This style of helpful communication means putting someone's words back to them in a slightly different format, perhaps with a questioning tone in your voice. If a silence continues in an uncomfortable way, you can ask, 'Are you still thinking about . . .?' or, 'Could you tell me what's on your mind?'.

- Keep your own questions open-ended – probably 'what?' and 'how?' rather than 'why?' questions. Leave the pace of the conversation to be determined by the child or young person.

- Answer with honesty the questions that a child or young person wants to ask you. But sometimes you will not know the answer, for instance, 'Why didn't Mum tell me that Dad's in prison?', or families will have their own way of answering questions like, 'What happens when you die?'

- Avoid rushing in with a solution that sounds right to you. You can consider with an older child or adolescent, 'Would it help to talk around what you could do about. . .?' or, 'Any thought about what you would find helpful right now?'

- Older children and adolescents often understand that there is no quick and easy way out of their current situation. Children or young people will sometimes communicate that they just wanted to talk around what they are currently facing. Sometimes, of course, they are unaware of possible sources of help that could make a difference to them or their family.

- You should respect the confidentiality of a confidence from a child or young person in the same way you would that of a colleague: confidences from children or adolescents should never fuel gossip in a staff group. However, you cannot agree to keep absolute secrets. You have a responsibility to share information professionally if you are concerned about a child's well-being or safety.

- On many occasions the issue will be more that you do not want parents to be left out of the communication loop. It might be appropriate to say to a child, 'I'd like to tell your mum about our conversation. She will want to know that you are worried' or to an adolescent, 'I really believe you should talk with your father about . . . If you think it would help, I'd be happy to talk with you about how you might start that conversation.'

If children and young people are seriously troubled, they may need more organised help, although that may still be at the level of basic counselling skills offered by a familiar adult (Lindon and Lindon 2000) and not long-term therapy offered by someone who is a stranger at the outset. A full- or part-time counsellor in a school may become a more familiar figure to whom some children may turn.

The other alternative, well documented by ChildLine, is that some children and young people choose to talk with a friendly stranger at the other end of a telephone helpline. ChildLine is sometimes assumed to be mainly, or only, about abuse and bulling. Some children do call about this kind of distress, but reports on www.childline.org.uk describe how many callers want someone to listen to other sources of worry.

Support between peers

Sometimes the best help from a concerned adult is to ensure that children and young people have the time, comfortable space and sufficient privacy to talk with their friends. Peer groups – male as well as female – can be very supportive. Helpful adults do not try to break into this privacy, but find ways to show that they are aware that a child or young person is carrying a heavy burden. You also need to be alert to the fact that a problem shared is sometimes a problem that then weighs down two people rather than one. Close friends – it happens with adults as well as children or young people – can begin to feel responsible for finding some solution. On the other hand, some children and young

Older children and adolescents support each other

people have the insight to tell friends that they just want to talk to someone who is not directly involved and do not expect answers.

On the other hand, children and young people are sometimes wary of talking freely with their peers, even those they count as close friends. They may be concerned, possibly for good reason, that private matters will not be kept confidential but will circle back as fuel for playground gossip and bullying taunts. Older children are also usually aware that parents talk with each other. So a confidence entrusted to one of their friends might be passed on, with assumed confidentiality, to that friend's parent and then into the local adult grapevine. Children and young people are often more aware of these dynamics than adults believe and, of course, they also listen to adult conversations and are alert to the messages of body language.

PERSONAL AND FAMILY LIFE

It is very unlikely that family life will continue through childhood and adolescence with no changes whatsoever. There is no set pattern for how children and adolescents react to changes with major consequences for daily life. A very great deal depends on:

- the temperament of the individual child or young person;
- how a change is anticipated, if that is possible, and handled when it arrives; and
- to what extent children and young people feel informed and involved in significant family change, or alternatively feel sidelined emotionally and/or in terms of information.

A range of possible sources of family change are covered in this section. Research studies often focus on only one type of significant life change, but there are common strands between different kinds of experiences and these are discussed from page 105.

New arrivals to the family

Some children will continue through childhood and adolescence with the same pattern of siblings, or their status as the single child in the family. However, a proportion of children will experience the readjustment that comes with one or more new babies. Additions to the family may arise from planned additional pregnancies or surprise arrivals. The reaction of older children varies: some are delighted and some are uncertain about what the change will bring. Some, especially adolescents, are anything from mildly embarrassed to seriously annoyed at this evidence that their parents must be having sex.

94

The same range of possible emotions arises when the baby is a half-sibling, from new adult relationships. Under these circumstances, much depends on children's feelings about the breakdown of the previous relationship and the security of their position within the new family dynamics. Calls to ChildLine about family change cover a wide range of issues, including life as a stepfamily. But some calls are about departures, rather than arrivals. One example was a caller's upset at the prospect of an older sibling about to leave home and the uncertainty that change brought.

Illness and disability in the family

Family life can be significantly changed when a new baby is seriously ill or disabled. Very premature babies now survive, due to advances in medical techniques and intensive care, and a proportion live with mild to profound disabilities. Serious illness or disability, either late developing or arising from an accident, can develop after infancy. There is now much more awareness that, as hard as parents try, healthy children can feel less of a priority than their very ill or disabled sibling. It was welcomed that the Children Act 1989, applying to England and Wales, identified all disabled children as 'in need'. But the Children Act (Scotland) 1995 went further and recognised in law that a child who has any family member who is disabled should count as 'a child in need'.

Illness does not only strike babies and children. Family life is significantly changed when a parent, or other important family adult, becomes chronically ill or has a serious accident. What has been normal life for children and young people undergoes major change for the foreseeable future until the adult recovers. But in some families there is no return to the previous 'normal', because a serious illness or accident has caused permanent damage. Under these circumstances there can be a great deal of uncertainty and continued stress in the family.

Family breakdown

Some children, for whatever reason, never live with both their birth parents, but many children do start in this way. A considerable number of these children will not reach adulthood with their two parents still living together under the same roof, whether married or not. It is estimated that at least one in three children will experience the separation of their parents before they reach their 16th birthday.

Some family loss is still created by the death of one partner but separation, and divorce between married couples, is the more common reason in the UK for this significant change. Children and young people have to deal with the breakdown of a relationship that they regarded as forever. It is also noticeable that by middle childhood, children in general become aware that parents can split up, because the family of at least one friend has become divided. So, children and adolescents living with both parents can be made very uneasy if the adults argue, or go through a sustained difficult patch.

When parents split up, children and young people need recognition that they have feelings too, and need to be able to voice them. As hard as it can be, the adults need to find emotional energy and time to listen to their sons and daughters. Some children and young people are relieved that obviously unhappy parents have finally called it a day or that an emotionally or physically cruel parent has left the home. But many others take the view that their parents could have sorted out their grown-up problems in ways that were less disruptive for everyone else. Children and adolescents do not want to be forced into making an emotional choice between their parents, nor be caught in the middle of adult distress and conflict.

People are often more concerned about the impact of separation and divorce on younger children, thinking that adolescents or young adults are emotionally more secure and independent. On the contrary, this age group can be devastated by family breakdown.

- Adolescents who are coping with the inevitable physical changes of puberty can be especially vulnerable to overload. Part of the distress seems to be that the last thing they need, during the major changes of adolescence, is for their apparently safe family base to be fragmented.
- An additional disruption for adolescents and young adults, especially when their parents seemed to be boring but happy, is to be forced to rethink the previous years along the lines of, 'But I thought you loved each other! Was it all just a lie?'
- Family breakdown is sometimes triggered by the infidelity of one parent. For continued family life after separation, the other parent has to find some way to get through the sense of betrayal. However, adolescents and young people explain that they too have to find a way to forgive a loved parent whose action precipitated the family breakdown, otherwise they do not hold onto, or regain, their close relationship with a father or mother.
- Young adults can also be very distressed. University counselling services refer to the 'January phenomenon': deeply sad young people who return after their first vacation break having heard their parents' announcement of separation. Even young people who knew their parents had relationship problems can be upset and sometimes angry

that 'they just waited until I was out the door!', whereas the adults assumed that holding on was better, because this timing would be relatively painless for their son or daughter.

The pattern for ChildLine (reported in the late 1990s) has been a relatively stable 15 per cent of calls about relationship problems within the caller's family. Not all calls relate to family breakdown, but many are from children and young people who want to talk about feelings of loss and the distress of family conflict. The ChildLine experience supports findings from research studies: that the experience varies for individual children and that family breakdown is a process, a sequence of linked events and not a single event of parental separation.

ChildLine reports that most of the family-related calls are at the beginning or at least early on in the process of family break-up. However, during the telephone conversation it becomes clear that about 20 per cent of these callers want to talk about family events that happened at least two years previously, some as much as ten years ago. For these children and young people, the passing of time has certainly not brought a new kind of stability. The callers represent that part of the young generation who feel very troubled because more disruption just keeps happening in their family. The callers have experienced serial family breakdown and have little confidence that it will end.

New family relationships

The future part of family breakdown can be that parents find new partners, who may become part of the household, forming a stepfamily. New partners may bring additional children of their own, either living in the same household or moving between two homes. Creating a stepfamily inevitably means a rearrangement of existing relationships. Research, and reviews of studies in this area, presents a picture that is variable – it all depends on the relationships and temperaments of the people involved.

- Broadly speaking, younger children seem to find it helpful to be part of a stepfamily, whereas older children can find it hard to adapt to changed circumstances. Older children or young people may have had longer as a small family unit and be uneasy about the role of this new adult.
- Sons or daughters can have been their parent's companion, and possibly confidant, for some years and may resent the intrusion of the new partner. From some reports, it emerges that children who have worked so hard to keep up the spirits of a sad parent are simply disheartened that this new adult appears to have made their parent happy so easily.

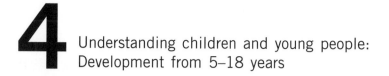

■ Adolescents in the family may also be absorbed with their own growing sexual awareness and the issues of attraction. They may feel it is not the ideal time for their parent to show an obvious interest in a sexual relationship. Some sons and daughters deal with their parent's greater honesty about their own sexual orientation, revealed through the sex of their new partner.

■ Generally speaking, older children require that a new partner finds a role that is not that of 'actual parent', becoming a friendly and supportive grown-up. Choice of names, or friendly nicknames, is often the way children and adolescents choose to distinguish between a birth parent and step-parent.

Many families work their way through breakdown to a new way of running a family life that is divided between households, but the adjustment takes time and feelings can run very high. Adults may feel there is no option but to split their relationship, but studies and anecdotal evidence from children and adolescents confirm that the transition is usually tough for them.

Temporary family separations

Families are divided for reasons other than the permanent breakdown of the adults' relationship.

Work and family life

Parents are sometimes absent for long periods of time because of their job, for instance careers that require extensive travel or postings without the family, such as members of the armed forces. Children and adolescents can feel the temporary loss of a parent deeply and worry about their well-being – a concern heightened by jobs and/or locations that are realistically dangerous. Younger children may be less aware of the details of their parent's or parents' job, although early-years practitioners describe how even young children are aware of the potential dangers for a parent in the military, especially at times when a conflict is regularly featured on television.

The demands of professional life may also bring about relocation of the whole family. Children with one or more parent in the military services often experience regular moves over their childhood and adolescence. A report in 2006 from Parliament's Defence Select Committee describes one primary school that served a large garrison. In the school, 90 per cent of the children were from service families and a similar proportion would move to a different primary school before they were 11 years old. These children had many more transitions to manage than the primary to secondary move of many of their age group (see page 113). Children and young people, who gave evidence to the Committee, described the difficulties of regular disruption of friendships and also of adjusting to a different school curriculum, even when the family had moved only within the UK. Parents gave evidence that this kind of disruption, for children and adults, was especially acute if children had special needs.

Family members in prison

A different kind of temporary family separation arises when a parent, sibling or other family member is in prison. As well as the separation itself, the fact of imprisonment creates other issues. Additionally, the time that a family member is in prison is only one part of the sequence. The events of arrest, being on remand and the trial happen before prison and the difficulties of adjustment outside the prison walls follow from release.

The whole situation may be a family secret if imprisonment is an unusual family event for the neighbourhood. Children may then be keen to avoid friends, teachers or anyone else knowing why their parent or older brother has been out of sight for a considerable amount of time. In some families, the children have been told a fiction, perhaps that Dad is working abroad. Children may be very wary about confiding in a teacher and they, with the rest of the family, will want to be confident that any sharing of the information is on a strict need-to-know basis. Children and young people can feel very isolated – Kelli Brown's (2001) report for the Action for Prisoners' Families Young People's Project is entitled *No-one's Ever Asked Me*.

Materials from Action for Prisoners' Families help to give an understanding of the variety in this family experience. Some children may be relieved that a violent relative, one who brings nothing but trouble to family life, is shut away for now – the anxiety is that he or she will emerge at some point. In some neighbourhoods, having a relative in prison may not be unusual and is viewed with annoyance for the disruption, rather than distress or shame. In some neighbourhoods, a spell in prison is seen as a badge of adulthood among young men, creating a corrosive effect on development into maturity and a major barrier for youth workers, as described by Shaun Bailey (2005).

Family life is inevitably disrupted with the absence of a parent. Visiting family members in prison can be very time-consuming in terms of travelling to the prison, and distressing during the visit. Some prisons have welcomed outside agencies who set up and support a play area over the family visiting times. For example, Marian Pearson (2004) describes the Humber Pre-school Learning Alliance initiative that provides play areas in

99

the visiting halls of three prisons in this area. These projects are not only for younger children and can make a huge difference to the experience of visiting for both children and adults. However, many prisons do not have this kind of facility and many do not have a proper visitors' centre.

Apart from the emotional impact on children and young people, there is good reason to make every effort for adults in prison to keep in contact with their families. For many, it will make the difference between re-offending or not. Some prison services are more open to easing communication between parents and their children and some combine parenting sessions inside the prison with practical help. The level of illiteracy is high among prisoners and projects to help parents write to their children are sometimes the vehicle to address low confidence in literacy – see the resources from the Literacy Trust, at www.literacytrust.org.uk/Database/prisonres.html.

Significant change in financial circumstances

Some major family changes are brought about by a significant loss of income. One of the related changes of family breakdown is that the joint income is very likely to be divided and spread more thinly. Intact families are disrupted by other sources of financial hardship, such as redundancy, long-term unemployment or serious problems in a family business. Children and young people are affected in two main ways when the family income is destabilised:

1 A serious drop in reliable income can make a significant change to what has so far been normal family life.
2 Seriously worried adults can have an impact on younger family members.

As with other major family changes, many children and adolescents cope better if they are informed about the financial situation, with details that will make sense given their age. They can be very supportive, although understandably sad when they have to make major changes to their lifestyle.

Refugee and asylum seeker families

Many parts of the UK now have at least some families who have reached the neighbourhood because of serious disruptions and fighting in their country of origin. Many children and adolescents face significant adjustments in order to cope with an unknown culture and language. Families who have migrated out of choice can still have significant differences in what was previously normal daily life. However, some refugee families seeking asylum status have emerged from extremely distressing circumstances. Even the children may have seen vicious fighting, witnessed the injury or murder of members of their family and experienced a terrifying flight out of danger. Some children and adolescents arrive in the UK as unaccompanied minors – neither with their family nor immediately joining family. In this case they legally become looked-after children and are the responsibility of the local authority – either at the point of entry to the UK or the area where they are relocated.

It is important to be able to call on specialist support in this situation, although much of what helps is basic good practice that is sensitive to children and young people.

- A great deal will depend on children's previous experiences: whether routines are familiar or very strange, and whether children have a shared language with local children or adults.
- Settling disoriented and possibly disturbed children and young people can be hard work in a school or after-school setting. Practitioners of all backgrounds need to be aware that children's experiences may make them vulnerable to what seems to the outsider to be over-reaction. They may be very easily distressed or hit out in self-protection. Children need emotional support and understanding, as well as guidance towards more appropriate reactions in a safe place.
- Like their peers, children from refugee families are likely to play out their experiences, whether through small world figures, active pretend play or within drawings or stories. Adults in the school playground or outdoors at club have sometimes had to re-think their choice to intervene in what they assume to be rough pretend play. It has become clear that children are re-enacting what they have previously seen and heard. Practitioners may still judge that it is wise to redirect play actions to an extent and children must be safe enough in your care.

Bereavement

Despite the many advances in medical science, some people die before reaching an advanced age. Parents die, as well as grandparents or other older relatives, and some children, for reasons of serious illness or fatal accident, do not live to adulthood.

Significant disruption and transition arising from bereavement during childhood and adolescence have tended not to attract as much research attention as family breakdown. Yet, many children and young people experience loss through the death of family members. Even when families manage to support each other well, the experience brings great distress, along with longer-term emotional and financial adjustments from the loss of an adult family member.

The experience of loss

Jane McCarthy and Julie Jessop (2005) estimate that the great majority (they suggest a figure of 92 per cent) of children and young people under 16 years of age will have grieved for the loss of someone they consider to be very significant in their life, which can include the loss of a family pet. Some children face the death of an adult such as a parent or grandparent, but they also sometimes lose a sibling, a friend or important non-family adult like a youth worker or play leader.

LOOK, LISTEN, NOTE, LEARN

Writing this section led me to reflect on my own family life. I realised that my son and daughter, before they reached the age of 18, had experienced the death of three grandparents, our next-door neighbour, the mother of one adolescent in the local friendship network and the father of another, and also my daughter's secondary school class teacher.

■ Look back upon your own childhood and adolescence and recall your own losses. You may wish to keep the memory private. However, if you are part of a supportive student or practitioner group, perhaps you could share those memories.

■ You are now a member of the adult population and it is important to avoid pushing bereavement to the very back of your mind. Read through the main points made in this section and consider how much they applied to your own experience of bereavement.

Studies of bereavement highlight a range of issues that can be helpful to adults who wish and need to be supportive:

■ Children who experience bereavement in childhood or adolescence are not necessarily at greater risk of emotional or behavioural troubles. Distress from loss can, of course, deeply affect children but support from their own family, trusted non-family adults and children's own friends can get them through this experience into another phase of their life.

■ Research sometimes overlooks children. For example, Jennifer Holliday (2002) mentions how studies of Sudden Infant Death focus mostly on the impact on parents. Few studies acknowledged the fact that some infants who died had one or more siblings, who also mourned the loss of 'our baby'.

■ Children and young people seem to be at risk when they have multiple bereavements and/or when their normal life is full of other disruption and lacks emotional or physical security.

■ Children and young people are highly vulnerable when they experience traumatic bereavement, for example witnessing the murder of a parent or finding a family member or close friend who has committed suicide. Serious emotional problems are likely under these circumstances, worsened often by media intrusion when a court case follows the event.

Many families will deal in private with their experiences of loss, although they may appreciate the discreet support of practitioners who know their family well. Children and adolescents do not usually need professional help and it is important that adults do not pass children or young people on to 'experts', because those adults are uncomfortable about death and bereavement. However, children and adolescents often do want to talk with someone familiar about their sense of bereavement – not necessarily close to the time of loss (see page 107).

Children faced with bereavement can struggle with the meaning of death and their emotions. However, some of the reactions attributed to children are often shared by grieving adults: apparent denial of the loss, temporary 'forgetting' of the death and expecting a loved person to come back in the front door, even anger at the person for having abandoned those left alive. Children and young people, just like adults, may cope with irrational feelings of guilt that their relationship was not better in what turned out to be somebody's last weeks or that they survived a car crash that killed their father or brother. Some families share a faith that reassures them they will meet friends and family again in an afterlife, or that dead souls will re-enter the world through a process of reincarnation. Such beliefs can be a source of comfort, although the sense of immediate loss is still powerful.

Bereavement may be anything from entirely unexpected – from sudden illness or accident – to the end point of a period of serious or recurring illnesses. Home-based or hospice care may create some level of support for the last period in the life of fatally-ill individuals. Hospices for children are very attentive to the needs of parents and siblings as well as the child who has a terminal condition. For more information, see the Association of Children's Hospices at www.childhospice.org.uk.

Loss in your setting
Death can have a very direct impact on a group setting like a school or club. You can experience the loss of a child or young person who attends your setting, the death of a member of staff or an event in the immediate neighbourhood. Professionals should take steps to be prepared in ways that would not be appropriate for families.

The experience of schools that have directly experienced loss suggests attention to these issues:

- It is advisable to have procedures in place for how you will deal with a critical incident, like death, that will disrupt normal daily life. The point about written procedures, or a policy, is to help you and your colleagues to cover all the significant practical issues at a time when emotions will make logical judgement and recall of priorities much more difficult. Louise Rowling (2003) gives the example of one school that reached the end of a very tough day only to realise that the one person they had not informed about the death was the part-time counsellor.

- Basic written procedures should not distance you from emotions. Guidelines are there to help you to act in ways that support the children and young people who are your responsibility, reducing their sense of anxiety. In times of stress, they need to feel reassured that the adults are not overcome by events.

- Attendance at the funeral of a child or staff member should be the choice of the family: the family who have lost someone and who may prefer a private funeral or the families of children who consider attending. Often, it will be more appropriate to organise a memorial service. The people who especially knew the child or teacher who died can be offered the opportunity to share memories – at the service or in a book of condolence.

- As far as possible, maintain the normal routines of your setting – allowing for children or adults who are especially affected by loss. Avoid any sense that there is one single way to express a sense of loss and recognise that some members of a large community, like a school, will not have been familiar with the child or adult who has died. There should be respect for those who are distressed, but grieving cannot become compulsory.

Schools and other settings need to be alert if the circumstances are likely to attract media presence, for instance the death of a pupil on a school trip. It is wise for the head in assembly, or class teachers, to alert children and young people to the situation and help them to be realistic about the risks of being misquoted and misrepresented. Even children can be met by reporters at the school gate or roving on local streets. Children and adolescents may be flattered that somebody with a microphone appears to be interested in them, or they may reply to intrusive questions in order to get the reporter to leave them alone. If children have the chance to talk more privately within your school or club, they are less likely to take a more public opportunity, which they may regret later (or not, of course).

TAKE ANOTHER PERSPECTIVE

Some discussion around this topic suggests that schools should approach some kind of 'death education'. The downside of this idea is that it risks packaging up bereavement as another school subject and therefore the responsibility of teachers. Loss is part of the experience of life and families need to support their children and young people.

- Jane McCarthy and Julie Jessop (2005) sum up well with, 'As a society, we need to understand that bereavement is a general feature of most young people's lives, without necessarily seeing bereavement as an issue for "experts" to deal with' (page 5 in the JRF *Findings* summary).

- Barbara Munroe, the Chief Executive or St Christopher's Hospice, London wrote, 'Grief is not an illness. It is a normal and inevitable part of human existence. All young people will have to find ways to incorporate the experience and its meanings into their lives (Foreword of Rowling, 2003, page v).

Schools and other settings share the responsibility with families to support children and young people. There will inevitably be opportunities that arise naturally – local and national events – to develop their understanding of loss and grief.

Shared issues for children and young people

It is useful to describe and to understand the different kinds of major change for children and young people. However, as I read the background research to support this chapter, it struck me that it was ultimately not helpful to approach support for significant family events as if they are completely different transitions. Some researchers have reached a similar conclusion. Mavis Maclean (2004) summarised from her review that, 'We need to move on from seeing the children of divorced and separated parents as having an experience which is essentially different from that of other children. All children experience a number of transitions that can be difficult for them, and for which they may require additional support' (page 1 of the JRF *Findings*). In terms of what seems to be supportive for children and young people, there is much in common across the different sources of family disruption.

Wanting information, including uncertainties
Children and young people want to know what has happened and not to feel on the outside of an important family event. They certainly do not

want to find out from peers or overheard adult conversations, especially from people who are neither family nor close friends.

- They need information in manageable chunks, often over several conversations that are attuned to their age and likely understanding.
- Children can cope with an honest 'I don't know yet what will happen about . . .' if this uncertainty is grounded in adult reassurance about what will not change. In family breakdown this may be as basic as, 'Your mum and I can't live in the same house together, but we are going to find a way to keep being proper parents to you'.
- Children and young people can be supportive when parents explain the likely consequences of redundancy or a severe downturn in the family business. On the other hand, they feel excluded and aggrieved if they are criticised for expecting outings or purchases to continue, when nobody had talked them through the necessary changes in the family finances.

Children and young people are not helped by adult beliefs – often convenient to those grown-ups – that a child or young person is ignorant of family troubles or would only be upset if they were told.

- Studies of family breakdown, that invite the views of children and young people, continue to show that a proportion are still not given honest information about what has happened and some sense of the future. Without enough information, children and young people are very likely to assume they must have done something to provoke stressed and otherwise unusual behaviour from family adults. There are good reasons why the NCH website for children and young people going through family breakdown is called *It's not your fault*.
- Some parents, or other family members, still choose to keep children in early and middle childhood ignorant of a significant family disruption such as a parent who is in prison. A series of increasingly unlikely reasons are given for a prolonged absence.
- Children and young people need to know about the serious illness, and particularly life-threatening condition, of any close family member. Adults do not always know what will happen when a sibling has bouts of chronic illness or a parent is slow to recover from a serious accident, but they need to share enough information so that sons and daughters feel it is definitely alright to ask, 'Will Mummy ever come home from the special hospital?'

Children are more aware than adults believe

A consistent theme across different studies is that children and young people know more about significant problems in the family, and they are aware at an earlier stage, than their parents usually believe.

- This is true about abuse of drugs and alcohol by parents (see page 320), who frequently believe they have managed to hide the extent of their addiction from younger members of the family.
- Children and young people often recognise that there are troubles between their parents, although they do not always realise that such problems are now beyond repair in the adults' view. So they can still be shocked by an announcement of separation and consequent family breakdown.
- Children and young people, just like adults who have only a partial picture of events, work to fill the gap. Even adolescents can be vulnerable to blaming themselves for events like family breakdown or a mysterious illness in a parent, perhaps because they know they have been less than easy to live with in recent times.

Space to talk and acknowledge feelings

Children and young people want time and the 'permission' to talk, express opinions, concerns and their feelings about major family change and possible upheaval. They may not want to talk when first invited to do so by adults and the time(s) they choose to open up on a sensitive subject may not be the most convenient from the perspective of parents or other trusted adults. Some prefer the anonymity of a telephone helpline, because it feels easier to talk to an unknown yet very supportive stranger – adults also sometimes feel this way. However, some callers to helplines like ChildLine appear to have nobody else with whom they can talk.

Children usually want to talk informally with someone they already know and trust. It is certainly not the case that children and young people should be swiftly passed onto 'experts' who 'will know what to say'. A minority of children and young people who have been severely distressed by unresolved family trauma may want, and need, eventually to talk to a supportive stranger in a counselling or therapeutic situation. The same possibility may apply to children and adolescents who have witnessed, or been directly involved, in a traumatic and violent event.

In terms of bereavement, ChildLine receives telephone calls and letters from some children and young people very soon after their loss, but sometimes not until years later, when an experience has, for some reason, brought the death back into the foreground. This information reminds you that bereavement is a process, like any other significant life transition. The sharpness of the emotions may fade but it is inappropriate, and disrespectful, to imply that children and young people (or adults for that matter) have to 'get over it' in terms of wiping the slate clean. A similar pattern also applies to calls about family breakdown and disruption. Children and young people do not always have that opportunity to talk, either with a person or at a time and place of their own choosing. Many report that they have not talked with anyone about their loss, or the separation of their parents, until this helpline call or until agreeing to participate in this research study.

Children are often overlooked, perhaps because it is more convenient for adults to assume that children 'do not understand', that young adolescents 'will be upset if we talk about it' or that stoic children and young people 'must be over it, because they have said nothing'. Children and young people sometimes keep quiet because they do not want to make matters worse for parents who are already distressed.

- Even 6 and 7 year olds can have an understanding of the strong and mixed emotions of their important adults. They grasp, for instance, that their father or mother is very distressed about the serious illness or death of their own parent. The loss of a loved grandparent also affects children themselves. But the disruption is that much greater if their parent is so overtaken by grief at the loss of their mother or father that daily family life does not get back on track.

- Children and young people are observant and often very concerned for the well-being of loved parents, whom they can see and hear are in emotional pain. Younger family members may draw back from expressing their own distress, anger or anxiety because they are worried about increasing the burden on a parent. A supportive practitioner may receive those confidences and your task is to listen to children or young people who trust you and encourage them not to give up on talking within the family.

- Perhaps a tentative attempt to talk about 'why our baby died' or 'what will happen when Dad comes out of prison' has been met with tears and incoherence from a parent. A child or young person may decide not to raise the subject again. They may then be seen later as 'not really bothered' by a parent or other family member, who could now cope with a conversation about the highly distressing event.

- Children and young adolescents understand that some family information is private, but they need to be supported in working out the nature of those boundaries. Children appreciate that everyone does not need to know that their elder brother is in prison – although in some neighbourhoods this event could bring social kudos rather than criticism. Closed family secrets can be a burden to children when the situation has an impact on daily life.

- Sometimes children will wait to be asked how they feel about an event. A project undertaken by Alexandra Troyna (1998) for the Child Accident Prevention Trust showed that, in accidents, understandably most attention is given to the child who has been directly injured. But friends and siblings are sometimes dealing with hidden and significant distress. They may have witnessed the accident, or just managed to jump back from the speeding car that hit their sister, and nobody seems to consider that they are very upset.

Support from peers

Parents and other family adults have to recognise that older children and young people may need to confide in a close friend, much as adults access this source of support and comfort. Children and young people may find reassurance in peer support groups – face-to-face or online – but they need to be sure that confidences are respected and that an online support chatroom is security-protected by a reliable host website. Older adolescents in further education may have access to peers who have been trained in basic counselling skills. Some sixth form colleges and many universities have a student-run counselling service – many belong to and have committed to the principles of National Nightline (www.nightline.ac.uk).

TRANSITIONS CREATED BY SERVICES

Some significant changes, experienced by most children and young people, are created by how services are organised. Some of the common transitions are created by the framework established for educational, health and social services. In any transition, there needs to be a manageable balance between the following:

- **Continuity:** that some aspects of daily experience remain the same for children and young people. Continuity may be achieved because familiar features of past experience are recognisable in the new setting or circumstances, or because there is stability in the rest of a child's or young person's daily life.
- **Progression:** that children and young people are enabled and helped to move on steadily and to recognise what they manage in their learning, increased maturity and other aspects of this transition.

(With thanks to Sally Featherstone who makes this key distinction in her conference presentations about transition into primary school.)

Older children become more able to cope when caring adults ensure that the experience of change is not too soon, too much or too fast. If it is any of these things, children still learn, but unfortunately they learn that life is unpredictable, important people and places change and adults expect children to tolerate this experience. The flipside to managing change is that healthy emotional development rests on attachment to an inner circle, usually including a child's immediate family and affectionate,

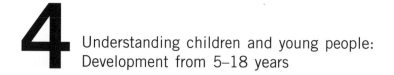

close relationships with friends. Children and young people need some aspects of their life not to change.

Transitions within the school system

Most children and young people receive their statutory education within the state or independent system. They cope with the move into the schooling system and between distinct parts of that system. Some home-educated children and young people enter and leave the schooling system at various points, so their transitions are of a different nature from their peers'.

■ The move into primary school still feels like a big step, even though so many young children have now spent time in some kind of early-years group setting. Hilary Fabian (2002) describes a caring approach to supporting children and their families into the years of formal schooling. The tone of her descriptions is set by the fact that an entire part of the book is called 'Preparing schools for children'.

■ In some areas of the UK, children in the state system have an additional transition between the infant and junior stages of primary school. Not surprisingly, children see this as another change, even if the junior school is on the same site or a very short distance away.

■ At around 11 years of age, children then experience the shift into the secondary part of the schooling system. Post-16, some adolescents

These children have at least two school transitions ahead of them

carry on with their education, either in the sixth form of their school or at a college.

- Children and young people in independent schools experience transitions at slightly different ages, entering the pre-preparatory stage at around 4 years, moving on to their Preparatory school at about 7 years and then to the next school at an age between 11 and 13. The exact age varies for children's move onto an independent senior school.

LOOK, LISTEN, NOTE, LEARN

Children are able to be reflective about their transitions in school. I am grateful to the ideas shared by the 6 and 7 year olds from Crabtree Infants School, who were at the end of their last term in Year 2 in the English system. They were to join the Junior school after the summer holiday. These young children were able to put into words their feelings about this transition and how the teachers had organised visits to help them with the move. These boys and girls highlighted that they had mixed feelings:

- They felt some excitement about moving on to join the older children, but it felt 'a bit weird' because they would be the smallest children again.
- Some children expressed sadness because their sibling would still be in the Infants school. Children also regretted leaving a liked teacher.
- This group, like many other children and young people with whom I talked, focused strongly on the social side of change. It was good to move on with your friends, but sad if they were not joining the same school.

The children all knew that they would be in the other school after the summer and took the trouble to explain the location to me – close but in a different building just up the road. Their current teachers had organised a steady process of familiarisation and the children all understood that their regular visits were to help to get to know the layout of the school and their next teacher, so it would not be all new in the autumn. They spoke with enthusiasm of having gone to see the Juniors' Christmas show and the regular Tuesday visits to do reading with Year 3 children. The two school teams organised several joint events and aimed to extend this initiative.

It seems to be rare now, fortunately, that children or young people are expected to cope with transitions within the schooling system with no support at all. They are clear about what helps.

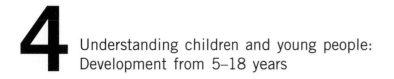

▧ At each stage, children and young people appreciate a chance to visit the next setting more than once, so that they become more familiar with the layout. Open evenings to meet their teacher are useful but it is even better if they can experience several visits, including feeling involved in some kind of activity at what will be their next school.

▧ The first days and weeks are that much easier when children or young people have already met their next teacher, who has ideally visited them in their current school as well as welcoming them to the new setting.

▧ A consistent theme for children and young people is the importance of friends: that any move is so much easier if you go with people you already know and that school life is much tougher if you find yourself without friends. The presence of siblings can be a help, or familiar faces among their friends, but children are clear that some older siblings are more trouble than support.

▧ A series of pre-visits, even one, is not always possible under some circumstances: when there is a delay in knowing which school the child will move to or for those children whose families relocate between the main school transitions. Children and young people were very clear that under these circumstances what they really need is friendly faces: that somebody takes the trouble to link them up with a buddy for support.

▧ Adjustment continues over the early weeks in a new setting. Children and young people are very clear that the process of transition stretches until they feel at ease in the new setting. The difference can be especially stark when they move into secondary school.

TAKE ANOTHER PERSPECTIVE

For various reasons, some children join a school later than their peers. Even children at the younger end of middle childhood appreciate that this situation can be difficult, because everyone else has already made friends. The groups of 6 and 7 year olds at Crabtree Infants School were very clear that what a 'new' child most needed was company. They homed in on how important it was to have a friend. If you did not already know someone at your new school, you really wanted another child to be nice to you and to help you in the early days. These young children explained the same priority that I heard from older children and from young people about the transition into secondary school. Life can be very lonely if you do not have friends.

Life at secondary school

The impression now is that many schools invite students who are in the first year of secondary school to visit pupils in the last year of primary. Adolescents from a range of school years are also sometimes welcomed to take on the role of buddy or mentor to individuals or are assigned to classes. When this system works well, the younger students are pleased to have friendly contact with the literally 'big' boys or girls.

Adolescents who have made the transition into secondary school are a source of practical and sensitive advice to younger boys and girls. I have asked many 12–15 year olds what advice they would offer to children about to make the move. They make the following points:

- You will be very tired: students at secondary school usually have more to carry in their bag and a normal day involves more movement around the school building than is usual for primary school.
- Be prepared for everything to look big. A frequent comment was that new students will almost certainly get lost in the new building and not to worry. Secondary schools are usually larger than primary schools, but some young people recalled that there were more students in their first secondary school year than there had been in their entire primary school.
- Even if a school does not include a sixth form, the older students look and are much larger. In a calm school atmosphere they are not intimidating, but 11 year olds can still feel uneasy.
- Young people talk sensitively about the reality that over the summer you go from being the eldest in your primary school, with the status earned over the years, to being the youngest and back at the bottom of the status pile. This shift in status is worsened if older students are allowed to harass younger ones. But even in a well-managed secondary school, this starting-over experience should not be under-estimated.
- It really helps to have practised anything you now need to know or be able to do. Examples included being confident about using public transport or knowing your landmarks on the walk to school. Secondary school may bring the first school uniform, or may have a more formal code of dress than a primary school. It is better to practise anything fiddly, like a tie, before you have to do it at speed, when changing for PE.
- It is really useful if you move on with friends, but that does not work out for everyone. Be ready to put yourself out to talk and show an interest in other people. New social groups will form and it takes a while for the social networks to settle into place.

113

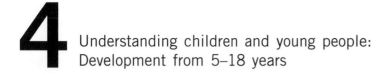

■ Overall the message is that the shift to secondary school is a big move but do not let people worry you unnecessarily – some older siblings and their friends appeared to enjoy telling horror stories.

LOOK, LISTEN, NOTE, LEARN

The views of children and young people summarised in this section are from individuals who are either still in the school system or who are within the early years of adulthood.

■ How far do the main points fit with your own memory of school transitions?

■ If possible, gather a range of accounts, including memories from people whose transitions were pre-1980s.

Young people emerge from their secondary school and the years of statutory education into early adulthood. Issues around routes for the transition into adulthood are discussed from page 280.

If you want to know more

✢ **Action for Prisoners' Families** Tel: 020 8812 3600. Unit 21, Carlson Court, 116 Putney bridge Road, London, SW15 2NQ; www.prisonersfamilies.org.uk. The national federation of services supporting families of prisoners – a wide range of materials for adults, including story books to use with children and advice for practitioners.

✢ **Bailey, Shaun** (2005) *No man's land: how Britain's inner city youth are being failed.* Centre for Young Policy Studies; www.cps.org.uk.

✢ **Bayley, Ros** and **Featherstone, Sally** (2003) *Smooth transitions: building on the Foundation Stage.* Husbands Bosworth: Featherstone Education.

✢ **Brookner, Liz** (2002) *Starting school – young children learning cultures.* Buckingham: Open University Press.

✢ **Brown, Kelli** (2001) *No-one's ever asked me – young people with a prisoner in the family.* Action for Prisoners' Families Young People's Project. Summary at www.prisonersfamilies.org.uk.

✢ **ChildLine** *Bereavement Information Sheet* and *Unhappy families: unhappy children – a ChildLine Study* (undated, published approx. 1998); www.childline.org.uk.

‡ **Child Bereavement Network,** information and directory of relevant services; www.ncb.org.uk/cbn

‡ **Cruse Bereavement Care,** 126 Sheen Road, Richmond, Surrey, TW9 1UR; Tel: general 020 8940 4818, helpline 0870 167 1677; www.crusebereavementcare.org.uk.

‡ **Dunn, Judy** and **Deater-Deckard, Kirby** (2001) *Children's views of their changing families.* York: York Publishing Services. Available for download at www.jrf.org.uk/knowledge/findings/socialpolicy/931.asp.

‡ **Fabian, Hilary** (2002) *Children starting school: a guide to successful transitions and transfers for teachers and assistants.* London: David Fulton.

‡ **Holliday, Jennifer** (2002) *A review of sibling bereavement – impact and intervention.* Report for Barnardo's. Summary available at www.barnardos.org.uk/resources.

‡ **Kidscape** *Moving up: going to Secondary School. Information for children.* See www.kidscape.org.uk.

‡ **Lindon, Jennie** and **Lindon, Lance** (1994) *Help your child through school: a parents' handbook.* London: Headway/Hodder and Stoughton.

‡ **Lindon, Jennie** and **Lindon, Lance** (2000) *Mastering counselling skills: information, help and advice in the caring services.* Basingstoke: Macmillan Press.

‡ **McCarthy, Jane Ribbens** with **Jessop, Julie** (2005) *Young people, bereavement and loss: disruptive transitions.* London: National Children's Bureau/Joseph Rowntree Foundation. Summary as a JRF *Findings* at www.jrf.org.uk/knowledge/findings/socialpolicy/0315.asp.

‡ **Maclean, Mavis** (2004) *Together and apart: children and parents experiencing separation and divorce.* See www.jrf.org.uk/knowledge/findings/foundations/314.asp.

‡ **National Children's Bureau** resources at www.ncb.org.uk. Using the keywords 'Asylum Seekers' and 'Refugees' takes you to a resource of discussion papers and useful organisations.

‡ **NCH** website for children and young people about family breakdown. See www.itsnotyourfault.org.

‡ **Parentline Plus** specialises in support for parents and families. Helpline 0808 800 2222. Information on www.parentlineplus.org.uk.

❖ **Pearson, Marian** (2004) *A welcoming visit – the Humber prison play project*. Children First (special issue) Pre-school Learning Alliance.

❖ **Parliament's Defence Select Committee** (2006) *Educating service children*. HC1054 (www.publications.parliament.uk/pa/cm/cmdfence.htm).

❖ **Rowling, Louise** (2003) *Grief in school communities: effective support strategies*. Buckingham: Open University Press.

❖ **Save the Children** resources about refugee children on www.savethechildren.org.uk.

❖ **Smith, Susan** (1999) *The forgotten mourners: guidelines for working with bereaved children*. London: Jessica Kingsley.

❖ **Troyna, Alexandra** (1998) *Providing emotional support to children and their families after an accident – Guidelines to professionals*. Child Accident Prevention Trust. Also other leaflets around the same topic at www.capt.org.uk.

❖ **Wade, Amanda** and **Smart, Carol** (2002*) Facing family change: children's circumstances, strategies and resources*. York: York Publishing Services. Available for download from www.jrf.org.uk/knowledge/findings/socialpolicy/772.asp.

❖ **Young Voice** (2004) *Tales of transition* (video and resource). Also edited by Adrienne Katz: the series *Parenting under pressure* (bereavement and parents in prison). East Molesey: Young Voice. See www.young-voice.org.

5 Moral development and pro-social behaviour

The behaviour of children and young people is part of a pattern of holistic development: actions are interlinked with feelings and thoughts. Children and young people learn patterns of behaviour. Their temperament acts as a filter on experience but nevertheless a very great deal depends on the sense they make of events and relationships during their childhood and adolescence. Practitioners in all the different services share a serious responsibility, along with families, of guiding children and young people towards positive and pro-social patterns of behaviour. That responsibility involves an awareness of your own adult behaviour: choices and consequences.

> **The main sections of this chapter are:**
>
> ✶ **Moral values, reasoning and actions.**
>
> ✶ **Encouraging pro-social behaviour.**
>
> ✶ **Helping children guide their own behaviour.**

MORAL VALUES, REASONING AND ACTIONS

Children of 5 and 6 years of age are already busy observers. They watch, listen and think, as well as act. They are ready to highlight adult inconsistency with, 'But you said . . .!' or 'But Jo lets us . . .'. Children and later young people have a strong sense of natural justice. Their first philosophical concept is possibly that of fairness, although it tends to be grasped first in the negative, as with, 'That is so unfair!'

MAKE THE CONNECTION WITH . . . LEARNING OVER TIME

You may have encountered the story poem that includes lines such as:

- If children live with criticism, they learn to condemn.
- If children live with hostility, they learn to fight.

And with plenty of positive lines too, like:

- If children live with encouragement, they learn confidence.
- If children live with recognition, they learn it is good to have a goal.

The full poem was written by Dorothy Law Nolte, who was a family counsellor and writer living in the USA. You can download the full version of the poem or the shortened version, for which Dorothy Law Nolte gave permission, on www.EmpowermentResources.com. There is a version for adolescence in Nolte and Harris (2002).

Understanding right: doing right

In terms of moral development, children move steadily forward in their ability to understand everyday moral issues. The main aspects to their learning are:

■ *Moral values*: values determine what is important, since they are key concepts that guide choices. Values also underpin ground rules – to indicate that 'it is important here that we . . .'. Values may be linked to reasons – 'why it is important that we . . .' or simply that 'this is the right way to behave'.

■ *Moral reasoning and judgements*: the thinking that lies behind why one course of action is preferable to another and in some circumstances how there may be a conflict in working out the better choice.

■ *Moral behaviour*: the choices that are made over actions – what people actually do, faced with a situation that requires a decision. Some choices, made in line with one person's values, may be judged immoral and wrong by someone else.

Younger children are guided by the moral judgements of key, familiar adults. Slightly older children may still take a simple line that something is 'good' or 'bad', 'right' or 'wrong' and may even echo the adult's favourite phrases, such as 'You must share' or 'Life isn't fair'. Children of 5 and 6 years old can understand a little of what lies underneath moral choices in behaviour. They will not grasp complex or lengthy reasons, but they often accept that life in a group, or the family, is much happier with some give-and-take. But children notice adult choices and are deeply unimpressed if some of their peers are allowed to get away with more take than give.

Habits of behaviour

Children's understanding builds from early experience in their family life and non-family early-years provision. Children at age 5–6 assume that the rest of the social world operates in much the same way as their familiar world.

■ Children, who have learned to talk through problem situations in their family or nursery, can be stunned to encounter peers in primary school for whom hitting is the first choice of action in any conflict.

■ Likewise, children whose family rule is 'hit them back', are surprised to be told in school or club that hitting is not acceptable as a way to solve conflict.

■ Children, who have already learned a habit of behaviour that 'I pick up what I drop', stare with surprise at peers who drop litter or leave resources in a mess that someone else has to tidy.

A great deal depends on the reaction of the adults in control of children's days.

It is useful to think of these patterns as habits of behaviour – established to some extent but still open to change. Practitioners need to reflect on what encourages habits you regard as positive, just as much as on the support for habits you would like to shift. Children and young people make moral choices about their own behaviour and a strand in supporting them is to talk in calmer moments about choices. Older children are increasingly able to talk through 'what else could you have done when ...?' and 'so, what will you do when ... happens in the future?' Helpful talking depends upon clear, shared values and ground rules if a school or club is to operate like a community. Conversations with individual children, with groups and within a proper exchange in a school council, all rest upon a clear agreement about 'what we do here if ...'. Childminders follow a similar approach in their own home. Genuinely helpful adults also realise that there may still be a gap between knowing and wanting to make the right choice and actually making it. Effective support with children and young people who struggle has to explore some strategies for what will help tip them towards doing the right thing.

Actions and intentions

Children and young people also make moral judgements about the actions of other people: their peers and adults. In middle childhood, their attention still tends to be held by the visible consequences of actions, although they begin to allow for invisible intentions. It is important to recall that adolescents, and even adults, still struggle sometimes to get past the fact that they have been hurt, physically or emotionally, to the possibility that the hurt was not intended. Older children become more able to allow for mistakes and unforeseen consequences. So long as similar actions are not blithely repeated, children may accept that their peers were carried away by the emotion of the moment and are now genuinely sorry.

Habits of courtesy

Behaviour, that may also be called 'good manners', is best established by making clear what counts for courtesy in your setting or home, and setting a consistent adult example of what 'courteous' looks like in practice. A great deal of this kind of behaviour connects with a ground rule of consideration for others and a practical value of treating other people how you yourself would like to be treated. These two ideas have to be supported by a developing sense of emotional literacy and emotional security (see page 58).

LOOK, LISTEN, NOTE, LEARN

A positive approach to guiding the behaviour of children and young people must always include adults' awareness of their own behaviour and the consequences of their choices. For example:

- The level of damage to people or property is not a good measure of malicious intent. But adults do not always set a good example to enable children to understand the need to distinguish the level of mess from whether somebody made a genuine mistake.

- Even the best behaved children and young people will not manage to be 'good' all the time. It is unfair if a child or adolescent cannot push the boundaries occasionally without being told they have disappointed the adult, 'because you are always such a helpful/sensible child'.

What do you think?

- Do you have memories from your own childhood to add insight? Were you perhaps a 'good' girl or boy?

- Can you reflect on recent incidents in your own adult practice where you, or a colleague, were perhaps too influenced by picking up the pieces to explore genuine intentions.

- In a friendly emotional atmosphere it is possible to discuss possibilities: how might you greet somebody else when they arrive, what does it feel like if you arrive at club or in the class and nobody seems to have noticed that you are present? In my experience, even 4 and 5 year olds can have learned confidence and courtesy towards visitors (like myself) in their setting.

- Is courteous behaviour from children different depending on whether they are communicating with a grown-up or a peer? Adults, who are attentive to words and body language, find out that some children try to follow rules of courtesy set by their family, for instance, that it is impolite to call adults by their first name.

- Courtesy around snack and meal time – table manners if you like – can be established with children in ways that show respect for different patterns of family eating. Adults sometimes need to resolve, away from the children, any inconsistencies that arise from their own background. Within the same team, some adults may have been raised with not talking at the meal table, some with social mealtimes and others with a limited experience of family meals at all. A team can agree on the basics like hand-washing, making space for everyone to be able to eat in comfort and what you do with food on your plate that you do not want.

A related issue about courtesy and food is that of sharing and hospitality. Children and young people can learn that the few remaining items on a plate are not simply grabbed – other people might want some. I have observed this aspect of consideration for others shown clearly by children younger than 5 years, who have been able to discuss with a familiar adult how to share out the rest of the fruit.

Older children and adolescents notice the differences that result from earlier experience. I have heard adolescents express surprise that a peer could eat an entire packet of sweets in front of them and not offer even one. Young people notice that what seems obvious to them – you offer the packet to your friends – is not a habit established with everyone.

The issue of hospitality was raised by some young people who described to me their experience of university. Some had been struck that their family habits – you offer a hot drink, snack or even make the evening meal stretch for unexpected friends – were clearly not shared by everyone, even friends who were otherwise good company.

MAKE THE CONNECTION WITH ... YOUR OWN HABITS OF BEHAVIOUR

My personal example is that I am effectively incapable of dropping litter. My mother had strong values that litter spoiled nice areas like the beach and it was not alright to expect somebody else to pick up your rubbish. I was encouraged to use bins and we carried our litter home if necessary. As an adolescent, I agreed with the reasoning and later behaved in the same way with my children.

But in no way can this family history be shifted to say, 'By 7–8 years of age, children will have learned not to drop litter'. Adult behaviour helps to build this habit for children. In schools, for instance, it is more effective to tackle litter as a shared responsibility, so that everyone has an enjoyable environment. One suggestion is to make litter patrol in the school grounds a privilege for children and young adolescents, who can be trusted, and not use the activity as a punishment. Special equipment helps, such as fancy litter pick-up prongs, black bin bags and proper gloves. If the school cook's best shortbread biscuits are also on offer for the patrol, so much the better!

■ Reflect on any of your own habits of what you feel to be courteous or thoughtful behaviour and consider sharing experiences with fellow students or colleagues.

■ How do you think these habits were established for you over childhood? Who influences you towards this behaviour and how did they encourage you?

Relationships with adults

Adult communication skills and positive attitudes underlie a wise approach to guiding the behaviour of children and adolescents. There are particular issues around different adult roles, for instance, parents should be emotionally involved with their children and adolescents. Parenting rests upon a different kind of relationship from the friendly commitment that needs to be felt by school staff or playworkers. Teachers need specific advice appropriate to dealing with large groups, because classroom management requires some different skills. Nevertheless, there is a great deal of common ground between the different adults involved in the lives of children and adolescents. Practitioners can learn from the useful advice offered in books and websites aimed at parents (see the suggestions on page 144). Foster and residential carers need to create a role that integrates genuine parenting.

Communication and boundaries

Children and adolescents need to feel that their parents are allies and not enemies. But a similar sense of working together is necessary in relationships between teachers and children or youth workers and adolescents. Part of a normal relationship is that sometimes older children and adolescents kick against a secure base, just to be sure that it is emotionally safe.

- Practitioners as well as parents can have difficulty in adjusting to girls and boys as they turn into adolescents. Adults know logically that a different approach is needed because these individuals are clearly no longer 'little children'. But teachers and other practitioners who know the boys and girls over this period of time can struggle to find an appropriate balance, especially since young adolescents themselves seem to change at random between wanting to be cosseted and rejecting this attention.

- Children and adolescents need to know that adults will be the grown-up, which means keeping to boundaries and agreed consequences, however hard a child or adolescent pushes to the limits. Wise adult behaviour is flexible and boundaries and rules need re-negotiation with adolescents.

- The few clubs and playschemes that are able to offer facilities for over 12–14s find that adolescents want an agreed framework that looks different from the club agreement with the under-12s. Leisure facilities for 14–17s need to reach a different agreement again. There are still boundaries but they reflect a relationship between young people and the older adults.

Older children and adolescents want time, attention and feelings of being connected with parents, but also with important and familiar non-family adults. They want a relationship, and practitioners resolve a lot of issues around behaviour through talking, listening and negotiation. A positive consequence is also that children and adolescents are far more likely to confide in adults about serious issues when there has been a backdrop of ordinary exchanges. Parents, foster and residential carers deal with the reality that older children and adolescents have a life that is partly separate. Some helpful conversations are about situations, in school for instance, that children face without their parent or primary carer. Children and adolescents want to feel confident that parents or carers will stand by them but that any direct intervention will be careful and will not cause more harm than benefit.

Life in 'ordinary' families

Much of the research literature about parents' keeping track of their children and adolescents is focused on troubled families and parents who fail to supervise their offspring. An understanding of what happens in 'ordinary families' is drawn from anecdotal evidence or assuming that parents follow practical advice in parenting books. In contrast, Stephanie Stace and Debi Roker (2005) explored the views of 11–16 year olds in families that were not troubled, nor under the eye of social care services. This study highlighted how the parents and adolescents exchanged information and the ways in which parents exercised their role of supervision over these years.

- Older children and adolescents were active within their own family over decisions for what they could do, when and unaccompanied by adults. It was normal that some of these discussions became argumentative.
- Monitoring by parents, about use of the internet as much as going out with friends, happened through family conversation, parents' setting boundaries and re-negotiation of rules as the years passed. Adolescents increasingly took over responsibility for decisions like what time to settle to sleep.
- Adolescents generally accepted the right of parents to ask about their movements outside the home. They were ready to volunteer information about where they were going and with whom. They respected their parents' right to ask, because they cared and worried about their offspring. Other adult family members were sometimes involved in this supervision.
- It was also normal in these 'ordinary families' that adolescents did not tell their parents everything. The young people did not necessarily lie, but they sometimes withheld information and their parents were aware that they did not hear every detail.

123

■ The process of keeping children safe took time and attention from parents and a willingness to let go steadily over adolescence. Parents had authority but were aware that they had to exercise that responsibility in different ways as time passed.

Practitioners, within school and after-school clubs, pick up the pieces when some children within a group have not been enabled to learn the give-and-take that is crucial for happy group life. Carole Sutton et al. (2006) describe the pattern that can set in by middle childhood when children have experienced the unsettling combination of experiences like harsh parenting, physical punishment, lax supervision and inconsistent discipline. However, it does not help anyone when children are indulged without limits.

Maggie Mamen (2006) described what she called the 'pampered child syndrome', created when parents have been reluctant to establish and hold to boundaries for their children's behaviour. Mamen acknowledges that her ideas have roots in the ideas of Alfred Adler, writing in the 1930s about the problems arising from what he called 'the pampered child'. Some parents seem unwilling to commit to the effort and patience required to guide children's behaviour. Others appeared to have followed one strand of parenting advice that claims saying 'No' (even only occasionally and for good reason) will permanently damage children's self-esteem. Unfortunately, the end result of such a pattern is a miserable family life. Children are a trouble to themselves, their peers and other adults, because they have no grasp that their immediate wishes and demands should not be met. Mamen suggests that parents who are unable or who will not behave as grown-ups, create behaviour from their children that mimics conditions like ADHD and minor levels of emotional and learning disabilities.

ENCOURAGING PRO-SOCIAL BEHAVIOUR

Much of the positive behaviour that practitioners want from children and young people falls within a general grouping of pro-social behaviour. Adults make requests that children 'take turns' with favourite equipment, 'think how somebody else feels', 'be helpful to other people' and just generally 'be nice to each other'. However, experience can have led older children and young people into learned patterns of antisocial behaviour – a phrase that I do not think should be applied until children have the capacity to think about the likely consequences of their actions.

Feeling kindly: kind behaviour

Children and young people are aware that other people have feelings, and choices arise from this awareness. The phrase 'pro-social behaviour' involves children's feelings and thoughts as well as their actions.

Friends will help each other

- A pro-social orientation arises when children have begun to learn empathy (the ability and willingness to tune into the feelings of others) and altruism (acting with a concern for the well-being of others). This outlook could be summed up as children learning to be kind to each other, to behave in a way that takes care of other people's feelings and concerns.

- Children have the capability to be caring. Young children can, and do, develop pro-social behaviour as a result of their early experiences, but it is not an inevitable step in the development of all children.

WHAT DOES IT MEAN?

- **Empathy**: the ability and willingness to tune into the feelings of other people, whether they are peers or of a different age.
- **Altruism**: acting with a selfless concern for the well-being of others, putting the concerns of somebody else before one's own wishes and preferences.
- **Pro-social behaviour**: patterns of actions that are voluntarily chosen, when the intention is to care for or benefit someone else.
- **Antisocial behaviour**: patterns of actions that harm, or could potentially harm others, and either the direct motivation is to cause distress or there is a lack of concern about negative consequences.

It is unrealistic to expect children and young people, or adults for that matter, to be kind all day long or always to put other people before themselves. Yet that statement is itself a statement of values – my own values. I do not think it is fair to ask this standard of anyone; everyone has the right sometimes to put their own needs and concerns at the top of the list.

TAKE ANOTHER PERSPECTIVE

I sometimes encounter firm statements in books such as, '5 year olds instinctively help other children when they are distressed', but instincts are inborn, automatic reactions; they are not learned habits. If helping upset peers were instinctive, then every child or young person would act in that way – clearly not true. Some children do move, without prompting, to help other children who appear sad or lonely. But some find the plight of another child amusing, or even act deliberately to create distress.

The words 'instinct' or 'instinctively' are now regularly used to stand in for more accurate phrases such as, 'without thinking much about it'. Careless use of these terms skates over the adult responsibility to create an environment in which children make the choice to support each other – all the ideas covered in this section. So use of language matters; I do not believe I am simply a nerd obsessed with definitions!

Children of 5–6 years old who show pro-social behaviour have almost certainly started at a younger age (see Lindon, 2005). The circumstances that provide fertile ground for developing pro-social behaviour in early childhood need to be continued into middle childhood and adolescence. Alternatively, you need to establish such an atmosphere if it is a novel experience for some children. The following factors are the most helpful and they all depend on adults' awareness of their own behaviour and putting their aims into daily practice.

- Create an emotionally warm environment in which children and young people feel they can get attention for themselves in positive ways. When they have to fight for the attention and approval of adults, children and adolescents have little emotional energy left to give to their peers. Nor are they motivated to consider the feelings and perspective of other people.
- Children who feel confident that their needs will be met are likely to be emotionally generous to others. It is important that class teachers

form a personal relationship with children. However, support and playground staff can be important adults for children, so these practitioners need to be valued as full members of the school staff team. There should be a home-like, friendly atmosphere in all after-school clubs.

- Create opportunities for children to do helpful things and take responsibility for care of equipment and the well-being of their peers. It is important to recognise helpful or considerate behaviour, close to the time, with words of encouragement that focus on what the child has done.

Marjorie Boxall (2002) observed that some children failed to cope with daily primary school life because of their early experiences. Within their early childhood, these children had not built up experiences that adult behaviour and daily routines were reasonably pleasant and predictable. The children were unable to manage in the large groups that are part of ordinary school organisation. They dealt with their confusion and distress through behaving in ways that disrupted the group and swiftly got them labelled as 'problem children'. Marjorie Boxall developed the concept of the nurture group to create a safe experience for children until they were able to guide their own behaviour and make pro-social choices.

Kindness as a moral value

Sometimes it is necessary for practitioners and teams to home in on a key value and work out what then evolves from that focus. For example:

- In my conversations with under 7s in Crabtree Infants School, these (still young) children were able to describe what they felt would support a child who came to their school after most children had settled in. They described that children would need to learn the school rules and know what happened if they did something wrong. But the entire tone of discussions was that of fair consequences, rather than punitive adult reactions. One child spoke up, and his peers nodded in agreement, that the 'new' child would be happy, 'because this is a kind school'.
- Hampstead Comprehensive School in North London appears as a case study in the *Bright Futures* report (1999) from the Mental Health Foundation. At that point the school team was working on a range of strategies from the single basic rule 'to be kind to each other'. Other initiatives, such as the tutors system, were linked back to this basic value in action. Strategies about behaviour evolved from the core value: student involvement in the school; an anti-bulling initiative; easing transition from primary school; creating a safe haven within an extended school day; and identification of students unable to cope without extra help.

Emotional awareness and choosing to hurt

Knowledge and understanding of emotions can work in either direction: to motivate a wish to be kind or to inform well-pitched intentions to be cruel. One way of looking at the problem of bullying between children and young people (probably between adults too) is to observe how children's knowledge of each other is used to guide choices over who to target and how. Bullying is a type of aggressive behaviour and children and young people can be seriously distressed by such treatment (see also Lindon, 2003 and Elliott, 2002).

Attacks or threats do not have to be physical in order to disrupt normal life. Children or young people can be very affected by persistent, verbal harassment: words intended to upset and ridicule. This kind of bullying may now use technological means, such as sending threatening text or voice messages to someone's mobile phone, or posting offensive remarks about someone on a website chatroom or blog (see page 296). Called cyber bullying, this form of personal attack also includes use of visuals, when photos are taken on a mobile phone, of peers (or adults, like teachers) while they have been harassed or under attack. The distressing images are then spread around by mobile phone messaging.

LOOK, LISTEN, NOTE, LEARN

Advice for children and young people has caught up with the technological approach to bullying. Readers can explore the ways that some children and young people cause trouble for their peers and the practical suggestions that can help. Access these resources:

- *An investigation into cyberbullying* written by Peter Smith and his team in 2005 for the Anti-Bullying Alliance. Summary and full report on www.anti-bullyingalliance.org.uk.

- The DfES guidelines on *Tackling cyberbullying* that can be accessed via www.young-voice.org/ through 'Links'.

Look for ways that discuss some of the issues, and advice, with older children or adolescents.

It is crucial that adults take bullying seriously, but do not abandon their skills of listening and problem-solving (see page 142) as soon as behaviour is labelled as bullying. The positive message that adults should never behave like uninterested bystanders needs to be seasoned with a sense of proportion. A heavily punitive approach, alongside some interpretations of 'zero tolerance', creates more problems than it solves.

For instance, the requirement to record and investigate certain types of bullying – such as behaviour alleged to be racist – must not become a substitute for action that will help children and young people. Children cause unhappiness and unpleasantness to each other for all kinds of reasons and not all distress has been motivated by a desire to bully.

TAKE ANOTHER PERSPECTIVE

Tim Gill (writing in *Nursery World*, 30 November 2006, page 31) made the important point that a high profile for anti-bullying initiatives can risk blurring 'the vital distinction between the troublesome and the trivial'.

He suggested that the word 'bullying' needs to be kept for describing behaviour that is persistent, systematic and intends to be cruel in some way. It is not helpful for children if they are encouraged to label minor and temporary unpleasantness as 'bullying'. This pattern also tempts adults to believe that they should intervene swiftly over minor altercations that children could, and need, to feel confident to deal with themselves. I agree with Tim Gill's views and with his concern that children need the chance to, 'sort out their differences for themselves, even if they sometimes fail and we have to pick up the pieces', otherwise they will not learn ordinary resilience.

Barbara Coloroso (2005) makes a distinction between teasing and taunting and describes bullying as a pattern of behaviour underpinned with contempt for the child or adolescent on the receiving end. Teasing another child can be friendly, but it may cross the line into unkindness. The difference is whether peers stop when a child or adolescent lets them know that they do not like this teasing. (They may need adult help with a phrase like, 'I don't like you saying that. Don't call me … any more'.) An insistence on continuing then crosses the line into cruelty – as one distressed 8 year old said to me, 'They know it upsets me and they don't care'.

■ I think that practitioners need to reflect on what behaviour can genuinely be called 'bullying' and the implications for different kinds of helpful adult intervention. What do you think?

From possible reasons to effective actions

There are different reasons underlying bullying, and adults who genuinely want to help need to keep an open mind about what is happening and why. Reasons are not excuses for unacceptable behaviour, but a better grasp of what is probably going on in the mind of a child or young person who moves into bullying can direct adults towards more effective help.

Children and young people who bully are not all 'thugs', although some individuals gain great satisfaction and feelings of status through intimidating others. Children who bully do not all experience low self-esteem, nor are they are all disadvantaged by circumstances. In fact, as Michelle Elliott has pointed out, some children are the original 'spoiled brats', indulged by their family, who have no conception that they should limit their demands. However, some children or young people who cause serious problems for their peers have a negative self-image and minimal confidence, despite the appearance of being strong.

The dynamics of bullying vary but the basic pattern requires three types of role: people who do the bullying, those on the receiving end and those who are the 'bystanders'. The same children and adolescents may take on more than one role at different times. Genuinely helpful practitioners in school or clubs need to become aware of the patterns in their setting. For instance, it can be difficult for children to leave a group that intimidates others. They will have to find new friends if they want to opt out of the bullying. Reluctant bullies may also fear, rather like bystander children who choose to do nothing, that they will become the new target.

The more effective long-term approaches to bullying do not leave all the responsibility with adults, although they definitely need to be effective leaders. It is essential to avoid adult behaviour that is bullying in its turn. There are, for instance, serious consequences for the atmosphere of a school or club when practitioners fail to resolve the fallout from what are later revealed to be false accusations of bullying.

- As reviews like that of Christine Oliver and Mano Candappa (2003) show, children and young people are usually the experts on times and places when they can be especially vulnerable to ill treatment from peers and they need adults to take effective action on this information. They are also the first point of call in evaluating whether anti-bullying initiatives actually work.

- Peer-group pressure can be mobilised by careful use of discussion in school councils, other kinds of problem-solving meetings in schools and group meetings in after-school clubs and residential homes. Guided group discussion, led by older children as well as adults, can highlight the feelings of the bullied child or young person in a way that the children who are tempted to bully will find harder to ignore.

■ Children or young people, in a variety of group settings, can be active alongside the adults in setting clear expectations for children who need to mend their ways. Group meetings, as well personal communication from adults, needs to be supportive when a child or young person, who previously bullied others, has made changes in how they behave.

Sandra Fowler (2004) shows that different types of peer-support initiatives can support action against bullying because they mobilise and encourage children's own skills. Children and young people can be effective in moving their peers towards taking responsibility for the consequences of unkind or cruel actions. Supportive adults take the situation seriously but create an atmosphere in which everyone gets beyond the label of 'bully' and homes in on the results of the behaviour. Peer-group pressure can also help to bring home the separate responsibility of every member of a group that bullies.

Children and young people who are being bullied need a sense of reassurance that adults in whom they confide will take them seriously and help them resolve the situation and not make it worse. Some individuals need support for ways that they can protect themselves, not least by reducing the satisfaction to peers who want to hurt them. This help is not the same as the ineffectual adult advice to 'ignore them and they'll stop'. A particular kind of 'ignoring' is needed that combines assertive body language, some sharp repartee and the help of friends if at all possible. Children need to find ways to hide their hurt from peers who get satisfaction from distressing others.

HELPING CHILDREN GUIDE THEIR OWN BEHAVIOUR

In the long term, children and adolescents need to be able to guide their own behaviour. They will not have adults looking over their shoulder forever. Young people will make their own choices about whether to do the right thing and the nature of that choice in any social situation.

Consistency from adults

As well as personal identity, the social and cultural context shapes children's views of what is 'normal' behaviour. The UK as a whole is a very diverse society and some neighbourhoods are striking in the level of diversity by ethnic group, cultural background and faith. However, there is always a great deal of variation within as well as between groups, in whatever way you create the divisions. Any practitioners working with children and young people need to be aware of the possible differences in values between school or club and home. But often you will have a lot of ground in common.

Children and young people learn to deal with different sets of rules in varied circumstances. Practitioners need to recognise differences and create an atmosphere in which it is easy for children to say, 'Well my Mum says I should . . .' or, 'In my other club, they told me to . . .'. Practitioners can show respect for parents' right to determine how they run family life and that not all clubs, or schools, run in exactly the same way. However, practitioners in school, playwork or youth work are responsible for being clear about 'what happens here'. The clear message needs to be that whatever a child's father says about hitting back, 'In club we sort out our problems with our words and not our fists'.

- I have encountered after-school clubs and playschemes that have successfully stepped aside from local norms for behaviour and simply said firmly 'not here'. For instance, older children and young people have accepted that language – swearing or racist phrases – that is common out on the street is unacceptable inside club and that persistent breaking of this ground rule will lead to loss of club membership.

- It is the primary responsibility of adults to ensure that children and young people do not have to deal with inconsistencies within a family, school or club. Some children and young people will happily exploit the gap when they are given a different key message from different adults in the same place. But not all children want to play one adult off against another: some are distressed by the anxiety created when life is too unpredictable.

- Children and young people object when adults within the same school, club or other context fail to behave in line with the official rules and underlying values. I have listened over the years to some very annoyed, and cynical, children and adolescents who were scathing about staff who behaved as if rules did not apply to them. These adults had lost their respect and considerable effort would have been necessary to earn it again. The current generation is no more impressed than previous ones with an adult strategy of 'never mind what I do, just get on with what I say you have to do!'

This age group apply their impressive thinking and communication skills to an analysis of whether 'life is fair around here'. Adults need to appreciate that several careful conversations may be needed to unpack some complaints about inconsistency, as perceived by children or adolescents. For instance, they can appreciate the impact of special needs on how peers are treated. However, I recall one lively group of 11 and 12 year olds who needed much more explanation than they were getting about the special treatment and facilities that appeared to them to be available for profoundly disabled peers in their school. A good starting point was their annoyance at the cavalier driving style of a couple of young male adolescents in their high-tech wheelchairs.

Workable rules that guide

If early experience has provided some consistency, then 5–7 year olds can have a sound basic idea of how rules for behaviour can work. They may well agree that rules are a good idea, for the benefit of everyone, and that it should be clear what happens if anyone breaks those rules. Many 5–11s, in primary school and out-of-school provision, are capable of talking through a specific situation that might need either another rule, or a clear application of one of the existing ground rules. These supported discussions happen in class groups, within school councils and in group meetings in after-school clubs. Even children and young people who have had very disrupted lives, respond well to guided discussion within the group meetings that are part of good practice in residential children's homes.

There is a place for basic ground rules in any setting and they are best started with 'we . . .' because this gives the public message that the ground rules apply to everyone within the school community or club, including visitors. Ground rules need to be phrased in a positive direction. A list of club rules dominated by 'Don't shout', 'No swearing' or 'No hitting here' are only half the message and a rather negative one as well. Written and stuck to the wall, the list looks daunting: a kind of laminated adult finger-wagging. At some point an alert child or adolescent will also identify what is not on the list, behave in that way and try for the justification that, 'but you didn't say not to . . .'.

It is equally relevant that the 'stop it' approach to school or club behaviour policy unbalances communication and guidance from the adults. Whenever I have encountered the 'don't' list, whether in a public space or a reminder about 'banning rough play' on the staffroom notice board, I have also noticed that adults are more alert to unwanted behaviour. They are far less attuned to 'catching children out being good'. Children and adolescents do sometimes need to be told to 'stop' an action, but something constructive has to follow.

Effective teaching depends on adult ability to hold the attention of a large group of children or adolescents and to deal with potential or actual disruptions. Bill Rogers (1997 and 1998) describes the importance of consistent rules within a class and across a whole school because it enables a teacher to guide by positive reminders. Adults can say, 'Please put your hand up, so I can see where your voice is coming from', rather than raising your voice to a child with, 'Don't shout'. Personal, rude

---

LOOK, LISTEN, NOTE, LEARN

It is wise to develop a short list of ground rules, and most positive behaviours can be reduced to no more than about ten basic messages. For instance, the Golden Rules in Crabtree Infants School were: 'We are gentle', 'We are kind and helpful', 'We work hard', 'We keep safe', 'We look after property', 'We tell the truth' and 'We listen to people' (see Mosley and Sonnet, 2005).

- Can you think of any behaviour you want to encourage from children that does not fit into one of those phrases?

- A positive phrasing also makes it much easier for adults to recognise and offer simple appreciation when children have been honest, especially if circumstances made that a tough choice.

I have seen other positive approaches in schools and clubs. Sometimes they are built around school mottos, such as, 'Help us to keep our school a happy place' or, 'Treat other people how we would like to be treated'. Of course, mottos do not work alone, but effective schools explore these basics through the personal and social part of the curriculum and through the way daily events are handled.

- If you are working with a set of negative ground rules, then please rethink them, ideally in cooperation with children or young people. They are responsive to discussions around 'What makes for a happy club?' or, 'How do we all need to behave so we feel comfortable in class?'

---

remarks to a teacher from a child or adolescent are met with, 'I don't make discourteous comments about your body or clothing and I don't expect you to comment about mine', rather than addressing any of the specifics of what has been said.

Adjusting to adolescents

The important issue is to build from general rules to which adolescents can relate, and which they judge show proper respect to their own feelings and perspective. It is then possible to talk around issues like feeling comfortable with unfamiliar people and that nobody likes to feel imposed upon by others. The general underlying principle is 'do as you would be done by'. It is a fair request that adolescents adapt how they behave so that other people do not feel that their personal space has been invaded. However, supportive practitioners need to acknowledge that the negative reaction of some adults is out of proportion to normal, lively behaviour from young people.

Newspaper headlines and vote-catching initiatives (see also page 13) have combined to present a great deal of ordinary adolescent behaviour as antisocial. Older children and young people have an uphill struggle if they are expected to be trouble by many adults. In 2006 the British Crime Survey quarterly findings (from www.homeoffice.gov.uk) reported that 32 per cent of people in their sample said there is a problem with adolescents hanging around on the streets. Standing on street corners is not an illegal activity, but adolescents are considerably more likely to be judged as 'up to no good' than an equivalent group of middle-aged women.

There is an increasing tendency to call the police for behaviour that is unacceptable, but which should be dealt with by the adults responsible for the children or young people. Careful reviews, like Andrew Millie et al. (2005) or Bernard Davies (2005) do not overlook the disruption and risk in some neighbourhoods, but do call for a balanced reaction to the younger generation. Carole Sutton et al. (2006) reviewed studies about criminality and described that many adult chronic offenders posed significant problems to others with their childhood behaviour, but the reverse was not true. Children and young people, whose behaviour could fairly be described as antisocial, are not all on an inevitable criminal career path.

Recognition and appreciation

Children are encouraged to make the effort to behave well when adults notice what a child has done and show appreciation of the wanted behaviour in a simple way, ideally as close as possible to the event. Older children and adolescents have a longer time perspective and so will not necessarily look puzzled if there is a delay before an adult says, 'I noticed what you did when .... Good for you, that was a considerate way to deal with ...'.

There is a place for symbolic rewards, like stickers or certificates, so long as they do not edge out basic communication skills that recognise a 'well done' and 'thanks for that' directly with children. Some teams in school, club or other settings have backed themselves into a corner and are effectively 'paying' children for ordinary pleasant behaviour. They are, as I choose to describe it, 'well and truly stickered'. Children and adolescents are the final judges of what is, or is not, effective as a reward.

- Some children do not enjoy public praise – some do, of course. Practitioners need to consider whether older children, especially boys, have their playground credibility undermined if they keep being awarded the 'best-behaved child of the week' certificate.

■ Children's feelings and interpretations also affect whether a reward – as seen from the adult perspective – backfires in some way. For example, children who are 'paid' with stickers to tidy up a room or the playground may – quite reasonably – decide not to join the tidy-up squad if they do not want to earn a sticker today.

I have encountered thoughtful systems in some primary schools where a limited number of certificates or other forms of written recognition are used to highlight what a child has managed that was a challenge for him or her. Careful use of whole-group reward can also be effective with primary school children, for example a jar for which individual children 'earn' the large marble or pasta shape. A full jar is traded in for an enjoyable activity or experience for the whole group. No record is kept of who earned how many marbles; it is a group enterprise and starts again with the empty jar.

LOOK, LISTEN, NOTE, LEARN

I advise caution over stickers, certificates, smiley faces and the like. Wise practitioners are alert to what is actually happening in their setting.

■ In what way do symbolic rewards genuinely guide behaviour? Do you really need them – will children behave well without the stickers? How do they feel about this system?

■ How prominent were stickers or certificates in your own childhood? If your school or club was a heavy user of symbolic rewards, in what ways do you judge that this approach affected your choices over how to behave?

Consequences

Children learn that their behaviour has consequences – sometimes positive and sometimes less enjoyable. Children and young people who show they can be trusted experience a loosening of adult supervision, because they are able to regulate their own behaviour in familiar situations and manage extended privileges. The reverse is true and children or young people who break rules find sometimes that loss of privileges and independent action are the consequence. It is important to deal with unacceptable behaviour in ways that do not suggest rejection of this child or adolescent as an individual. The approach is summed up by using actual words such as, 'I like you, Darren; I don't like the way that you . . .' or, 'How you spoke to Moira was a rude way to tell her that . . .'.

MAKE THE CONNECTION WITH ... THINKING ABOUT BEHAVIOUR

With help, 6 and 7 year olds can make a start on their ability to reflect on choices they made. If children and young people are to inhibit some behaviour choices, and take a different option under times of stress, then they need to be clear about that option. Adults need to help that process and give children practice, without the experience being unpleasant.

A group of 7 year olds in Crabtree Infants School talked about 'filling in the forms' – a phrase that I had to ask them to explain to me. In their school it was fully understood that, if you had done something wrong (more than just minor), children went see the head teacher. They had to write down what they had done that was not alright. But the routine was also to think about, and write down, what they should have done instead. The writing was part of a firm but friendly conversation with the head about what had recently happened, but also about 'next time'.

'Filling in the forms' was not these 7 year olds' favourite activity, but they understood the reasons why adults wanted them to do it. The routine links with conversational approaches I have encountered in late primary and early secondary school when an adult talks through with a child or young person, 'What could you have done when ... that would mean we wouldn't be having this conversation right now (or that you wouldn't be in trouble like this)?' This type of private conversation has a chance of provoking children to 'think about what you do', so long as the emotional tone is 'firm yet fair', avoiding further reprimands or any attempt to embarrass a child or young person in front of their peers.

Adults are responsible for considering the consequences of their own actions. Are any sanctions reasonable and fair, do they improve a situation and make it easier for a child or young person to 'do the right thing' next time? Or do they worsen an already fraught situation? Two examples given to me were:

- Teachers who removed marbles from the group jar after they had been legitimately earned. This is unacceptable adult behaviour. A tough day with children can bring a regretful comment that nobody has earned a marble today – 'let's start afresh tomorrow'.
- Playground supervisors who made children, who were judged to have misbehaved, stand with their faces to the wall. The consequence of this demand was that children were regularly banged by balls that landed on their back. They turned around to be able to dodge any

more balls and were given further punishment for failing to stay in the required position.

Bill Rogers (1997 and 1998) highlights how teachers need to keep the good-natured majority on their side. Frustrated adults, who feel under verbal attack, turn to sweeping whole-group punishments or are ill-tempered with the whole group. Teachers then alienate the well-disposed children or adolescents, who may gravitate towards those individuals whom Bill Rogers described as 'the catalysts' for disruption in a class.

Children's behaviour: adults' feelings

Support for practitioners who feel hard-pressed often has to address issues around adult emotional literacy and who is feeling what in this situation. It is very uncomfortable for adults to fear losing power to children and this anxiety is often linked with feeling incompetent as a playground supervisor or playworker. In some cases, children are active in creating a power battle, because they are individuals who very much want to win. But some win–lose scenarios are set up by adults – in the role of parent too – when they cannot separate their feelings from children's emotions and intentions.

TAKE ANOTHER PERSPECTIVE

Adult feelings can become entangled with perceptions of children. Behaviour is labelled as 'challenging' when children or adolescents are not being seriously confrontational. They may be less than courteous, even cheeky on occasion, but they are just being 8 or 14 year olds. I think some usage of the word is to avoid 'naughty' or 'bad', but it is important that 'challenging' is kept for behaviour that is definitely out of the ordinary for the given age group. Adults who apply 'challenging' to behaviour that is within normal range for the age group should address who feels 'challenged' and on what grounds?

An assertive, rather than an aggressive, response from practitioners (or parents) sets a good example to the younger generation. Rebellion or secret non-compliance usually follows the uncompromising adult stance of, 'Those are the rules and you obey them, or else!' It feels very different to open a discussion with phrases like, 'You don't think it's fair that …?', 'You can't see/don't agree with my reasons for …?' or, 'You believe it's time we had a conversation about …?'

Andrea Clifford-Poston (2001) describes a slippery slope of adults who feel powerless with a child because they cannot directly control the behaviour that they do not want. The feelings then move to include anxiety, arising from belief that a competent adult would and should be able to control a child. Then, often, the feeling of anger takes over: anger with the child for behaving in this way, but often also hidden anger with oneself. I think that the feeling of resentment is often tangled up in the mix and that is how some grown-ups reach a point when they directly blame children. Bill Rogers (1997 and 1998) describes how fear of loss of control undermines teachers' behaviour when they slide into power battles with individuals. Part of effective classroom control is to deal simply with low-level disturbances and to avoid resorting to attempts to ridicule or intimidate children or adolescents.

Life also becomes more complicated if practitioners focus on single events classified as 'behaviour problems', and also when adults feel their own sense of competence is under threat. Many issues around the behaviour of children arise within their play – in the school playground, in after-school club or playscheme. Wendy Russell (2006) describes an approach within playwork in which she supported practitioners to draw up play profiles, as a way to look carefully at what was happening within the pattern of children's play. The team was able to home in on 'critical incidents' that were significant for what followed. But these times were also a possible turning point if adults made a different behaviour choice, sometimes to watch and not intervene. Some actions from children that adults labelled as 'challenging' were normal testing of boundaries, or could be resolved by adult involvement as a playful but grown-up companion. Much of children's lively behaviour was not disruptive, so long as the adults no longer felt being a 'good playworker' depended on their ability to manage through direct control.

When practitioners feel more comfortable over control, they may also be more able to judge which incidents need to be discussed with parents. I had a useful conversation with the leader of one after-school club (thanks to Jackie Clasby of the Balham Family Centre) about how they used a Feedback Book to help practitioners distinguish between recorded issues over children's behaviour that were minor and those which were more serious. The team discussed, before the end of the day, which events needed to be discussed in a constructive way with a child's parents. It was unhelpful for everyone if parents were met at the end of the day with accounts of insignificant wrong-doing that children thought had been completely resolved.

Children and young people are often a good source of ideas about what works and what matters most. Sue Cowley (2006) has a chapter entitled 'What the students said', and many of her points are similar to what I have heard in conversations with children and adolescents about life in the school classroom. The advice is also consistent with recommendations from Bill Rogers (1997 and 1998).

- Children and adolescents appreciate and want teachers, or other adults in authority, to be a combination of firm and fair, with reference to agreed school rules.

- Teachers are not 'one of the kids' and should not pretend to be in this role. The real 'kids' appreciate someone who is friendly and has a sense of humour, but does not give up proper authority. Be enthusiastic about your subject and look as if you are reasonably pleased to be there.

- It is best to state what is wanted in an assertive way; there is no mileage in pleading with a class to behave better. Adults need to start out firm – not ferocious – and can then ease up if appropriate. It never works to start soft and then try to get tough with the same group.

- Show respect to children and young people and keep control without resorting to ridicule or shouting. Step away from power battles that you will either lose or only win by behaving in ways that would attract criticism if class members behaved in that way.

- Avoid making threats that you cannot or will not carry through. If you make a promise, then keep it or have a good reason for letting the group down and explain that reason. If there is a reason to apologise, then say 'sorry' genuinely – behave in line with what you expect from the children.

Alternative strategies for children

Adults need to think carefully about the behaviour they would like to encourage from the children as much as those actions that they do not want. But simply telling children 'stop fidgeting' or 'you shouldn't call people names' is not enough. If 'telling off' is all you do, children will dismiss you as a boring nagger, but also they have no real idea of what to do instead; they are left with a puzzling detective job to find what has not been explicitly banned.

Children are much more likely to be able to redirect their behaviour when adults show insight over why it is so hard to stay still in assembly. Is there some kind of 'official fidgeting' that could be permitted, like fiddling with a piece of ribbon? Children who have called one of their peers names, may well have put immense effort into not giving this child a hefty shove or slap. They may revert to fists next time, since their efforts to use words still led to a reprimand. Supportive adults explore other ways in which

Children will sort out many issues without adult help

children who feel cross or hurt can use their words: phrases like,
'Don't . . ., I don't like it!' or, 'That's a horrid word, don't call me that!'

Limits for 'telling an adult'

Some schools and out-of-school provision require that, instead of hitting
or shouting, children should always approach and tell an adult what has
happened. However, 'telling' is not useful as the main, long-term strategy
for children or adolescents to resolve problems and it feels like a weak
choice to many children. Their peers often complain that the child who
tells has 'grassed' on them and retribution can follow. I have also
encountered too many children, who have followed the telling rule, only
to be criticised by teachers or playworkers for 'telling tales'. Children are
told to 'stop whinging and sort it out yourself' by adults who give no
help for ways that children could resolve the problem. Adults also soon
feel overwhelmed by a stream of 'telling', often for what are minor ups
and downs of playground or playscheme life. One can understand their
irritation but, as children say, 'it isn't fair' to blame children for obeying
the rule set up by the adults.

Problem-solving with children

Children are able to learn skills of conflict resolution so long as adults are
clear about the skills that they wish to share. A basic bottom line is that

practitioners set a good example by using those skills when helping children to resolve ordinary problems in class, playground and club life. The skills of conflict resolution can be described as what works for problem-solving under pressure, when the emotional temperature has risen.

The basic context for adults is that you are alert to what is going on with children and make a judgement about whether they can resolve the problem themselves. You do not allow troubles to escalate but you do not impose adult 'help', if children are sorting matters out themselves. The sound of raised voices does not necessarily mean trouble: how do children appear, do any of them look intimidated or able to lose emotional control? Helpful support follows a similar pattern, which children are steadily able to use themselves.

- Be close to the children, without crowding them, and stop any hurtful behaviour by calm use of your voice and body language.
- Acknowledge children's feelings with statements like, 'You both look cross' or, 'You look very unhappy about something'. Supportive adults show respect for what troubles children, even if it seems minor to an outsider.
- Help children to listen to each other by asking 'What has happened?' or, 'What's the problem here?' These are more productive questions than 'who started it?' (everyone else!) or, 'Why did you ...? (greeted by silence or 'because ...' followed by an explanation unwelcome to the adult).
- Enable each person to be heard and ease the interaction by using your own words, for instance, 'I think Harry is angry because you joined the game without asking first'. A wise adult does not repeat the rude name that Harry called the other child.
- You ease the discussion from, 'So the problem is that ...' into, 'What could we do about it?' Listen to what children suggest and avoid filling a silence. If there is an impasse, then offer, 'I have an idea, do you want to hear it?' or, 'Shall I make a suggestion?'
- You reach an agreement and commitment from all the children about what will happen now and how the problem can be resolved. In some cases, the simple fact of a calm discussion means that children head off in different directions. Keep a friendly eye on whether children would appreciate any follow-up. Be ready to say later, 'well done, you have sorted ... out by ...'.

This approach to conflict resolution works because adults address the feelings and choices of children and young people. For example, the message is not a blunt, 'you mustn't feel angry'. The key issue is about what is done with angry feelings: they do not have to be expressed through cussing and fighting. Sometimes you will need to move swiftly to ensure that everyone is safe. You need clear team guidelines about using your adult strength wisely to keep children safe. Practitioners who work with very troubled children need proper training in safe restraint, for the well-being of everyone.

Problem-solving by children themselves

Schools, even early-years settings, that have taken the time and trouble to coach children in these skills, find that soon adults are not needed all the time. Children resolve a lot of minor disputes on their own behalf. Some schools specifically build conflict resolution skills into the personal and social strand of the curriculum. In a process sometimes called peer mediation, some children are given additional coaching to act as a support to their peers in the playground. You can find more detailed descriptions from Margaret Collins (2005) and Hilary Stacey and Pat Robinson (1997).

The pattern is usually that trained mediators are available at predictable times, especially within school breaktimes. They may have a badge or a hat. Children and young people are most likely to have assigned days when they are on duty, since the aim is not to use up all their breaktime. They are available for peers to approach with a request that the mediator help two or more children to resolve a disagreement that they have not managed to sort out for themselves. However, the mediators can also offer their help when they see unresolved disputes or observe an incident that would be described as bullying. Some mediators double as a playground buddy, to keep isolated children company.

Many children may use their skills of conflict resolution within play, but the role of mediator needs to be actively accepted by the child or young person. Effective mediators are not exclusively the well-behaved children or young people. Part of a positive behaviour policy in any setting is that boys and girls are enabled to reflect on and change their own reactions. Children and adolescents who have struggled with a positive approach to conflict can be especially effective as the playground mediators, because they genuinely understand how hard it can be to do the right thing.

If you want to find out more

❖ **Adlerian Workshops and Publications** – useful books and booklets on this approach. Tel: 01296 482148; www.adlerian.com.

❖ **Boxall, Marjorie** (2002) *Nurture groups in school: principles and practice*. London: Paul Chapman Publishing.

- Briers, Stephen and Baveystock, Sacha (2006) *Teen angels: how to find calm in the storm of teenage years*. Harlow: Educational Publishers LLP.

- Carr-Gregg, Michael and Shale, Erin (2003) *Adolescence: a guide for parents*. London: Vermilion.

- Clifford-Poston, Andrea (2001) *The secrets of successful parenting: understanding what your child's behaviour is really telling you*. Oxford: Pathways.

- Clifford-Poston, Andrea (2005) *Tweens: what to expect from – and how to survive – your child's pre-teen years*. Oxford: Oneworld. (Good ideas – I just wish writers would not use the term 'tweens', partly because it originated with marketing to this age group, see page 15.)

- Collins, Margaret (2005) *Young buddies: teaching peer support skills to children aged 6 to 11*. London: Sage/Lucky Duck Publishing.

- Coloroso, Barbara (2005) *The bully, the bullied and the bystander*. London: Picadilly Press.

- Cowley, Sue (2006) *Getting the buggers to behave*. London: Continuum. (This book has good ideas, which is the reason it is here. However, I think it is unacceptable to refer to children and adolescents with a term that would attract a reprimand if they used it to teachers or other adults!)

- Davies, Bernard (2005) *Threatening youth revisited: youth policies under New Labour*. See www.infed.org/archives/bernard_davies/revisiting_threatening_youth.htm.

- Elliott, Michelle (ed.) (2002) *Bullying: a practical guide to coping in schools*. London: Pearsons.

- Fowler, Sandra (2004) *Making schools safer using effective anti-bullying strategies*. Spotlight Briefing London: National Children's Bureau. See www.ncb.org.uk.

- Hand in Hand – an organisation based in the USA and led by Patty Wipfler. See www.handinhandparenting.org.

- Hartley-Brewer, Elizabeth (2004) *Talking to tweenies: getting it right before it gets rocky*. London: Hodder and Stoughton.

❖ **Lindon, Jennie** (2003) *Child protection.* London: Hodder and Stoughton.

❖ **Lindon, Jennie** (2005) *Understanding child development: linking theory and practice.* London: Hodder Arnold.

❖ **Kidscape** – practical materials on bullying, as well as personal safety. See www.kidscape.org.uk.

❖ **Mamen, Maggie** (2006) *The pampered child syndrome: how to recognise it, how to manage it and how to avoid it. A guide for parents and professionals.* London: Jessica Kingsley.

❖ **Mental Health Foundation** (1999) *Bright Futures: promoting children and young people's mental health.* London: Mental Health Foundation.

❖ **Millie, Andrew; Jacobson, Jessica; McDonald, Eraina** and **Hough, Mike** (2005) *Anti-social behaviour strategies: finding a balance.* Bristol: The Policy Press. Summary and report at www.jrf.org.uk/knowledge/findings/housing/0305.asp.

❖ **Mosley, Jenny** and **Sonnet, Helen** (2005) *Better behaviour through Golden Time.* Cambridge: LDA.

✳ **Nolte, Dorothy Law** and **Harris, Rachel** (1998) *Children learn what they live.* New York: Workman Publishing.

❖ **Nolte, Dorothy Law** and **Harris, Rachel** (2002) *Teenagers learn what they live – parenting to inspire integrity and independence.* New York: Workman Publishing.

❖ **Neall, Lucinda** (2002) *Bringing out the best in boys: communication strategies for teachers.* Stroud: Hawthorn Press.

❖ **Oliver, Christine** and **Candappa, Mano** (2003) *Tackling bullying: listening to the views of children and young people.* Available from www.childline.org.uk.

❖ **Rogers, Bill** (1997) *Cracking the hard class: strategies for managing the harder than average class.* London: Paul Chapman Publishing. (For this and other useful books, see www.PaulChapmanPublishing.co.uk.)

❖ **Rogers, Bill** (1998) *You know the fair rule: strategies for making the hard job of discipline and behaviour management in school easier.* Harlow: Pearson Education.

❖ **Russell, Wendy** (2006) *Reframing playwork: reframing challenging behaviour.* Nottingham: Nottingham City Play Service. Tel: 0115 915 8630.

❖ **Stace, Stephanie** and **Roker, Debi** (2005) *Monitoring and supervision in 'ordinary' families: the views and experiences of young people and their parents.* London: National Children's Bureau. Summary at www.jrf.org.uk/knowledge/findings/socialpolicy/0165.asp.

❖ **Stacey, Hilary** and **Robinson, Pat** (1997) *Let's mediate: a teachers' guide to peer support and conflict resolution skills for all ages.* London: Sage/Lucky Duck Publishing and other titles from www.luckyduck.co.uk.

❖ **Sutton, Carole; Utting, David** and **Farrington, David** (2006) 'Nipping criminality in the bud', *The Psychologist* 19(8) – part of a Special Issue on criminality. See www.bps.org.uk/publications/ thepsychologist/search-the-psychologist-online.cfm.

6 Developing the skills of communication

Children and young people extend the ways in which they are able to choose to use their abilities in spoken and written communication. Talking and listening connect with cognitive development and are one way in which individual thinking becomes explicit and is shared. Children's impressive skills in communication enable them to operate with confidence in more structured or public situations. Responsive communication is closely linked with emotional development and can therefore support initiatives in which children and young people help each other.

> **The main sections of this chapter are:**
>
> ★ **Talking and listening.**
>
> ★ **Using skills of communication.**
>
> ★ **Understanding and using written language.**

TALKING AND LISTENING

Children of 5 and 6 years of age can already have extensive skills of communication: expressing themselves through spoken language, an ability to listen and process what is said to them and a continuing awareness of non-verbal communication. With suitable encouragement, these abilities continue to develop over childhood and into adolescence.

Making their language work

Most children will have abilities to express themselves in words, especially in familiar situations and with familiar people. Children of 5–8 years of age usually have a significant vocabulary. Readers with time on their hands might like to explore just how long it can take to make a comprehensive list of all the words used spontaneously by this age group, followed by the vocabulary that they clearly understand in context. Researchers in this area do not agree on a total figure for words, but it definitely reaches into the thousands. As you listen to children, you will also hear words and phrases that reflect their special interests, like an absorption in natural phenomena – volcanoes, dinosaurs, big spiders, special forms of transport – anything that has provoked their curiosity.

Talking to think out loud

Children use their words to express what they are thinking or to work through an idea out loud. Children may find it harder to be active thinkers if they are blocked from speaking or even muttering under their breath.

- They can tell, describe and recount what has happened to them or the events in an enjoyable story, film/video or television programme. Children, who feel relaxed and not under time pressure, often give a connected account of direct or indirect experiences.

- Talking and listening connect with thinking skills as children become more able to weigh up information and come to judgements, expressed in spoken and later written words. A great deal depends on their experience through childhood, much of which is mediated for most children and young people through schooling (see also page 191).

- They are active in using questions, and comments phrased as an implied question, in an active search to find out more about a topic or to seek an explanation of something that has more than one potential explanation.

- Children express opinions and argue their case when they are in disagreement with another child or an adult. Strong emotions can overwhelm clear communication and helpful adults guide in ways to disagree without fierce argument.

- Children are increasingly able to monitor the understanding of their listener(s), perhaps to ask, 'You know what I'm talking about?' However, older children may still assume adults share the same basic knowledge base, unless they are asked, 'Please explain the bit about . . .'.

Communication to amuse

Children younger than 5 years have a sense of humour. Their verbal jokes are largely physical in origin, like going 'boo!' to make people jump or

---

LOOK, LISTEN, NOTE, LEARN

Some years ago I was told a joke by a 7 year old that went as follows. 'Why was the sand wet?' (Required reply of 'I don't know. Why was the sand wet?') 'Because the seaweed.' (Say it out loud – the sea wee-ed!) The jokes told by 6–11 year olds frequently involve reference to toilets or bodily fluids. The essence of a good joke for children is often that it crosses a perceived boundary into mild rudeness. But also notice that this example requires understanding the double meaning from the sounds of the words: the joke is a play on words.

- Collect some jokes that amuse children.

- Reflect on what the humour tells you about their grasp of language as well as the conventions of telling a joke or funny story.

laughing at minor mishaps like falling. Over middle childhood they develop an ability to use words to make other people laugh and understand the principle of a joke communicated mainly or completely by words.

Older children come to understand the conventions of a joke and learn particular formats, such as the 'Knock knock ...' variety. Their vocabulary has limitations and they sometimes repeat a joke or a funny poem/song that has raised a laugh elsewhere, without knowing the meaning of every word. Sensitive adults allow for the loop of, 'Do you know what ... means?' and avoid leaping straight to the assumption that a child or young adolescent intended to offend.

TAKE ANOTHER PERSPECTIVE

The great importance of jokes and puns was highlighted by a research project in Scotland. New software was developed for the computerised speech aids used by children and young people with severe disabilities affecting their communication. The team was aware that children who can speak, typically use humour through language to experiment with words and to hone their social skills with peers.

The STANDUP project (System To Augment Non-speakers' Dialogue Using Puns) created a means for disabled young people to generate jokes that depended on bringing together words in a novel way. The software provided a dictionary, information about words and simple rules about puns. A small group of young people with complex communication needs from a Glasgow school tried out the programme. They created groan-worthy jokes on their own initiative, such as, 'What do you get when you cross a car with a sandwich?' – answer, 'Traffic jam'. The young people were able to be more active in their communication and showed great delight in their ability to entertain others.

Find out more on http://groups.inf.ed.ac.uk/standup. My thanks to *Children Now*, and the journalist who writes their 'Hound' news column, who helped me track this project.

Bilingual children and young people
Some children learn two or more languages over the same period of time in early childhood. However, some become secure in a single family language and then encounter another language as they enter early-years

provision or school. Some children who relocate with their families as refugees seeking asylum, then encounter the language that is new to them at any point over childhood or adolescence. Depending on the language proficiency of their parents, some older children act as the family interpreter in communication with educational or other services.

Sometimes children and young people reach a similar level of fluency in their languages, possibly using one language more at home and another at school. The difference may mean that children operate a rather different vocabulary in each of their languages, because they serve different purposes.

- In any language, children and young people need a large vocabulary and it is important that practitioners are ready to help them gain plenty of words. Of course, children need to put words into phrases and sentences, but when children are coping with more than one language and possibly coming later to one of them, adults can overlook that a child is operating with a much narrower range of useful everyday words than their peers.

- Bilingualism can bring many advantages and hopefully the time is gone when monolingual adults assumed that bilingual children and young people inevitably faced and posed 'problems'. However, the more optimistic approaches to bilingualism can be rather blasé about the hard work of building up vocabulary and grammar in more than one language.

- Children who would welcome some specific help to extend their vocabulary, through conversation, play and stories, are thinking like 6, 10 or 14 year olds. So helpful input is nothing like supporting young children who are talking and thinking at 3-year-old level. Older children and young people have knowledge – of abstract ideas as well as the more tangible aspects to daily life – but they do not always know the relevant words in each of their languages.

World languages do not share the same alphabet and not all are written in the left to right direction of English. Some children and young people are therefore busy with two distinct ways of writing for their different languages. A child's home language has significant connections with personal and family identity. When families send children to special language classes, the experience is sometimes linked with instruction in the family faith, for instance in Hebrew (Judaism) or Arabic (Islam).

When talking is difficult

Children and young people vary as individuals over their willingness, and enthusiasm, for talking. Any concerns about children need to be placed within a context of informal observation by familiar adults. For instance, not all children are that keen to speak up in larger groups. Children who are more reluctant to speak with adults at the moment may be at ease with their peers. However, some problems will not ease with simple encouragement and time.

Stammering

This type of disfluency is not only a difficulty with communication. Stammering can undermine children's confidence and affect their outlook once they go to school or during their time in an after-school club. Check with the child and their family whether they are receiving help from a speech and language therapist. You can then link with advice from that specialist.

■ The main aim is to reduce the emotional pressure that makes stammering more likely. But do not achieve this aim by cutting back on children's involvement in ordinary classroom or club activities.

■ Find out by observation and talking with the child what helps this individual. Some children and young people find it easier to speak up in a group if they have something visual to add to the words. Some find it less stressful to read aloud or present to a group if they work with a peer who reads in unison or who takes relaxed turns with the presentation.

■ Allow for the fact that struggling children may not be able to hold eye contact and get their words out at the same time. However, note the study on page 183 that found many children needed to drop their gaze when they were thinking hard.

■ When children cannot express themselves easily, for whatever reason, adults can be uncertain whether the child has understood an idea or body of knowledge. Time and attention will be needed to find out if stammering has covered up a child's confusion or is even a handy strategy for avoiding study tasks that are difficult.

A child with any kind of dysfluency can be a target for teasing or even more sustained bullying. Children will be better equipped if adults – parents or practitioners – have helped them with some assertive responses, verbal and non-verbal. However, children who stammer are not inevitably bullied. Like children whose speech is not easy for unfamiliar people to understand, they can have friends who are patient and understanding. Peers sometimes wish to be kindly helpers and have learned the social skills to balance easing the communication with avoiding a take-over of speech.

Adolescents who stammer can face what the British Stammering Organisation (www.stammering.org/teens_info.html) calls 'double trouble'.

The anxiety about disfluency can heighten normal adolescent concerns about social communication. Supportive adults, including a speech and language therapist, need to help a young person with appropriate strategies. Friendly support may remind adolescents that many of their peers also lack confidence in the same situation. The British Stammering Organisation offers information and practical advice on stammering across the age range (Helpline 0845 603 2001; www.stammering.org).

Silent children

Children who do not to speak other than to their immediate family can risk being labelled as un-cooperative or very shy. However, selective mutism is now recognised as a condition that goes far beyond shyness and arises from a sense of extreme anxiety in children, more often girls than boys.

It is tough to tell the difference in early childhood between a young child who is very anxious about unfamiliar people and places and one who is 'slow to warm up'. The situation becomes more serious when children do not emerge from their silence once they enter school. Children are then on the outskirts of classroom experience and can be socially isolated. Even the most kindly of their peers cannot relate to a child who does not communicate, and sometimes does not even use nods or other gestures.

Children with selective mutism are not so much choosing not to talk as opting to deal with their extreme social anxiety through silence. It becomes harder for them to work with other strategies the longer being a 'silent child' has become part of their personal identity outside a very small, emotionally safe inner circle. You will find a useful source of advice at Selective Mutism Information and Research Association (SMIRA) 13 Humberstone Drive, Leicester, LE5 0RE. Tel: 0116 212 7411; email smiraleicester@hotmail.com.

Disability that affects communication

Some children live with disabilities that mean spontaneous communication is less straightforward for them.

- Serious learning disabilities can slow down the pattern of language development so that an older child is operating at a level much younger than their chronological age.
- Some physical disabilities directly affect children's capacity to make the sounds of spoken language, to hear what is said to them or see the messages from body language.
- Some children with delayed or unusual language development have a disability that affects only communication. Sometimes even detailed

observation cannot identify why language skills have been disrupted, only that the child is faced with an uphill struggle and needs significant help.

■ Some disabilities, like autistic spectrum disorder and Asperger's Syndrome, affect the pattern of social interaction and communication.

Each of these areas of disability has practical books, organisations and supportive websites of their own. The only practical option in this general book is to advise readers to explore further on their initiative, starting with reliable websites like that of the National Deaf Children's Society (www.ndcs. org.uk), Down's Syndrome Society (www.downs-syndrome.org.uk), National Autism Society (www.nas.org.uk) and I Can (www.Ican.org.uk).

Children and young people living with communication difficulties can be supported by adults, and active peers, who are willing to use visual as well as spoken means of communication, signing systems and appropriate technological aids to communication. Children and young people need methods that enable them to get across the practical requests of daily life, but also the subtleties of feelings and what they like. Sally Millar and Stuart Aitken (2003) describe the idea of Personal Communication Passports that belong to the child or young person. Words and photos are built into a personal resource that enables less familiar adults to understand for individuals 'how I tell you if I don't like something' or 'what it means when I shut my eyes'.

The skills of social conversation

The point about conversational skills is that social interaction involves turn-taking, in other words, what you say links at least a bit with what the other person has just said. Children learn initially when adults set a good example of how a conversation flows and how to manage turn-taking without interrupting. With suitable early experiences of many conversations with one adult or a very small group (what I call a sofa-full), 5–6 year olds can show they definitely understand the concept of a conversation. They use their skills to initiate and continue this kind of communication.

The skills of conversational exchange are built for children through experience. However, some children and young people will continue to find conversations a mystery, along with other aspects of social interaction with peers or adults. Children living with disabilities like Asperger's and autistic spectrum disorder find daily life very perplexing and often a source of significant anxiety. Depending on the severity of disability, some children and young people learn the give and take of conversation almost as an intellectual exercise. So they can operate in social situations,

LOOK, LISTEN, NOTE, LEARN

It is worth exploring what older children and young people like to talk about during personal conversation – not structured, adult-led group times. Think about what I like to call 'kitchen table conversations'. This kind of relaxed chatting can happen within children's own families, but it also develops with staff in the playground at school and with practitioners in club, youth work and residential homes.

- What conversations have children or young people wanted to hold with you in recent weeks? I mean 'ordinary' conversations rather than confidences about something that worries them.

- What do they want to talk about when they start a conversation or show interest in continuing if you start one?

- Reflect on children and young people with whom you spend time. What really enthuses some of these individuals? Have you watched an episode of their favourite television programme or read their favourite author?

- Are there some children or young people who rarely, if ever, initiate a conversation with an adult? With anyone else? What may be getting in the way for them and what might you do to encourage relaxed exchanges?

Children enjoy chatting together

without necessarily being in tune with the reasons why other people like this activity so much. For an insight into this world, try Mark Haddon's *The curious incident of the dog in the night-time* (2003, London: Vintage). This novel is regarded as an accurate portrayal of an adolescent living with Asperger's Syndrome.

Supportive adults

Relaxed, unplanned exchanges – just chatting – are an important part of joint social life between adults and children. Studies, supported by anecdotal information, show that this generation of children and young people are pleased to chat with adults – friendly practitioners and their parents – as well as wanting generous opportunities to communicate with their peers.

- Children and young people want conversations with adults about their own current interests. Younger people like familiar adults to show an intelligent interest in what absorbs them: books, computer games, leisure pursuits, sports – whatever matters to this child or adolescent.
- Children and young people want to talk about issues and decisions that affect them in school, club, drop-in services or youth and leisure groups. They want to be kept up to date with information that could affect their daily life and have a chance to express their views.
- Children and young people are aware of current affairs, not least because news is spread over all the different types of media. They often want to talk about what they can see for themselves on television and in the headlines. Sometimes they want to talk seriously about how an event affects them or raises anxieties provoked by distressing news.
- If children and young people are old enough to ask tough questions, they have the right to straight answers from adults. Even 5 and 6 year olds may want to talk about what has happened and why, could it happen here, what do the adults think about it, what is their opinion?

The more personal issues and opinions are likely to be raised in circumstances when children and young people feel especially at ease. Emotionally safe situations are more likely to be their own family – so long as parents and other family members are generous with their time and attention. However, home-like circumstances can be created in after-school clubs, holiday playschemes and youth services where children and young people feel at ease with well-known and trusted practitioners. Some of the practical books written for parents are equally useful for any adults who should develop a personal relationship with children and young people – see, for example, two books by Adele Faber and Elaine Mazlish (1999 and 2005).

MAKE THE CONNECTION WITH ... FAMILY DISCUSSIONS

This section covers ways in which children and young people are capable of discussion in non-family settings. Individual families vary considerably and not all parents judge that it is appropriate to involve their sons and daughters in serious discussion and decision-making – or possibly that it is too difficult to find the time in a hard-pressed life. Children and young people are capable of such discussions and are denied valuable life skills if they are excluded.

Ian Butler and colleagues (2005) report a study of 8–11 year olds (69 children in four different locations). They found that these older children were able to talk about the issues of decision-making as they operated in their own family. They generally welcomed feeling a part of decisions and appreciated that, after hearing the views of younger members of the household, parents sometimes made a final, big decision. However, some children had been actively involved with significant changes like finding a new home.

The 8–11s were clear about issues on which they definitely knew more than their parents, such as choice in new clothes for the children. The theme arose again, as in so many studies that invite children's views, that fairness was crucial: everybody should have their say and one person's preference or perspective should not always win. Children also emerged as sharp observers of family interaction, being alert to, and critical of, inconsistency from parents over time or decisions that depended on the adult's mood today.

Good practice for residential workers is to create a home-like feel, and for foster carers to use the advantages of care in a family home. Looked-after children should all have a personal social worker, but even those professionals, who are not weighed down by impossible case loads will never see a child or adolescent for as much time as their foster carer or key person in a residential setting. Informal conversation lays a strong foundation of trust so that worried children or young people feel able to broach a sensitive topic. Practitioners, whose role includes elements of parenting, will need to respond to unexpected conversational openers. It is not unusual for children or young people to start talking about something serious while being driven somewhere or while they are busy with an adult on a shared task. The joint activity, plus sometimes the reduced eye contact, seems to help a reluctant child or adolescent to start the discussion.

Should adults talk about themselves?

Children and young people are often interested in the childhood and adolescence of familiar adults – either their own parents or trusted club or youth workers. Non-family adults need to decide about boundaries to personal details that they disclose. However, there is good reason to respond with some sharing when children and young people ask straight questions. There is also a place for considered self-disclosure from adults when sharing will give children or adolescents an alternative perspective. One example given to me was to let adolescents understand that familiar adults, who seem very confident and well established now, did not necessarily have an easy early life. Careful self-disclosure can be a friendly challenge when adolescents are currently taking the tack of 'how can you possibly understand!' and wanting tough times to be a good excuse for making life miserable for everyone else.

Any kind of simple sharing of personal experiences needs to be done with care, and links in with the basics of good helping skills (see Lindon and Lindon, 2000).

- Any kind of self-disclosure needs to arise because there is a good reason to add your experience to the current conversation. Children and adolescents are irritated if lengthy adult narratives take over a conversation.
- Any contributions must be authentic. Never make things up – you will be found out often enough and what happens then?
- Keep the telling of your experience brief, because your example should not over-shadow what the child or young person wants to say, whether that is lightweight or more troublesome.
- Keep it distinct – your experience is not the same, nor does it make you an expert on another person's feelings. The contribution is undermined if adults are tempted to say, 'I know exactly how you feel'.

Conversations between peers

Children talk differently with each other than with adults. They need relaxed time for social communication with friends and acquaintances, some of whom will be age peers. Some conversational exchanges are part of their play: discussions about what to play, how, where and the ground rules of a game or imaginative sequence. Increasingly, children, often but not always the girls, like comfortable places to sit, indoors and outside, where they can simply chat and be sociable. The best playground make-overs include attention to this issue about places and spaces for being together, as well as important issues of play spaces and simple equipment for play.

In middle childhood girls and boys take the view that some topics of conversation are just between peers, because adults are not interested in this subject or not to this depth of discussion. By age 5–7, children have usually worked out that adults do not always share their sense of humour or have a limit on jokes about toilets and poo. Older children and adolescents sometimes talk among themselves when they judge adults do not need to hear about this issue: because they will worry, interfere and/or not understand.

Children and young people also sometimes choose to use a different accent and vocabulary with peers. Over middle childhood, boys and girls who live in a diverse neighbourhood become aware of different accents and versions of the same language, even where there is not a range of distinct languages. Older children may start to use a different accent and style of speech when talking with friends, compared with speaking up in class or with their families. Their ability to shift in style may not always be welcome to their parents. Children who live in less diverse neighbourhoods are more dependent on the media for imitating accents and words that they do not hear locally.

Older children and adolescents may be conscious of shifting deliberately to a different accent, because it feels more appropriate with their peers. Sometimes a playground or street accent increases social acceptance and reduces the likelihood of taunting for being 'posh' or some other 'wrong' social background. In diverse city areas there is anecdotal evidence that adolescents deliberately blend words from local languages, for instance young people whose family language is English have started to use Punjabi or Bangladeshi words as part of street and peer interaction. The reverse is also true.

USING SKILLS OF COMMUNICATION

Children and young people can learn about the different patterns and ground rules for communication that is more structured than spontaneous conversation with chosen partners.

The school classroom

Good primary school practice includes a significant effort to balance learning within small groups with whole-class work. But even when alert teachers bring in every child or adolescent as much as possible, classroom communication is different from the skills of conversation. For many 5–8 year olds there is still a relatively short window of time between thinking something interesting and needing to say it out loud. Children become steadily more able to hold a thought or other contribution to a conversation or group discussion, but some individuals still struggle and it is not unusual for a child to have lost hold on the thought by the time their turn has arrived in group or classroom discussion.

When adults are patient and supportive, children learn how to communicate appropriately in the classroom situation. They understand about ways to indicate that they want to speak. Group discussions within school often follow the social convention of putting up a hand, although some circle times use props like passing a 'talking stick' or similar symbol. With help, children also steadily manage to link their contribution more tightly to the topic that is under discussion today. Effective teachers create the atmosphere in general and the content for today in particular. A lively classroom or group discussion can then be guided but not dominated by the teacher (see some of the examples from page 192).

The speaking and listening skills of children and young people should not be judged only or mainly through the classroom model. However, it is important that children gain the ability in primary school to operate within this more structured situation, otherwise they will be at a loss in secondary school, and a source of grief to those teachers.

Assembly and other audiences

Children vary in their level of confidence in what is actually a form of public speaking in the classroom. However, some older children have gained the confidence to speak up appropriately, even in very large groups, such as school assembly.

- In primary schools children are often given the opportunity to make a presentation to the whole school through a themed assembly. With support and a chance to practise, many children manage to make their contribution to a class account about a trip or a project. Even in a small primary school, the size of the audience creates a large sea of faces, so it is impressive that 7 and 8 year olds have started on this kind of communication.

- Some older children and adolescents gain confidence within school assembly and become adept at the turn-taking of public debate. Some young people are enthusiastic about public speaking and are ready, with discreet adult support and practice again, to speak up at inter-school conferences.

- An increasing number of conferences for adults about services for children and young people welcome representatives from that age group, who are able to make their presentation, sometimes with the technological backup that eludes a proportion of the adults.

Communication in meetings

Children and young people also learn ways to communicate within the format of a group meeting. The three main types that I have encountered are weekly house meetings in some residential homes, after-school clubs that hold regular club meetings, and school councils in primary and secondary school.

The coming together times in residential homes work rather like a family kitchen table discussion, with the added support needed for children and young people who have experienced severe disruption in their lives. These sessions are welcomed by children, who are confident that the adults keep the discussion even-handed, fair and emotionally safe. Older children and young people use this kind of 'house meeting' to discuss issues of what is happening in the residential home – sometimes problems but sometimes decisions that need to be made as a small community.

Any kind of group meeting works best when there are some basic ground rules to ensure courteous yet open communication. The main guidelines are about listening to other people, finding ways to be honest without being hurtful and not being obliged to speak right now. Some residential homes and after-school clubs use a prop like a 'talking stick' or a teddy that passes from speaker to speaker, including the adults. In after-school clubs, practitioners find that 7–8 year olds can be well able to talk around club issues and set an example that younger children learn to follow. The older children, who are usually no more than 11 years old, are often adept at making conversational space for the younger or less outspoken children. They have learned a style of communication from practitioners, school or from the pattern in their own family.

Many primary and secondary schools in the UK now have a school council, although the pattern of operation varies between schools. The main point is that children and young people are able to participate in discussion and decision-making in this more business-like way. They can understand and follow the structure of communication as it works for a meeting. They are also able to fulfil a wide range of roles. Older children and adolescents become adept at the skills needed to chair school council meetings, lead and manage discussion, organise an agenda and minutes and report back to peers. Like any other development in communication skills, it is crucial that adults understand the skills needed for effective meetings and coach children or young people in those skills. These are the same skills and ground rules needed to ensure effective meetings between adults.

It is also important that adults – teachers, club or youth workers, anyone involved in meetings with children or young people – follow the ground

MAKE THE CONNECTION WITH ... CHILDREN'S POTENTIAL

Children as young as 5 and 6 years old are able to act as the class representative and discuss issues with the adults. In my conversations at Crabtree Infants School, a group of the class representatives were confident enough to explain to me what they did and how.

They described their role as listening to other children who wanted to say that something was the matter. The representatives would try to help if they could, but felt able to bring in an adult if necessary. In meetings, with the head teacher or another senior member of staff, they talked about problems that needed solving within school life and reported back to their class. The eldest of this group were 7 years of age, but they were already able to explain that some problems were not solved easily and that they sometimes needed to explain this to their class.

The council representatives were elected by their classmates and served either a term or half a year. These children were willing to give their time also to help raise money for the school and served the refreshments to special visitors. They explained to me that, because the monthly meetings happened on a Friday, new representatives needed to know that sometimes they lost their Golden Time – the special time for choosing at the end of each week.

rules themselves. Group meetings or a school council have to be established and run in an honest way. Children and adolescents soon use their observation and thinking skills to assess whether a council or any regular meeting has no real power for decision-making. Rather like adults, children and young people are irritated by a situation in which, 'nobody wants to know how we feel'. But they are infuriated by a pattern of, 'they pretended to be interested – then they just did what they'd already decided!'

Communication and the media

In different ways children and young people can find themselves in a very public arena. Consultation exercises (see page 281) sometimes bring active involvement in local issues. Children, young people and their families can be approached by journalists and reporters for the many television channels. Contact can be especially sensitive if the school has become the temporary focus of media attention as the result of a tragedy (see page 104). Adults need to be clear-eyed about how even the more responsible sections of the media world operate. They need to share a well-informed understanding and suitable wariness with children and young people.

■ In the end, it is the choice of a young person, alongside their family, whether to give an interview, agree to be a 'case study' in a magazine or take a public stance in other ways. However, everyone needs to know that 'case studies' plus photographs may not be used in the final feature. Entire articles or sections of a television programme may never appear.

■ There is always an angle, because a journalist or reporter has to fit the brief they have been given and independents have to craft something they can sell. Responsible journalists will explain the context, or their line of questioning will show the dominant perspective.

■ Adults need to be ready to support a young person if the pattern of interview diverges from what was expected or promised. Personal concerns can risk being sensationalised, for instance a journalist may not be interested in the 'ordinary' aspects of life for a young carer. Vulnerable young people may be pushed into delivering only the bad news stories.

■ The person who conducts the interview or gathers the examples is very unlikely to control the final shape of a feature and therefore the tone of a child's or young person's contribution. Headlines and sub-headings set the context in the written media; the introductory words do the same job in the visual media.

There is no need to become terminally cynical about every form of media, but older children and adolescents need to develop knowledge alongside useful skills to make an informed choice about any kind of involvement. All the points made above apply also to involvement in any kind of television programme: documentaries or the different types of 'reality television'. Ill-considered words or actions continue with a recorded life of their own.

Communication within peer support

The phrase 'peer pressure' is often used in a negative way by adults to refer to behaviour that can range from the mildly inappropriate to seriously unacceptable. Undoubtedly the way that children and young people sometimes back up one another can be disruptive, especially if they are leading one another into risky choices. However, peer pressure also works in a positive way and the initiatives around peer support demonstrate the impressive communication abilities of children and adolescents.

The idea of peer support is relatively new to the UK, with active development since the 1980s and 1990s. There is a longer history of such

---

LOOK, LISTEN, NOTE, LEARN

- Consider the examples of peer support in this section and find out more using the resources on page 177.
- If possible, make a visit to a local school with a peer support scheme.
- Reflect on how these schemes highlight the potential abilities of children and adolescents. What do they tell you about development?

---

initiatives from the 1960s in Canada and the USA. A range of initiatives draws on the potential skills and motivation of many children and young people to help their peers. The adult responsibility is to create fertile ground to encourage such abilities. Additionally, it is crucial that all the involved adults have a thorough understanding of the skills they seek to transfer. Any schemes in primary or secondary school need to be open to any pupils or students who show an interest, or whose motivation is provoked by a discreet suggestion. Children and adolescents who have struggled with their own study skills or behaviour in the playground can be effective in peer support at a later date.

WHAT DOES IT MEAN?

- **Peer support**: a wide range of initiatives that draw on the willingness of children and adolescents to help each other.
- **Peer pressure**: the process by which children and adolescents persuade each other towards a course of action – with positive as well as negative consequences.

Peer mentoring

This term is used to describe supported developments when a child or young person acts as a positive role model for another child, maybe a peer but possibly a younger child. Peer mentors blend in some schools or play settings with the idea of a 'buddy' or a 'befriending' scheme. In this instance the pupils called 'mentors' are linked up with a new school intake, or individual children or young people new to the school, to ease their entry into the school environment and the pattern of the day. Volunteer play leaders can be helpful advisors to younger children who look up to the 'big boys and girls'.

Mentoring also merges with encouraging older children to be a supportive role model for young ones – in a school or play facility. Some primary schools enable the older children (who are still only 9–11 years of age) to listen to younger children read. Some schemes link together a primary and local secondary school. The older primary school children are also encouraged in some schools to organise games for younger children in playtime breaks.

The Mental Health Foundation report (2002) describes the peer supporters in 'A Space', an out-of-school learning centre located in Kingsland secondary school, but also serving the last two years of the feeder primary schools. Peer supporters were active in supporting children through their transition from primary to secondary school. The supporters made presentations to their peers and younger children about dealing with bullying and other significant issues for emotional well-being in school. They were also active in training new peer supporters. As a result of clear links between A Space and the secondary school, the peer supporters were a familiar figure, helped by the fact that they wore badges in school time, and were used by Year 7 (the first year of English secondary school) students as a source of support and help.

Some peer support schemes are called peer tutoring or peer education. Older adolescents in sixth form or college may work together to support one another in study, sometimes from the direct suggestion of a teacher or tutor. Peer educational initiatives arise when children or young people are trained in a given subject or topic, so that they can then deliver the content to their peers. Examples have included education around health issues such as drug use, sexual activity or awareness of the issues around bullying. The term is used in some rather different ways, but the common features are that children and young people are trained to deliver workshops to peers of a similar age, status and background to themselves.

Peer listening

Children and young people often listen to friends who wish to express worries, and sometimes attempt to offer support and advice. The peer listening projects build on that motivation to help and the reality that sometimes children and young people would rather talk with a peer than with an adult. Children or adolescents are trained in listening as part of a basic helping relationship. Initial training covers the skills of active listening, attention to verbal and non-verbal communication, the steps of problem-solving and boundaries for confidentiality. The peer listening services in school are face-to-face, whereas peer counselling services in university can be a combination of face-to-face and anonymous over the telephone (see page 96). Listening skills are also central to schemes of peer mediation (see page 143).

The peer-run service depends upon supportive supervision, just like any helping service run by adults. Issues can arise around confidentiality, including the circumstances under which peer listeners need to bring in a trusted adult. Like any helpers, children and young people need to be able to leave the role behind. Clear times and a place for talking and listening are non-negotiable for this service to work in school or college. Peer listeners also need the opportunity, in a confidential situation, to unload distress that may have grown upon them as they listen to a peer's complex problem.

The Mental Health Foundation's *Peer Support Manual* (2002) describes projects in secondary schools and colleges of higher education. The examples show not only the great potential of the skills of children and young people, but also that any peer support service has to be responsive to the school population.

- The peer listening service set up in Wanstead High School was run by trained listeners from the sixth form who ran a lunchtime drop-in service. Peer listeners were also attached to the first three year groups of the secondary school and became familiar to those young adolescents. An individual peer listener was later linked with each Year 7 (first year of English secondary school) tutor group. The sixth former became well known to the younger students, acted as an older friend and joined in activities such as hearing the children read.
- A second example, from Kingsbury High School, shows how an effective service is ready to change in response to use. The timed peer listening service was not used much and so was changed to be a more informal playground-based opportunity. The trained peer listeners took their skills out of the building and operated as befrienders for students who looked to be without company in break or lunchtime. As they became familiar figures, the peer supporters used their skills to mediate in disputes and disagreements.

It is important in co-educational schools that boys and young men are involved in the peer listening project as much as girls and young women. Males are potentially as able as their female peers, but without active encouragement there is a possibility that the service could be female-heavy and then give the impression that listening and support is a female preserve.

Peer advocacy
Children and young people sometimes attempt to speak up for a friend in an informal way. Depending on their social skills and the outlook of the adult involved, children and adolescents can find their input either welcomed and the beginning of a more informed dialogue or treated as

an interference and unacceptable challenge. Children and young people are sometimes enabled to speak on behalf of peers in different ways.

- Children and young people represent their class within the school council. However, under-18s can also be associate governors on the governing body of their own school, often through the route of being on the school council. However, they can also be invited to join the governors of another local school. Student governors do not carry the same kind of responsibility as the adult (over-18s) governors.
- Other initiatives include the idea of support groups for children or young people who have similar experiences – of distress or disruption – who are empowered to speak on behalf of the other group members. The aim is usually to communicate the nature of their experience and perhaps to work towards some practical improvements. Sometimes a few children or young people will speak up to represent the views of a larger group, for example over a consultation about local developments or changes.

Some children and young people have no choice but to be the spokesperson and advocate of their parents. Young carers (see page 274) may have to speak for, or offer effective support for, parents who are less able to seek help, information or exercise their rights to a service.

Children and young people as observers in lessons

School Councils UK has a project (ongoing in 2006) in some London secondary schools that acknowledges and uses these observational skills. The idea of student observers in lessons is part of an exploration of the impact of effective school structures for student participation.

- There is discussion before each time of observation because students and teachers together decide upon the particular features of the lesson that will attract close observation. The observer then sits in on the lesson, recording teacher performance and student reaction on pre-prepared time charts.
- The agreed pattern can include issues like the teacher's use of closed and open questions, balance of positive and negative comments, gender patterns in participation and individual student behaviour.
- Children and young people then give feedback in a private conversation to the individual teacher. Trust needs to be established on both sides for this communication to work. Students describe that it can take more than one conversation for them to find a constructive way to give potential criticism, for instance that use of sarcasm by one teacher upset some students.
- The initiative works to promote discussion about education and gives children and young people some insight into the hard work of

preparation behind lessons. There also seemed to be some increased empathy about the effects of disruptive behaviour on teachers' work.

Teachers who are uneasy about being observed in this pre-planned way sometimes need reminding that the children and young people in their class already observe them and reach a judgement. The School Councils UK website (www.schoolcouncils.org) is a useful source of information on many of these initiatives and a report of this particular project will be available online from autumn 2007 (my thanks to Lois Canessa for the information).

UNDERSTANDING AND USING WRITTEN LANGUAGE

UK society needs a literate, as well as a numerate, adult population. So, there is no argument that children need to read and write with confidence before they leave primary school. But there is plenty of disagreement about when and how children are best taught the specific skills that enable them to become independent readers and writers.

Realistic expectations

It was not possible to write this section unless I took a clear stance on the current (2006) debate in England over some recommendations from the Rose Report: the *Independent review of the teaching of early reading* by Jim Rose, 2006 (www.teachernet.gov.uk/publications). Along with a considerable number of reading specialists, researchers and experienced teachers, I consider it is developmentally inappropriate practice to require that children should start being taught formally to read no later than the age of 5. Many children in other European countries start school later, and are not formally taught to read until around 6 or even 7 years of age. They are also often learning a language that is less complex than English.

The Rose report also requires that children are taught exclusively through the systematic method known as synthetic phonics. Children need to learn ways to decode the English language so that they can read, but also so they can become confident writers. However, key claims within the report about the success of synthetic phonics over other methods are not supported by research, see, for instance, Dominic Wyse and Russell Jones (2006) or Carole Togerson et al. (2006) – a review commissioned by the Department of Education and Skills. Early literacy matters, and Sally Featherstone (2006) offers many ways to build firm foundations towards the time when children are developmentally ready for formal instruction.

It is developmentally realistic to expect 7–8 year olds to be able to read and write, although some find the skills easier or more enjoyable than others. If 8 year olds are not making noticeable progress, then there is reason to make careful assessment of the source of their difficulties and plan appropriate help. This slide downwards of two years through unrealistic early learning goals for 5 year olds in the Foundation Stage (and now the Early Years Foundation Stage – England) has nothing to do with significant changes in observed developmental norms. Legitimate concerns about later literacy were pressed down the age range, with minimal understanding of how skills are built and the additional problems of becoming literate in English.

WHAT DOES IT MEAN?

Literacy skills: competence in reading and writing. Literate children and young people are able to cope with ordinary life situations that require use of the written language.

Emergent writing: deliberate mark-making by children that has the general appearance of written script for their language. Children may also say that it is 'my writing'.

Phonics: approaches to the teaching of literacy that focus on the relationship between the written letters of the alphabet and the sounds of speech.

Learning to read and write English

English is a very rich language, which historically has drawn from many other languages across Europe and Asia. These origins mean that English is especially complex: for almost every grammar or spelling rule children also have to learn exceptions. Languages like Welsh or Polish look difficult to the non-speaker, but the structure is far more consistent, once you know the rules. A further complication for children is that English is spoken with such a wide range of accents. This diversity adds to the lack of consistent rules on how to transform the way that a word sounds in everyday, local speech into how it is spelled through single letters of the alphabet.

This situation means that it is especially unrealistic to expect English-speaking children to attain levels of proficiency in reading and writing at similar ages to their peers in other European countries, whose language is considerably simpler in terms of predictable rules. There is no evidence to support claims, for instance in the Rose Report, that the complexity of English means that formal teaching of reading and writing should therefore start in early childhood. Usha Goswami (2003) sums up the situation as, 'The main reason that English children lag behind their European peers in acquiring proficient reading skills is that the English language presents them with a far more difficult learning problem' (page 462). She also notes (2005) the irony that so many research studies of the process of learning to read have been undertaken by English speakers and the linked models of teaching have exerted a lot of influence in non-English speaking countries. There is no good reason to suppose that what works for our rich, but extremely difficult, language would necessarily be the best approach for languages that are much more straightforward to decode.

Apart from enthusiasm for books and meaningful mark-making, children need to become attuned to the sound patterns and rhythm of English. Studies, including those reported by Usha Goswami (2003), suggest that beat detection is really useful for children in early and middle childhood. This kind of vital experience is offered through music, singing, rhymes and story-songs with a clear beat. Ros Bayley (see page 170) has developed a range of materials that support this learning for children, partly emerging from her experience with children who are struggling with literacy skills.

Keen readers?

Literacy really does matter. Children need to be taught how the language works and have plenty of practice in decoding until they are confident to read independently. Secure literacy skills for adulthood require that children and young people want to use those skills themselves once they have left school. Literacy skills are deeply insecure if children become convinced, within primary school, that the only reason to learn to read or write is to stop the adults nagging them.

Children can already have decided in their early primary years that they are 'no good' at reading and/or writing. These negative attitudes can emerge through patterns of behaviour that enable the children, more often the boys than the girls, to avoid the disliked task but which label them as being 'disruptive' or a child 'with poor concentration'. Struggles with literacy then easily become intertwined with issues in school around unacceptable behaviour from children. Children may form strong social bonds with other children who have similarly 'failed' and peer pressure develops against even mild enthusiasm or effort about school work.

Some children, it will become clear, have specific difficulties such as dyslexia or dyspraxia that complicate the task of literacy. However, problems that arise are not always about special needs related to reading and writing. There is serious concern that, when children are fast tracked through the process, a proportion are being made to feel like failures at a young age, and/or being thoroughly bored by experiences that seem to have no payoff for them.

Christina Clark and Amelia Foster (2005) report a survey of the reading habits of children and young people from primary and secondary schools

---

LOOK, LISTEN, NOTE, LEARN

There are serious risks for future learning if children are switched off the task of reading at an early age. Children's interest can be recaptured so long as adults find a suitable route back towards literacy.

Ros Bayley and Annie Clews worked with one advisory service in the Birmingham area (England) that supported some primary schools in disadvantaged neighbourhoods. Ros Bayley describes meeting 6 and 7 year olds, most of them boys, who had already decided that they were failures at reading and avoided books. These children seemed unable to retain information in the classroom context, but they could recall complex song lyrics and really liked the rap format.

Ros Bayley linked up with Steve Scott, a musician who had become interested in writing songs for his young daughter. Ros wrote the text of *Maurice the Mouse*, a story that flowed like a song, and Steve put the words to music. They made a CD in which Maurice's search for a suitable house is told with a rap rhythm. This style seized the children's attention and they were keen to explore the song and the illustrations in the book, to try out role play around the story and finally to address the written text.

The children discovered that they could read and they transferred their skills and sense of success to other books. Children in the same schools, who were not seen as problem or slow readers, were equally enthusiastic about the special song/books. So there was no risk that these were marginalised for the 'struggling' readers.

Thanks to Ros Bayley for describing the project (personal communication) and the many ways in which she uses music and the importance of beat to bring children into reading and enthusiasm about stories.

- Three books with CDs have been developed so far and are available from Lawrence Educational, tel: 0121 344 3004; www.educationalpublications.com.

- A wide range of CDs is available from Steve Scott and Greg Bone, from their company Keeping the Beat, www.keepingthebeat.co.uk.

that were part of the National Literacy Trust's Reading Connects initiative.

- They describe a younger generation with many children and young people who are enthused about books and other reading matter and who do read out of choice and for pleasure. The survey does not support the gloomy pronouncements of some adults that 'kids don't read any more!'
- Enthusiastic, rather than reluctant, readers of both sexes were also more likely to talk about what they read with family members as well as school staff. The majority of the children and young people in the survey saw reading as something that should be encouraged by home as well as school.
- However, there were differences between the sexes in that girls and young women were more likely to read because they enjoyed the pastime and less likely than their male peers to express negative views about reading. Many boys and young men read for pleasure, but they were more likely than their female peers to give reasons such as they had to read books, or reading would improve their job chances.

The survey and the Reading Connects initiative both rested on the conviction that literacy teaching has to create enthusiastic readers, and not simply children and young people who are technically able to read. The team point to three main strands that are important in schools:

1 Create a culture in which all pupils are encouraged to be enthusiastic readers.
2 Consider how to engage boys with reading. There is nothing the matter with concluding that different tactics may be needed for one sex within an overall strategy that works for most children.
3 Seek to support parents in encouraging reading at home.

The craft of writing

Learning to write requires that children understand how words are formed with a sequence of specific letters: the nightmare that is spelling for English. Children need to be confident and competent in the technical skills of handwriting, because this method has not disappeared completely in favour of typing on a keyboard supported by a word-processing package. As the years of middle childhood pass, children are able to get to grips with punctuation and that correct use does matter to bring meaning to written materials.

However, the skills of writing do not begin and end with technical issues of handwriting. Literacy in terms of writing is not achieved through

MAKE THE CONNECTION WITH . . . THE PLEASURE OF STORIES

It is important to keep reading to older children, even adolescents if they would like, long after they have become independent readers. There is a phase when children can read but it is still hard work. However, it is enjoyable to hear someone read out loud while you relax and listen.

There is a tremendous choice of books that work well for reading in episodes. I have read modern books by Terry Pratchett, Roald Dahl and Judy Blume, along with less recent publications like Charlotte's Web (by E.B. White), The Secret Garden (by Frances Hodgson-Burnett) and books of myths and legends.

Always read a book or long story to yourself before you start: you'll avoid folk tales that are too bloodthirsty for the younger end, or you'll know about a sad or scary section.

If you have already tried the episode reading with children:

■　What have you found that works well?

■　What books did children or young adolescents choose?

If you are not in the habit of reading to children who are independent readers, then make some plans to change that situation.

Children need plenty of relaxed practice

being a competent copier of existing pieces of written work. Children also need the ability and motivation to be able to plan what they will write. They can become aware of the many different styles of using the written word, much like a wide use of spoken language (see page 148). Good primary school practice steadily provides experiences in planning and writing for different purposes.

- Children enjoy writing their own stories and are often especially motivated by the narrative style of writing. They are well served by experiences in their early years that have created enjoyment of story books and story telling with puppets, other props and simply by recounting out loud.

- By 10 and 11 years of age, children can have grasped, and some really enjoy, the pattern of how to use writing for poems or the layout of a simple play with characters.

- They can grasp the different style that is needed to tell somebody about something, which might be through the genre of writing a letter, a simple account, report or wanting to describe something of interest. Telling and describing interesting information rests as well on early experience of non-fiction books (books about . . .) and on plenty of opportunities to tell adults and other children through oral language about interesting events.

- Children move into the style of writing, with the additional vocabulary, of simple news reporting. Under 11s are capable of organising a simple news sheet – handwritten or using some of the facilities of a computer.

- Children often like making lists, and pretend play around shopping builds the understanding of how writing is very useful for this practical purpose. Happy list-making can evolve into other kinds of writing as a way to plan ahead, including how to give instructions to somebody who needs to be clear about the steps in a process, like a recipe or how to build something.

Children are often interested to share their own interests and then to use their literacy and research skills to find out more. Of course, it is the job of teachers and the task of all adults to extend the interests of children and young people into a range of books, art forms, music and other aspects of what is summed up as 'culture'. However, this younger generation is no more likely than previous ones to be motivated to try suggestions from adults if the same people are dismissive of what enthuses children and young people themselves.

Jackie Marsh and Elaine Millard (2000) make a strong and practical case for inviting children's interests into the classroom. They describe a variety

**MAKE THE CONNECTION WITH . . .
CONTINUED SKILL IN ORAL LANGUAGE**

Children's understanding of variations around the written format continue to develop alongside their skills of spoken communication. For instance, Jeni Riley and David Reedy (2000) discuss the ability of children to move into the kind of writing needed to support putting your side of the argument and writing to persuade others. They explain how language for debate and persuasion has to be explored through the oral route, so that children understand in spoken terms how to express opinions, gather their supporting information and be ready to answer any counter-arguments.

They then describe a long-term project by one of the authors (DR) with 5 and 6 year olds who were able to explore and document whether zoos were, overall, a 'good or a bad place' for the animals ('A case study: on zoos', Riley and Reedy, 2000, pages 147–57).

of long-term projects that supported literacy and evolved from children's interests from a wide range of media. The whole approach shows respect for children, avoiding setting up stark contrasts between 'good ' and 'bad' culture, or books that are judged to be 'classics' and those that are dismissed as trivial. Of course, allowing time for projects that start from children's interests does not stop adults sharing interests in their turn and planning for tasters from books or the visual media that extend children's experience.

Mobile phones and texting

Communication between peers is supported by mobile phone technology, writing text messages and sending visual images by phone and by email. There are issues around mobile phone etiquette in any shared spaces such as a school or college classroom. Adults, including those in the teaching profession, have also expressed concerns about the possible impact of texting on children's cognitive and linguistic development.

It seems that enthusiasm for texting can co-exist with ability to spell and write full-length words. However, children and young people do need to learn appropriate context: that texting is not acceptable for writing essays, nor answers to exam questions. Anecdotal evidence from examination boards and the teaching profession suggests strongly that some young people have not made that distinction, or have not been given a sufficiently clear message by adults. I would add my experience of reading a considerable number of adults' evaluation forms for my training days, a proportion of which now include text-style writing, along with variable spelling of full-length words.

A research study is in progress at Coventry University, run by Beverly Plester and Clare Wood. So far they have considered a group of 10 and 11 year olds who regularly use texting and who had also performed well in the Key Stage 2 assessments of writing and spelling (national assessments at the end of primary school in England). These girls and boys were keen texters and well able to write and spell for their age so their enthusiasm for texting by mobile phone had not undermined their ability to spell. The researchers are cautious about generalising too much from a small sample (26 girls and 9 boys), but point out that children's phonological awareness might be enhanced by the practice of texting, since many text abbreviations are phonetic in nature. This form of written communication requires a grasp of the link between how words are said and how they are spelled letter by letter or, in the case of texting, by sometimes putting in a number (like 4 to stand for 'for').

Beverley Plester and Clare Wood also suggest that, at least with this group of able children, their familiarity with language for texting has not undermined their knowledge of standard English – the children seem able to switch between the different forms of written language. (Look at page 158 for a discussion of children's ability to alternate between ways of speaking.) But it is uncertain whether the same is true of less able English users, or younger children with less sure knowledge of the conventions of the language. A growing number of 7–9 year olds are now being given their own mobile phone.

With thanks to Beverly Plester for providing me with information about this research in progress (presented to the British Psychological Conference in London, September 2006). Readers who are interested to find out more can contact her on b.plester@coventry.ac.uk. If you want to improve your knowledge of the language of texting, there is a handy dictionary resource on www.text.it/text/text_dictionary.cfm.

If you want to find out more

❖ **Attenborough, Liz and Fahey, Rachel** (2005) *Why do many young children lack basic language skills?* Discussion paper for National Literacy Trust, www.talktoyourbaby.org.uk.

❖ **Basic Skills Agency** – a source of information about literacy and numeracy, practical examples. Tel: 020 7405 4017; www.basic-skills.co.uk.

❖ **Butler, Ian**; **Robinson, Margaret** and **Scanlan, Lesley** (2005)
Children and decision making. London: National Children's Bureau.
Summary at www.jrf.org.uk/knowledge/findings/socialpolicy/0365.asp.

❖ **Clark, Christina** and **Foster, Amelia** (2005) *Children's and young
people's reading habits and preferences: the who, what, why, where and
when.* See www.literacytrust.org.uk/Research/readsurvey.html.

❖ **Faber, Adele** and **Mazlish, Elaine** (1999) *How to talk so kids will
listen and listen so kids will talk.* London: Piccadilly Press.

❖ **Faber, Adele** and **Mazlish, Elaine** (2005) *How to talk so teens will
listen and listen so teens will talk.* London: Piccadilly Press.

❖ **Featherstone, Sally** (ed.) (2006) *L is for Sheep – getting ready for
phonics.* Husbands Bosworth: Featherstone Education.

❖ **Frater, Graham** (2000) *Securing boys' literacy.* London: Basic Skills
Agency.

❖ **Gorman, Tom** and **Brooks, Greg** (1996) *Assessing young children's
writing: a step by step guide.* London: Basic Skills Agency.

❖ **Goswami, Usha** (2003) 'How to beat dyslexia', *The Psychologist* 16(9);
www.bps.org.uk/publications/thepsychologist/search-the-psychologist-
online.cfm.

❖ **Goswami, Usha** (2005) 'Synthetic phonics and learning to read: a
cross-language perspective', *Educational Psychology in Practice* 21(4)
December, pages 273–82.

❖ **Hughes, Anne** and **Ellis, Sue** (1998) *Writing it right? Children
writing from 3–8.* Available for download from www.ltscotland.org.uk/
earlyyears/resources/writingitrightchildrenwriting38.asp.

❖ **Learning and Teaching Scotland** – plenty of useful information and
downloads for anyone across the UK involved with children and
young people, for instance, online resources about study skills at
different stages of education; www.ltscotland.org.uk.

❖ **Lindon, Jennie** and **Lindon, Lance** (2000) *Mastering counselling
skills: information, help and advice in the caring services.* Basingstoke:
Macmillan.

❖ **Literacy Trust** See www.literacytrust.org.uk.

❖ **Marsh, Jackie** and **Millard, Elaine** (2000) *Literacy and popular
culture: using children's culture in the classroom.* London: Paul Chapman.

❖ **Mental Health Foundation** (2002) *Peer Support Manual: a guide to setting up a peer listening project in education settings.* Available for download from www.mentalhealth.org.uk – includes a useful description of the different types of peer support as well as initiatives within peer listening projects.

❖ **Millar, Sally** and **Aitken, Stuart** (2003) *Personal Communication Passports: Guidelines for good practice.* Edinburgh CALL Centre, University of Edinburgh. See http://callcentre.education.ed.ac.uk.

❖ **Owen, Pamela** and **Pumfrey, Peter** (1997) *Children learning to read: International Concerns Volume 1: Emergent and developing reading: messages for teachers.* London: Falmer Press.

❖ **Riley, Jeni** and **Reedy, David** (2000) *Developing writing for different purposes: teaching about genre in early years.* London: Paul Chapman.

❖ **School Councils UK** – a source of information about all aspects of a school council, also student governors and for a range of projects and initiatives. Tel: 0845 456 9428; www.schoolcouncils.org and explore through the sub-sections of 'resources' or 'network/best practice'.

❖ **Togerson, Carol**; **Brooks, Greg** and **Hall, Jill** (2006) *A systematic review of the research literature on the use of phonics in the teaching of reading and spelling.* See www.dfes.gov.uk/research/data/uploadfiles/ RR711_.pdf full report or a summary RB711.

❖ **Wyse, Dominic** and **Jones, Russell** (2006) *Teaching English, language and literacy.* London: Routledge.

7 Developing the skills of thinking

Young children show clear evidence of thinking within early childhood and some of their intellectual power is shown through what they do as well as what they say. During later childhood and adolescence, boys and girls continue to develop their powers of thought and reasoning. A considerable amount of this kind of learning can happen within their educational experience. However, cognitive development is definitely not restricted to the time and place boundaries of school life.

> **The main sections of this chapter are:**
>
> * ⭑ **The development of children as thinkers.**
> * ⭑ **Supporting thinking skills.**
> * ⭑ **Thinking and learning at school.**

THE DEVELOPMENT OF CHILDREN AS THINKERS

As the years pass, children and adolescents show significant development in how they think. However, more sophisticated thinking skills do not emerge simply from the passing of time; a great deal depends on experiences to encourage thinking. Efforts to fast-track children towards higher-order thinking are likely to be derailed by the fact that their brains need time to develop. The human brain is ready to make another leap during adolescence and studies of brain activity have identified a sustained burst of activity and neural reorganisation over the years of adolescence and into early adulthood.

The influence of Jean Piaget

In the UK, views of cognitive development through childhood and adolescence have been very influenced by the stage theory of Jean Piaget, who proposed that children moved from a strong dependence on their senses and tangible objects towards the ability to process complex ideas and abstract methods of reasoning. Jean Piaget's detailed description of qualitatively different stages remains thought-provoking, but any practical application of his ideas has to allow for research that challenges some of his conclusions.

Susan Isaacs, from her observations in the Malting House School, challenged Piaget's conviction that 5–7 year olds struggled with certain kinds of logic or patterns of cause and effect. Margaret Donaldson, and her team in Edinburgh, established that 3–6 year olds had a much better grasp of abstract ideas than Piaget claimed. Young children were very busy thinking: trying to make sense of the rather odd questions and experimental scenarios. Slight changes of materials enabled children to make sense of a situation, such as how somebody might see a small-world layout from a different angle. In many ways, Jean Piaget was right about the thinking power wielded by children younger than 7 or 8 years old, he just seemed to overlook the possibility that they continued to think and try to make sense of adult behaviour during his own experiments. For a summary of some of this research see Lindon, 2001 and 2005.

Explorations of Piaget's ideas applied to older children and adolescents have raised several areas of criticism.

- The most practical drawback to the theory is that Piaget was not really interested in individual differences, such as those explained by temperament and particular life experiences. Nor was he motivated to explore any possibility that girls and boys, on average, might develop different patterns of thinking.

- Some theorists take exception to fine details of Piaget's stages and his view of information processing (see Sutherland, 1992). But a more general problem is that Piaget's view of abstract thinking rested largely upon observations of children and young people from families within his own academic community in Geneva, Switzerland.

- Piaget proposed that 12 year olds were ready to begin the qualitative shift into formal operations, a way of thinking that uses a systematic consideration of possibilities and deductive logic (see page 189). Adolescents show that they can move into this kind of higher-order thinking, but studies have regularly found that the significant shift for most young people in industrialised countries is more around mid-adolescence, 14 or 15 years of age, and not the early period.

- Furthermore, even older adolescents and adults are not necessarily at ease using the more abstract forms of logic and reasoning, especially applied to problems that do not connect to familiar experiences or context. Helen Bee and Denise Boyd (2004) suggest that most adults do not spend a significant proportion of each day operating at the level of formal operations, unless their profession demands that kind of intellectual rigour.

- A great deal seems to depend on relevant experience and specific instruction, most likely through schooling. The details of an educational system in turn depend on economics, but also on whether a given society wants or needs a population that is able to operate at the abstract level. Studies of non-industrialised countries have found limited evidence of young people progressing into the level of thinking described by Piaget's formal operations stage.

MAKE THE CONNECTION WITH ...
THE NEED FOR CONNECTIONS

In many ways Jean Piaget has been proved correct in some of his descriptions of children from 6 to about 12 years of age, who are in what he called the concrete operations stage.

■ Children need a familiar context in which to apply their growing understanding of rules that can be applied to objects, the natural world, relationships and mathematical or scientific thinking.

■ They need to ground their thinking in some way and can be puzzled, uneasy or bored if they are prevented from making connections to experiences, their existing ideas and the rich data from all their senses.

■ Many of the projects around thinking skills (described in this chapter from page 192) depend upon creativity from adults, who have found the hook of understanding for individual children or a group.

■ Many educationalists have serious concerns about more formal and highly structured approaches to children in some primary schools, precisely because children become disconnected from direct, first-hand experiences that enthuse and support learning (see Diane Rich et al., 2005).

Application to practice

In a nutshell, when Piagetian theory is put to the practical test, he seems to have under-estimated the thinking power of children who were some way through what he called the pre-operational stage, from 2 to 6 years of age. Later observers have criticised the way in which Piaget seemed to judge these younger children often in terms of their apparent failure to understand – called the deficit model – especially since he required logical answers to some rather obscure questions.

On the other hand, evidence has generally pointed to his over-optimism about the age at which young adolescents manage very abstract levels of complex thinking: his stage of formal operations. There is no solid evidence that formal operations is a universal stage of thinking reached by everyone. There is every reason to argue that a great deal depends on specific instruction and experience to open this door for adolescents to operate comfortably with higher-order, abstract thinking.

The sheer level of complexity within Piaget's formal operations is daunting. It is possible to feel one's neural pathways creaking just from reading detailed descriptions of thinking that is allegedly typical of this final stage of cognitive development. Furthermore, most of his examples were drawn from the kind of research problems and logical reasoning typical of a scientific laboratory. So there is also a sound basis for arguing that complex, more mature thinking will present itself in some ways that do not fit the model of an experimental scientist.

Knowing and thinking

Given adult support and a positive environment for communication, children are potentially able to manage many skills by middle childhood. At 7–8 years of age, children are already making progress within these broad strands of thinking skills. Consider in what way you observe this productive thinking in busy children you know well.

- *Information processing*: children's ability to take in and work on bits of knowledge. They may receive information in different ways: through listening and looking or the results of direct exploration and experimentation, often through play in childhood, as well as by direct instruction from adults.

- *Putting thoughts into tangible form*: children's thinking is closely linked with communication. Children, like adolescents and adults, can do solitary thinking, but nobody knows unless their thinking is shared: spoken, written, drawn, danced, sung or displayed through other channels of communication.

- *Finding and making connections*: thinking involves bringing together facts and ideas, reflecting on whether new information fits existing assumptions and beliefs. The thinking skills of weighing up information, interpretation and evaluation can lead to new connections and serious rethinking about what previously seemed certain.

- *Thinking connects with creativity*: because open-ended information processing sometimes takes a leap, links with guesses and 'let's find out if . . .'. The point about helping children to share ideas in guided small-group work is because the give-and-take of a group discussion sometimes propels thinking into a whole new sphere.

In middle childhood you can see evidence of children's ability to gather and recall knowledge.

- Some boys and girls have already developed specialist interests in which they are very knowledgeable, sometimes more so than the adults around them. You may be struck that some children already have more general knowledge than their peers. A great deal seems to depend on family experience: talking together, enjoying television together (but avoiding non-stop viewing) and a home with plenty of books and other written materials.

LOOK, LISTEN, NOTE, LEARN

Sometimes adults judge that children are paying attention only when they are looking steadily at the adult. However, Gwyneth Doherty-Sneddon (2004) has shown that many 5–8 year olds learn a strategy of looking away (gaze aversion) to support their concentration when they are thinking hard. Children looked away from the adult most often when they found the verbal or arithmetical questions difficult, but not impossible. They seem to use gaze aversion to control a situation that would otherwise be a cognitive overload. If they could look away, children then sometimes produced partially correct answers.

It makes sense, within reason, to ask children to look at you while they are listening, although adults need to allow for cultural variations in what children are told is polite behaviour. But this research implies that practitioners should not require the same 'evidence' of attention when children are considering their answer. Younger children use visual clues a great deal to fill in the gaps when what an adult says does not make sense. Their awareness of non-verbal communication is very useful and continues as part of full language skills. However, by middle childhood this strategy is less often needed, unless children have disabilities in communication. Most children need the time, and an adult tolerance of silence while they think, if they are to be able to do the hard thinking before they answer.

- In what ways can you apply this practical research to your own time with children or adolescents?
- Be alert to how much adults use gaze aversion when they are thinking. Gwyneth Doherty-Sneddon suggests that children almost certainly learn the strategy by watching us.

- By middle childhood, many 7 and 8 year olds can access their own knowledge in an active way by saying, 'I know that' or, 'I don't know that'. They can be aware of the effort to locate what they know, with 'I can't remember', and may have already learned some simple strategies for trying to memorise information and to recall. They may follow the model set by an adult or older child and use specific words and phrases that flag up their thinking, such as, 'I think that ...', 'I'm sure/fairly sure' or 'I guess ...'.

- By middle childhood, many children are able to voice the link between their opinion or statement of fact and the supporting knowledge. Children who are already keen users of books may say, 'Every creature does not go to sleep. Sharks don't go to sleep; I read it in my book about marine life.' Of course, 6 and 7 year olds are just as likely to say, 'I'm just right and you're wrong!' or, 'Because my Dad says so.'

Children have already built a framework around knowledge and may talk with certainty about 'what I know' or 'it's true/not true that . . .'. Barbara Tizard and Martin Hughes (2002) describe the twin tasks for children of building up a strong base of knowledge and the conceptual framework in which to make sense of new information. Sometimes new information simply will not fit the existing framework and a serious rethink has to follow about how the world operates. Supportive adults remember that an ordinary childhood is full of finding out just how much you do not yet know.

Fantasy and reality

By middle childhood, many children have a sound basis of what is real and what is not real and can be very clear about 'just pretend' in their own play. They are adept at stepping in and out of role in their chosen imaginative play. Older children may be running complex pretend play scenarios that last over weeks, with serious discussions about characters and working scripts. However, there are significant gaps in children's knowledge and they are open to explanations that may seem illogical or bordering on the magical to adults.

- Researchers, like Eugene Subbotsky (2004), who study the development of an understanding of reality and fantasy, show that up to about middle childhood, girls and boys may sometimes state firmly that magic is not possible. But they remain open to magical explanations, especially if adults have introduced the idea to children through a story or sleight of hand.

- Children can understand the nature of a story, yet they may still be wary that characters in books or on film/video are hiding in the shadows. They have blurred boundaries between fantasy and reality, but adolescents and even adults can be scared by films or books they know to be fiction.

- Adolescents, and adults, may be firmer on the logical stance that magic does not occur, but many people still allow the 'just in case' gap for superstition. Strongly held spiritual (see page 80) and political/philosophical belief systems are often not amenable to rational thinking and appear illogical or magical to the outsider.

In my opinion, some of the research into children's magical thinking specifically fails to allow for the reality that children are sometimes deliberately misled by adults. Father Christmas does not exist, yet every year a proportion of the UK adult population tells children that he does and gets very agitated if other adults fail to support the façade, even with 8 or 9 year olds. So it is not surprising if children keep an open mind about other unlikely explanations of how daily life works.

TAKE ANOTHER PERSPECTIVE

Children can be perplexed because of their strategies to deal with situations when adults appear to be talking nonsense. Amanda Waterman et al. (2001) followed up earlier research that suggested under-8s would often try to answer nonsensical questions from adults, especially when an initial 'don't know' was followed by an adult repetition of the question. A series of studies suggested that under-8s were more likely to answer nonsensical questions, like, 'Is a jumper angrier than a tree?' when they were phrased as a closed question to which children could answer yes or no.

Most of the children said 'no' to this question, but could later say clearly to researchers that it was a 'silly' and not a 'sensible' question. Further conversation showed that individual children meant something different by their negative reply. Some produced a creative reason for their answer, such as trees would not like people climbing up and breaking branches. But some children who said 'no' explained that the question did not make sense because jumpers and trees could not get angry.

Even in middle childhood some children try to answer a question even if they do not have the knowledge to give an informed reply. The research team found this effect when children were asked about a story and sometimes had not been given the information to answer a question one way or another. Children still replied with a yes or no, when 'I don't know' was the only logical route. They seemed to be influenced by the pattern that when adults ask a question they like to have a clear answer.

Reflect on the practical implications of this research for classroom discussion, and any kind of interviewing of children, whether over playground troubles or more formal situations.

Thinking about possibilities

Children become more able to think through possibilities, so long as they are familiar with enough aspects of the task.

- Children can sometimes work through possibilities in practical tasks, such as where they might have left their school bag. So long as they do not feel nagged by an adult, older children may be able to consider where they have been in the recent past, think logically through possible locations for the lost bag and maybe even go and find it.

Many games require children to think and plan a strategy

However, there are limits and a tired child may well prefer the option of, 'Somebody must've stolen it!'

- They can think ahead into the future in ways that make sense given their experience so far, perhaps planning what they might do next week. However, older children within middle childhood become adept and enthusiastic about predicting 'what might happen if we . . .' for various practical experiments.

- They can also suggest alternative actions that could have been taken in the past, although thinking backwards in an open way seems to be more difficult for children than adolescents. Open-endedness is perhaps more of a challenge when children's knowledge tells them what has definitely happened.

Children also show their skills of logical thinking, planning and weighing up possibilities through their ability to play games with rules.

- By middle childhood boys and girls can have learned to play games with pieces, like draughts, dominoes, chess, backgammon. They are sometimes very adept at games with simple equipment, like Connect 4™.

- Well before adolescence, children can play card games and board games like Snakes and Ladders. But, with prior experience with adult players, 10 and 11 year olds are perfectly capable of playing a game like Monopoly™ without help.

■ Children, especially boys, are enthused by games that work on the computer, through a television or on hand-held systems. It is unwise for adults to permit them to play for significant amounts of time, or without checking the content of a game. However, moderate use of the games technology can support the thinking skills of strategy, recall and a particular kind of quick reaction attention.

LOOK, LISTEN, NOTE, LEARN

Children and young people show their thinking power through games, but they need to be taught how to play in the first place. Adolescents may be patient enough to teach each other card games or how to play chess; but children are less likely to be able to explain the rules and get cross with peers who persist in playing the wrong way.

It is worthwhile teaching a range of games to older children, and to adolescents who have no prior experience. They learn and enjoy games that work on luck, a sharp eye and sometimes (like pairs) on recalling what has already been briefly revealed. But children can also be taught games that need them to work with different possible strategies to win. In terms of card games, I have successfully taught under-11s a range of the simpler card games that involve the concept of a suit for trumping and tricks.

■ What card or board games have you introduced to children in your class, club or home?

■ Look carefully as they play. What can you observe about children's or adolescents' thinking skills?

■ If you know that you do not have a wide repertoire of games, then first build up your knowledge and then introduce some ideas to the children.

What can adolescents manage?

The shift to more complex thinking is a steady process, not a sudden change. Adolescents become more able, potentially, to think about possibilities without having to use direct observations at the time of working through alternatives. Children often find it difficult if they cannot actually do something, move objects around or link a direct experience with abstract thinking.

■ Older children learn about the many ways that symbols can represent ideas, for instance through arithmetical signs, diagrams or the symbolism of a map. Adolescents progress further in their grasp of symbolism and it becomes clear that some individuals have a talent for handling the abstractions of higher-order mathematical or scientific thinking.

- It becomes more possible for adolescents to think through different hypotheses of a 'what if . . .' nature. This kind of thinking does not only apply to scientific enquiry but also to social issues and ethical discussions. Educationalists who work with the Philosophy for Children approach (see also page 195) describe how adolescents are more able to talk around ideas like justice. Children can be very involved in discussions about fairness, but need to connect their proposals with specific examples that make direct sense to them.

- Adolescents can think conceptually in terms of planning and weighing up possibilities. They can be more able to consider the likely consequences of different options, but not all the time and not if emotions are running high (and nor can adults!).

- Adolescents are potentially able to do a great deal more thinking about their thoughts – what is sometimes called metacognition. On issues that matter to them, they may have strong views that relate to higher-order rules, for instance, under what moral circumstances it could be right to break the law.

- Adolescents are more able to think systematically than children, following through a line of thought and going to and fro between strands. Nevertheless, adolescents still get bogged down in some decisions and problem-solving, just like adults. They can learn handy techniques for exploring different angles thoroughly before moving onto another, especially when they face hard-to-resolve dilemmas. This kind of decision-making is difficult, because a person faces a choice when either both (or more) options are equally attractive or both are equally uninviting.

WHAT DOES IT MEAN?

Metacognition: in brief, the ability to think about thinking. Metacognitive abilities include awareness of your own ideas and reasoning; knowledge about what you know and, equally important, the gaps in your current understanding; and the ability to make deliberate choices for strategies for extending knowledge and resolving uncertainties or problems.

Different types of logical thinking

Children can use their powers of reasoning to work something out or to argue their position. But they have a different starting position from the way that adolescents can think. Children are most likely to use inductive logic. This pattern of reasoning starts with direct experience and moves on to develop a general principle or rule.

▓ Plenty of hands-on experience shows children that whenever they add another brick to a tower and then count up the separate bricks, there are always more. So they can reach a general mathematical principle that adding items always makes more in terms of number. They have a great deal of experience to come about different ways to measure 'more'.

▓ Children use their thinking skills about social relations and in middle childhood they have the broader experience to wonder about their own family life. One child may consider, 'Mum and Dad argue a lot, so does that happen in all families? But my cousin's parents don't shout at each other, so maybe it's only my parents who get so cross with each other – why?'

WHAT DOES IT MEAN?

■ **Inductive logic**: a form of reasoning that starts with direct experiences and progresses to the principles that appear to be supported by that evidence.
■ **Deductive logic**: a more abstract approach to logical thinking that starts with a principle or prediction and moves to anticipate what should follow from that ruling.

Adolescents become more able and likely to use deductive logic, at least sometimes. This form of reasoning moves from the general to the specific, rather than the other way round.

▓ Once adolescents can work with deduction, they can think forward from a general principle towards predicting a particular event or reaction, or choosing an interpretation that makes sense from the principle.

▓ They use the concept of a rule to decide the more appropriate choice between actions, for themselves or another person. This type of deductive thinking leads to moral decisions, as well as a rationale behind what is 'the right thing' to do in a given situation.

▓ A great deal of scientific experimentation works with deductive logic. A theory or basic principle is stated and then a prediction is made on the basis of that principle. The prediction is then tested by a careful study and should be able to be disproved, as well as proved.

■ Deductive logic also allows adolescents to take the leap into creative thinking that depends on following through an imaginary situation that has no connection with their familiar daily life. An example might be to explore how society would function if any adult who wanted to have a baby had first to pass a parenting exam.

In daily life for children, adolescents and adults there is usually an interplay between inductive and deductive logic. Even children sometimes work from principles, such as 'promises must be kept', because this value is central to their family life. Experience will unfortunately show them that everyone does not keep their promises. On the other hand, vulnerable adolescents have often experienced serial disappointment over commitments to them. They will predict that even an apparently trustworthy adult will probably let them down at some point. If that adult proves their worth, then adolescents may develop a limited principle of, 'all adults let me down except Jon'. It will take more time and other positive experiences to change to a working principle of 'some adults can be trusted and some cannot and here are some ways that I might be able to tell the difference between the two groups.'

TAKE ANOTHER PERSPECTIVE

The results of thinking by children and adolescents are not always welcome to adults. Even when they deliver their views with care, children and young people sometimes find that their spoken thoughts are experienced as 'cheek' or 'challenging' of the authority of adults.

The logic and consequent 'why?' from a child, even more so from an articulate young person, requires adults to think and to explain or justify their position. Less confident adults, especially those who are anxious about losing control of a group (see page 138) find it hard to deal with this situation. It is appropriate for adults to guide children and adolescents towards courtesy in discussion or argument. However, it remains an adult responsibility to set a good example, even when older children and young people challenge cherished beliefs or confident facts.

Cause and effect

Even adults struggle sometimes with the logical thinking and weighing up of evidence that underpins an accurate judgement of cause and effect. It is easier to assume a simple pattern of causality and this kind of logic supports animosity between groups. Classroom or club discussion may start with the apparently logical argument that, 'my mum says our family has got worse off as this group of people moved into the neighbourhood, so our troubles must be caused by them'. However, the explanation of the family troubles is independent of the arrival of the group whom it is easy to blame. The two events have just happened over the same time span. The example that used to be given for statistics was that over a period of time in Sweden the increase in the population of storks was very similar to the increase in the human birth rate. But these charts were not proof that storks had anything to do with the arrival of babies.

LOOK, LISTEN, NOTE, LEARN

Media discussion about education, health issues and diet is sometimes over-simplified. It is worth exploring some news stories with adolescents and tracking back, if possible, to the piece of research that provoked the headlines. Adolescents and young adults need the logical thinking skills to make sense of possible misunderstandings and half-stories.

For instance, discussion about health can get side-tracked when the message is reduced to a simple cause and effect. One of the health risks of smoking is that smokers develop lung cancer, but the health warning is about an increased percentage risk. Every smoker does not die of lung cancer and some non-smokers nevertheless develop this disease. Somebody will always have a grandfather who smoked 100 cigarettes a day and lived to be 90 years old.

SUPPORTING THINKING SKILLS

There has been a great deal of interest, even concern, about how to make the most of children's potential for full cognitive development over childhood and adolescence. Many of the initiatives have been undertaken in school, at both primary and secondary level, and you will find more detail about those projects from page 200. However, the insights into development have a broad application for any practitioners involved with children and adolescents.

Independent learners

A team led by David Whitebread (2005) explored the nature of independent learning within early childhood. The study established that, with suitable experiences, 5 year olds could already be aware of their own learning, be able to organise themselves and how they approach activities for learning and could view themselves as learners. The Cambridgeshire

Independent Learning project showed that young children were capable of self-directed thinking, given a suitable learning environment. The key points that emerged from the research are useful for practitioners in any setting with children across the age range.

▩ Children learned a great deal by watching each other – so time and space were important for them to observe and learn. Given the opportunity to make their own choices and decisions, children were remarkably focused and organised. They pursued their own plans with persistence and over long periods of time: an observation that surprised some of the adults who thought they knew the limits for these 3–5 year olds.

▩ Sometimes when an adult became involved in an activity the children were more inclined to say they could not do something, but if they were working with another child they were less likely to question their ability and often imitated the other child, gaining confidence in their abilities. This finding does not imply that practitioners should back away from helping; the practical point is for adults to be alert to whether their direct input is needed this time. Also, confident children will know they can ask.

▩ Often, the most effective response practitioners could give to a child asking for help was to refer them to another child, who had greater competence or expertise in that particular area. Of course, again the implication is not that practitioners always pass on a child's request. Alert observation of individual children will inform practitioners of the full array of skills within a group, and not just those resting with the adults.

Individual differences were also clear by 5 years of age. Some children responded well to open-ended, child-initiated tasks, whereas others really wanted a supportive structure established by an adult, before they were comfortable to develop their own explorations. Support for independent learning required both kinds of opportunities to be provided; good practice is not to abandon children.

Encouraging thinking skills with children

A focus on thinking skills within the educational process has led to useful summaries of research and probably the most influential review has been that undertaken by Carol McGuinness (1999). These main points emerge from her review and a range of subsequent projects.

▩ There is no inevitable pattern for the cognitive development of children and young people. A great deal depends on their experience, and since most children and young people gain their education within schools, their thinking skills are shaped by the dominant messages from classroom priorities and values in practice throughout primary and secondary school.

- Thinking skills need to be made explicit within a school curriculum. It is crucial that teachers are supported to find time and see how thinking skills apply across subjects and subject content. Without this framework, only the outstanding students at secondary level will make connections between school subjects.

- Adults need to recognise and bring out the transferable thinking skills that cross subject knowledge. There has to be time for discussion, and at secondary level that is likely to be through a review or plenary at the end of a lesson or block. Children and young people need to have time and encouragement to reflect on not only what they have learned this time, but also how they learned it. Not every lesson needs review time, but the process needs to be part of each student's learning career over all the years of formal schooling.

- The idea of review and helping children and young people to reflect on what they have learned is not limited to the material on thinking skills and certainly not to the secondary years. Helping children to step back from what they have learned is an integral part to helping children to develop as independent learners.

Adults – teachers or not – need to be aware of what they are doing, and a whole-school approach is required if a value for thinking skills is really to take root. The more successful classroom interventions have been clear about the theoretical underpinning (why, what and how). They had well-designed materials that fitted into a favourable context: appropriate learning environment, explicit and shared understanding about pedagogy and commitment to continued professional development for the adults, often but not always teachers.

WHAT DOES IT MEAN?

- **Pedagogy**: a term that describes the craft of teaching and which covers the choice of actions, prevailing values and attitudes of adults who set out to support learning. Pedagogy can be seen as an interactive process involving adult teacher, learners (who might be children, young people or fellow adults) and all aspects of the learning environment.

Successful developments take time and address the value placed on active learning and habits of good thinking. This fact has repercussions for adult views and habits of thinking, talking and the teaching role. Carol McGuiness sums up this point with, 'Developing better thinking and reasoning skills may have as much to do with creating dispositions for good thinking as it has to do with acquiring specific skills and strategies. For this reason classrooms need to have open-minded attitudes about the nature of knowledge and thinking and to create an educational atmosphere where talking about thinking – questioning, predicting, contradicting, doubting – is not only tolerated but actively pursued.' (1999, page 2 of the summary brief).

How do adults model being a thinker?

In order to think about thinking, children need to be supported as they develop a language about and for thinking. Adults, in any situation with children, can create friendly circumstances for exploratory talk and airing ideas.

- Make your thinking explicit through talking out loud to children: 'I'm thinking about your question', 'That's a puzzler . . . I think the answer could be . . . but that depends on . . .', 'This is a tricky problem, what might we do?', 'Let's think about that'.
- Children may like the simple structure that comes from, 'Can we take some thinking time on . . .' and 'I need a turn with our Thinking Hat', even with an actual, special hat used exclusively for generating Big Ideas.
- Make your learning explicit with, 'That's a new idea to me', 'I wouldn't have thought of doing it that way – that was very creative of you and Harry'.
- Acknowledge your belief that children and young people are thinking: 'You look like you're thinking that over', 'I'd like to hear your ideas on . . .', 'Jessica, could you please talk us through your good idea about . . .'.
- Explicit thinking time – flag to children that this is time to think and they will become accustomed to this quiet time to generate some ideas. Thoughts can then be shared with a small group or partner, which lifts the pressure for those children who are not keen to speak up in front of large groups like a class or the whole club.
- You can model that there are different ways to share your thinking, one of which is to say your ideas out loud, but it is also possible to use writing and drawing skills, simple diagrams and visual maps. Children will respond when you model, 'I need to write those ideas down before we lose them' or, 'I think we could be ready to do one of our spider web diagrams'.
- Important projects, in school and in other settings, merit a research display board or other ways of documentation. Thoughts are shown

respect because they are written down, even when they lead somewhere else: the journey to the answer is as important as the solution itself. The process can include key questions, big ideas, what we found out and how one idea links with another.

- You can model, as well as show in these different ways, that useful thoughts may not be the final answer, but are an essential pointer onwards. You might say, 'Let's not forget that the idea from Ulric was what I meant by really useful "wrong answers". If we hadn't spent time talking around the practical problem with Ulric's suggestion, we'd never have got to . . .'.

In many ways you are showing in practice what metacognition is all about: thinking about thinking, reflecting on thinking and understanding that everyone can step back from their own thought processes.

Children and philosophical enquiry

Children show, through their conversations and questions, that they are ready for some complex issues about how the world works and relationships. David Whitebread (2006) led a study to look at the effectiveness of several methods of supporting children's thinking skills, including the Philosophy for Children approach, TASC and Mind Mapping, all of which are described briefly in this section. Each approach had strengths as a way to give 3–8 year olds a means to discuss their own thinking and learning. All of the methods had an impact on children's confidence to try out ideas and take intellectual risks when they were not certain of the answer. (Some searching questions do not have a conventional right answer.) A further consequence of using any of the methods in the nursery or the primary school classroom was that the adults had been stimulated to reflect on their own practice and style of pedagogy (see page 193).

Philosophy for Children

During the 1960s, in the USA, Matthew Lipman became interested in the thinking capacity of children and young people. He proposed that children were curious and ready to wonder and those qualities were the basis of a philosophical approach through questioning and reasoning in the style of the philosophers of ancient Greece. Lipman developed a curriculum for 6–16 year olds called Philosophy for Children, sometimes abbreviated to P4C. This new approach to learning, and education in schools, used what Matthew Lipman called 'communities of enquiry', in which teachers and students collaborate in understanding and exploring the world: material, personal and ethical aspects. Interest and application spread to the UK over the 1980s and 90s.

WHAT DOES IT MEAN?

■ **Philosophy for Children**: an approach developed by Matthew Lipman to support and extend the learning of children and adolescents through creating an atmosphere and strategies of philosophical enquiry in collaboration with adults.

See www.sapere.org.uk for the approach as used in the UK

Philosophy for Children is a distinct approach which nevertheless has much in common with other ways to focus on the thinking potential of children and young people. (With thanks to Ruben Kuyper for some of the examples that follow.)

▨ Philosophical explorations with 4–6 year olds need to be closely linked with events, objects or experiences that are meaningful in their social world. These younger children can manage some more abstract ideas, like feeling ill or what is painful, so long as the concept relates closely to a familiar experience. There are parallels with the ways in which children begin to make sense of emotions (see page 58).

▨ Soon, 6–8 year olds have enough familiar experiences to tackle more abstract ideas, like lying and truth; how you forget things; inventing unusual uses for a familiar object; and how things begin and end.

▨ The literacy skills of 8–10 year olds mean that they use what they have learned from reading as well as direct personal experience. They can be keen, with encouragement, to launch into very thoughtful discussions, such as talking about happiness. Adults may ask some questions but these older children generate philosophical questions on their own, for example, 'Is being happy boring after a while?' or 'Can you teach someone to be happy?'

▨ Older children of 10–12 years of age have less need of playful exchanges and tangible objects to provoke discussion. They are able to talk about and around concepts like responsibility and to think through imaginary scenarios.

TAKE ANOTHER PERSPECTIVE

Some readers may have worked in adult group discussions when you have to decide on a set number of items you need on a desert island, or other survival scenario. Ruben Kuyper (personal communication) describes his exercise of asking 10–12 year olds to imagine that a serious disaster means they will have to stay in school for the next ten years. They have a short time gap in which they can have 15 items brought into the building – what should these be?

The discussion that always follows shows that this age group, with a few adult prompting questions, can deal with the challenge of thinking beyond their immediate need. Children, often bouncing ideas off each other, work out how old they will be before they get rescued from their school. They will be old enough to have babies, so maybe some items should anticipate that situation.

MAKE THE CONNECTION WITH . . . IT'S SO UNFAIR!

Children have a concept of fairness as a forerunner to the philosophical concept of justice. They are very able to talk about what is fair or just, although they are more articulate, or annoyed, about what they judge to be unfair. Jean Ruddock et al. (2006) explored how 6–10 year olds were able to talk about specific instances of unfairness in their school experience and to explain clearly why the event, or an adult's handling of what happened, was unfair. They also demonstrated an ability to see an incident from more than their own perspective, even having an insight into the viewpoint of a child who had done wrong towards them.

- ■ What examples have you encountered from your own time with children?
- ■ Access the research paper (details on page 208) and discuss with colleagues the possible implications for your own practice.

TASC

Belle Wallace (Wallace et al, 2004) developed the framework of TASC: Thinking Actively in a Social Context. The approach supports adults to guide younger children through a project or other long-term exploration. But the framework also enables older children to track and evaluate their own thinking and research. The pattern can work as a cycle, rather than as a linear progression, as children realise that interesting questions often lead to more lines of enquiry. Some of the main strands of the TASC framework include the need to identify the task, recognising what is already known and what has to be researched, generating and assessing possible ideas, trying out the possibilities and evaluating what has been managed and finding ways to share discoveries with other people.

The TASC approach is supported by appropriate questions from adults. With younger children the guidance from an adult needs to be basic: questions like, 'What are we trying to do?', 'Is our plan working?' and 'How can we show other people?' There is also an important recognition that children and young people grow in confidence when adults allow the time in any project for reflection on 'What have we learned?' and 'What are we proud of?'

Mind Mapping

The concept of Mind Maps was first developed by Tony Buzan (www.mind-mapping.co.uk) as a way of helping adults to learn and recall more effectively by using a diagrammatic layout to connect related ideas or strands of an area of knowledge. Mind Mapping (a registered trademark idea with Tony Buzan) has been used and modified to work well with children and young people. Children often respond well to working with the combination of visual, diagrammatic and written methods. Nicola Call and Sally Featherstone (2003) describe how younger children are able to touch and see the connections by sometimes using actual objects on a large sheet of paper and connecting them with lines and emergent writing – or dictating to their adult scribes.

THINKING AND LEARNING AT SCHOOL

Some projects about thinking skills have focused on how children can be best supported to understand mathematical or scientific concepts and become confident in this kind of thinking. Children can decide in their schooling that they are 'no good at maths' or that science is 'very boring'. A particular kind of abstract thinking is required for advanced comprehension in both these subjects and not every student will have a specific flair for maths or science, but children need to feel mathematically and scientifically able. The conviction of being a maths failure lasts into adulthood and can undermine practitioners' work with children or young people in a professional life outside the boundaries of school.

Mathematical thinking and practice

In recent decades there has been more than one overhaul of the teaching of mathematics in the UK. The problems and choices are well discussed for non-mathematicians in a series of publications from Learning and Teaching Scotland – in particular by Dorothy Cadell (1998), George Wilson (1999) and Effie Maclellan et al. (2003). The key points include:

- Children need a firm foundation of hands-on mathematical experiences. Abstract concepts, like shape, weight, speed and many others, make sense from how they appear and can be manipulated in action, often through play. Good practice over the first years of primary school is dominated by authentic experiences of maths in action. Liz Marsden and Jenny Woodbridge (2005) documented how much 5 and 6 year olds showed that they understood about mathematical concepts and operations through the medium of designing and playing games.

- Children need plenty of reasons to be convinced that it is useful to be able to count – reasons to use their numbers – to measure, to estimate and be accurate and so on. Only the children with genuine mathematical flair will relate to the abstractions without some grounding in 'that's what it's for' and 'that's what it looks like in real life'.

- Children need experiences and practical activities that home in on using their mathematical knowledge in a range of authentic, real-life situations. Children are usually the best judge of whether a mathematical problem is relevant to daily life, and their physically active engagement with a mathematical problem is the best sign. Older children and young adolescents also need experience of more abstract problems.

- Children, as they say clearly themselves, need plenty of practice with putting any mathematical operation or idea into practice. Reviews of effective teaching of mathematics have stressed that children and young adolescents need more practice at mental mathematics than often happens within the curriculum across the UK. Children need to use paper and pencil and, in time, understand the effective use of calculators. But the pendulum has swung back to an understanding that children and young adolescents need to be able to do maths 'in their head'.

WHAT DOES IT MEAN?

- **Mental mathematics**: the ability to work in your head with numbers, calculations and basic arithmetical operations. Mental mathematics depends on understanding and memorising key numerical facts.

A great deal of mathematics has to be grounded in experiences that make sense to children. You will find a range of practical examples on the Learning and Teaching Scotland website (www.ltscotland.org.uk/5-14/problemsolving). An example from Invergowrie Primary School with 6 and 7 year olds shows how their teacher brought alive the logical process of reasoning by elimination and use of categories. The lesson started by the teacher asking the class to stand up. Children were then asked to sit down if they fell into a particular category – wearing a grey jumper, having black hair and the like – until only one child was left. Then they worked collaboratively in small groups to identify 'Rosa's robot', which they had to select from six possible robots, using the clues to eliminate those robots that could not be the correct one.

On the same website, examples are available for secondary school practice taken from CAME (Cognitive Acceleration in Mathematics Education). Even in mathematics with adolescents, the examples still focus on the importance of hands-on exploration, talking about maths and sharing ideas within the class. Secondary school mathematics has progressed to a challenging level of abstraction and one strategy is to ask students who understand a concept or process to explain it to their peers. The explanation needs to cover not only what you need to do for a mathematical operation or solution but why the steps matter or why the strategy works.

Rethinking science in schools

The recent (2006) overhaul of science within the national curriculum for England and Wales has been underpinned by the objective that teachers should satisfy the curiosity of children and young people with knowledge. This conceptual approach requires that teaching methods engage children, and the approach in practice draws on many of the ideas in the more general study of thinking skills in action.

The proposal for a new Science GCSE (for England and Wales – www.21stcenturyscience.org) developed from the recognition that most 14–16 year olds are not going to work as scientists. But British society needs young people to be scientifically literate. The new approach to Science GCSE is to attempt to support scientific thinking, so that young people have a basis for understanding science in their life and judging scientific findings that become widely discussed. Similar approaches to children and younger adolescents are led by the aim to show how science works, how the scientific method creates a body of knowledge and also that issues in science connect with other subjects, including moral decisions and ethics.

TAKE ANOTHER PERSPECTIVE

The approach of the new Science GSCE raises the big question of the purpose of education within schools. The practical recognition that every young person studying science will not go on to be a scientist has parallels with other school subjects.

- The purpose of teaching mathematics cannot be exclusively, or even mainly, to give the best grounding for young people who will go on to be mathematicians as their profession.

- What about the purpose of physical education and experience of sporting activities? Is it to create sporting stars for the future, to rack up the medals for the UK? How much should P.E. be balanced towards creating healthy habits that young people might continue in their own leisure time?

- What about English as a school subject? Children and young people need to be literate (see page 167) but they will not all go on to be novelists, poets or book reviewers. What about music or art?

What do you think?

Scientific thinking from under-11s

The approach of the network of Science Learning Centres across England (www.sciencelearningcentres.org.uk) has been to find ways to connect with the undoubted thinking power of children and young people. The aim is not to simplify science, but to identify ways that will excite students' curiosity about phenomena and the events of the world around them. The underpinning framework is the observation that children and young adolescents need interesting things to talk about, otherwise why should they bother to think scientifically? The focus that stimulates talk, and therefore thinking, may be tangible objects, like bones, or ideas that make sense because the conceptual exploration develops from an absorbing, direct experience. I am grateful to Jane Turner (Deputy Director of the Science Learning Centre East of England) for sharing her own examples of the impressive scientific thinking of children who are still in primary school.

For instance, a class of 5 year olds visited the Science Learning Centre East of England planetarium: a domed room with a 'magical box' (my words to convey my own, adult delight at the experience – visit it if you can!) that projects onto the ceiling. The software programme allows the presenter to home in on anywhere in the known astronomical universe. The programme can also go backwards or forwards in time. This group of children were expected by their teacher to manage about ten minutes in the planetarium, but they happily spent an hour with the centre astronomer. Boys and girls asked a stream of spontaneous questions: How big is the sun? How hot is the sun? Do stars live forever? Why don't aeroplanes get sucked up into space? What stops them? Is there life on other planets? And many other searching questions.

It is very easy for adults, teachers and other practitioners, to underestimate the thinking skills of children and their thirst for enquiry. Jane Turner also described her session with 10 year olds that started with information about how people can be logged in to databases through their personal DNA. These children were intrigued and wanted to understand how this process worked. They also raised ethical issues through their spontaneous comments and questions. The children moved on from the fact that it was possible to keep records of people by their DNA to whether it was right to keep records of this kind and what it meant for the individual as a member of society.

LOOK, LISTEN, NOTE, LEARN

Keep alert for your own examples of children, or young adolescents, who are curious to extend their factual knowledge and understanding of science.

- **What has provoked, and sustains, this interest?**
- **What kind of materials provoke this interest while the children are with you – in class, in club or your own home, in the outdoor area?**

Interesting scientific projects tend to engage children because they are rich opportunities for playful investigation. In fact, good scientific investigation has a lot in common with play because many scientific 'facts' are not entirely certain. A good test of theories follows what is effectively a pattern of 'let's pretend that … works this way' or, 'let's hold this factor constant …' and, 'If that were true, what would then follow?' Scientific enquiry can be experienced as a conversation – both literally and figuratively as thinking in your own head. Children will do this kind of exploration if they have meaningful experiences and adults model science in conversation.

Science presented as active and open-ended investigation seizes children's interest and imagination. For instance, Jane Turner documented an investigation with primary school-aged children that started with the question, 'Do tall people have big feet?' To reach a supported answer to this question, children needed to organise themselves to undertake a series of direct investigations. They needed to collect measurements (with permission of the owners of the feet), record their findings, analyse the data and reach supported conclusions on the basis of their evidence. As well as action, there were plenty of opportunities for questions, predictions and explanations.

TAKE ANOTHER PERSPECTIVE

Jane Turner promotes a view of science as something that is worth arguing about. If science matters and engages children, then it is worth arguing about in words, as well as exploring that constructive argument into writing, drawing or singing.

■ I think this view provides good food for thought. What do you think?

■ Perhaps this point could be made as a goal for any school subject or area of knowledge for children and young people.

Coming in through stories

The curiosity of children and young adolescents is often provoked by stories, either fiction or the narrative of true events. Effective use of stories depends on having good books, but also on adults allowing enough time for proper discussion and being ready with open questions to provoke thinking and language for thought. Even 5 and 6 year olds can be very thoughtful about fictional tales.

Adult language needs to be adjusted appropriately for children's age, and there is a great advantage if some of this kind of discussion can sometimes happen in groups smaller than a whole class. Children can be supported to consider and think about these kinds of questions (not all at once and not necessarily applied to every story):

■ What happened in the story? Is there any reason to be uncertain; for instance, are some of the 'facts' dependent on the perspective of one character?

■ Why did such and such happen? Do children feel there were particular reasons? What are their theories?

■ What might have happened if such and such had not happened or if the character had not made that choice? This kind of thinking arises from a counter-factual suggestion: children are asked to reflect on an alternative to something that happened. This kind of thinking is usually too hard for under-7s, but older children relish the speculation.

- What does such and such a character think has happened and is there reason to be sure that s/he is mistaken? How do we know this and s/he does not?
- What could happen next in the story? Some stories are written in ways that make it easy for an adult reader to pause and encourage children to think about hypothetical choices of action. This kind of 'I wonder ...' is straightforward with oral story-telling supported by a puppet, because the story unfolds one scene at a time.

Children need reflection time as well as listening time, so it is important that adults deal with any of their own habits like rushing to fill a silence. Children may be busy thinking.

Readers can find more ideas from *Thinking through stories* and case studies on www.standards.dfes.gov.uk/thinkingskills. One example describes how a group of 6 and 7 year olds heard their teacher read a story twice, then were given what the class called 'Thinking Time' to come up with anything they thought was strange, interesting or puzzling about this story. Their teacher listened to all the comments and, where necessary, helped the child to turn a comment into a question. Each question was then written on the board against the child's name. The class as a whole then chose a question for everyone to explore. A child's comment that a character was unkind would become the question of 'Was ... unkind?' and could be discussed: Did other children feel the character had behaved in an unkind way and what might be the reasons?

This kind of group discussion, whether in a school classroom, after-school club or family home, is best supported when adults help children with the way of giving an opinion that follows the format of 'I agree with Tony because ...' or, 'I disagree with what Rona said about ... because ...'. A similar pattern works for thinking about poems as well as stories. Another example on this website resource described how 8 and 9 year olds were able to pursue a similar discussion in small groups. They had less need for an adult to guide potential questions and generated their own in groups of four before putting their ideas to the whole group. With support, these older children are able to debate through the format of 'I agree with ... because ...' and 'I disagree with ... because ...'.

Using true stories

Jane Turner and Grant Bage (2006 and Bage and Turner, 2004) have explored scientific issues and knowledge with children through stories of what has actually happened. For example, older children were absorbed by the true story of William Burke and William Hare who, over the 1820s, supplied bodies to Edinburgh Medical School. They became known as

MAKE THE CONNECTION WITH . . . PUPPETS AS A FOCUS

Stories may be explored through books, but often with the addition of props including puppets. A single puppet can be the focus of attention for a story told through this character. Children engage with the puppet, watching him or her rather than the adult, even when they are fully aware logically that it is the adult speaking and not the puppet. Well into middle childhood, boys and girls are happy to make the leap of imagination, to suspend their disbelief. They exercise their thinking skills through communication that revolves around the puppet and what happens to this character and his or her friends.

I have learned most of what I understand about the use of puppets from watching two specialists in action:

■ Ros Bayley – see www.educationalpublications.com; and

■ Peter Lockey – see www.puppetsbypost.com.

the body snatchers and progressed from raiding graveyards for dead bodies to murder. Nine and 10 year olds were keen to discuss the ethics of the original grave robbing and the conversation led to serious moral discussions around, 'If people were dead, was it alright to use their bodies for science?' The historical context of the true story led to further discussion: 'Could something similar happen today and do people sell bits of bodies?' One child knew that some people donate a kidney to others.

The effective use of true stories, like fiction, depends on adult preparation to support the discussion and an understanding of the use of open-ended questions from adults. Jane Turner and Grant Bage help this process with pre-written cards that extend from simple agree–disagree, to statements like, 'It's a true story' or, 'It's a scary story', through to more complex questions that aim to help children connect two ideas.

Organising and planning

Children within their primary school years need to build skills of how to track and use different kinds of resources. Knowledge about ways to document and the skills of effective research have to be continued through the secondary school years and are crucial for further independent study. Thinking skills are necessary to support learning about study skills. For instance:

■ How do you find information, but also how can you know it is reliable? Children and young people nowadays still use books and

Adolescents need to have learned skills for study

libraries, but they also need specific skills for using the internet and how to judge the reliability of the many sources that can be brought up by a general search.

▪ How do you use this information within your own written work? Even under-11s need to be learning that legitimate use is not simply to copy materials wholesale. Adolescents and students in higher education need a clear understanding of how to access, use and reference materials properly, and what is regarded as plagiarism.

▪ How do you plan a larger piece of work? Is there a logical sequence and how do you manage your time to avoid last-minute panics? This generation of school pupils, and students in higher education, have been expected to deal with the study skills required for project work. This method of being assessed is not necessarily an easier option than testing by sit-down, fixed-time exams.

If you want to find out more

❖ **Bage, Grant** and **Turner, Jane** (2004) *Mud and mountains.* Cambridge: Mill Publishing.

❖ **Bee, Helen** and **Boyd, Denise** (2004) *The developing child.* Boston MA: Pearson Education.

- Caddell, Dorothy (1998) *Numeracy in the early years: what the research tells us.* Dundee: Scottish Consultative Council on the Curriculum. Available for download from www.ltscotland.org.uk/earlyyears/ resources/numeracyintheearlyyears.asp.

- Call, Nicola and Featherstone, Sally (2003) *The thinking child resource book.* Stafford: Network Educational Press.

- Cottrell, Stella (2003) *The study skills handbook.* Basingstoke: Macmillan Press.

- Cowley, Sue (2004) *Getting the buggers to think.* London: Continuum. (I have serious reservations about the title but the ideas are sound.)

- Department for Education and Skills, the Standards website www.standards.dfes.gov.uk/thinkingskills provides a range of briefing papers, case studies and suggested further reading. See for instance *Excellence and Enjoyment: learning and teaching in the primary years* (2004).

- Department for Education and Skills (2004) *Pedagogy and practice: teaching and learning in secondary schools Unit 16: Leading in learning.* See www.standards.dfes.gov.uk.

- Doherty-Sneddon, Gwyneth (2004) 'Don't look now . . . I'm trying to think', *The Psychologist* 17(2). Available for download from www.bps.org.uk/publications/thepsychologist/search-the-psychologist-online.cfm.

- Fabian, Hilary (2002) *Contexualised learning for 5–8-year-olds.* See www.ltscotland.org.uk/earlyyears/resources/contextualisedlearningfor58 yearolds.asp

- Learning and Teaching Scotland has plenty of examples in print and visual/video clip format. The organisation of schooling in Scotland and the curriculum is not identical to the rest of the UK, but the materials here are relevant for anyone. See www.ltscotland.org.uk/ 5-14/problemsolving.

- Lindon, Jennie (2001) *Understanding children's play.* Cheltenham: Nelson Thornes.

- Lindon, Jennie (2005) *Understanding child development: linking theory and practice.* London: Hodder Arnold.

- Maclellan, Effie; Munn, Penny and Quinn, Victoria (2003) *Thinking about maths: a review of issues in teaching number from 5 to 14.*

Glasgow: Learning and Teaching Scotland. See
www.ltscotland.org.uk.

❖ **McGuinness, Carol** (1999) *From thinking skills to thinking classrooms.*
London: Department for Education and Employment. Download
Research Brief 115 (RB115) from 'publications and downloads',
www.teachernet.gov.uk.

❖ **Marsden, Liz** and **Woodbridge, Jenny** (2005) *Looking closely at
learning and teaching – a journey of development.* Huddersfield: Early
Excellence. See www.earlyexcellence.com.

❖ **Mitchell, Alison** (2001) *Study skills for early years students.* London:
Hodder and Stoughton.

❖ **Sutherland, Peter** (1992) *Cognitive development today: Piaget and his
critics.* London: Paul Chapman.

❖ **Rich, Diane; Casanova, Denise; Dixon, Annabelle; Drummond,
Mary Jane; Durrant, Andrea** and **Myer, Cathy** (2005) *First hand
experience: what matters to children.* Clopton: Rich Learning
Opportunities. See www.richlearningopportunities.co.uk/fhe.htm.

❖ **Ruddock, Jean; Demetriou, Helen** and **Hopper, Bev** (2006) *How
pupils deal with incidents of unfairness.* See
www.educ.cam.ac.uk/randd/proj5.html.

❖ **SAPERE** – a website to inform and guide anyone in the UK who is
interested in the Philosophy for Children approach. See
www.sapere.org.uk.

❖ **Science Learning Centres** – a network of centres across England. See
www.sciencelearningcentres.org.uk.

❖ **Subbotsky, Eugene** (2004) 'Magical thinking – reality or illusion', *The
Psychologist* 17(6). Available for download from www.bps.org.uk/
publications/thepsychologist/search-the-psychologist-online.cfm.

❖ **TASC (Thinking Actively in a Social Context)** developed by Belle
Wallace and part of the website of the National Association for Able
Children, with explanation of the approach, diagrams and illustrated
case studies from schools. See www.nace.org.uk/tasc./tasc_home.htm.

❖ **Taggart, Geoff** and **Ridley, Kate** (2005) *Thinking skills in the early
years: a literature review.* Slough: NFER. Summary at
www.nfer.ac.uk/research-areas/pims-data/summaries/thinking-skills-
in-the-early-years-a-literature-review.cfm.

❖ **Tizard, Barbara** and **Hughes, Martin** (2002, 2nd edition) *Young children learning.* Oxford: Blackwell Publishing.

❖ **Turner, Jane** and **Bage, Grant** (2006) 'Real stories: real science', *Primary Science Review* 92.

❖ **Wallace, Belle; Maker, June; Cave, Diana** and **Chandler, Simon** (2004) *Thinking skills and problem-solving – an inclusive approach. A practical guide for teachers in primary schools.* London: David Fulton. (Materials also on www.nace.co.uk/tasc/tasc_home.htm.)

❖ **Waterman, Amanda; Blades, Mark** and **Spencer, Christopher** (2001) 'Is a jumper angrier than a tree?', *The Psychologist* 14(9). Available for download from www.bps.org.uk/publications/thepsychologist/search-the-psychologist-online.cfm.

❖ **Whitebread, David; Anderson, Holly; Coltman, Penny; Page, Charlotte; Pasternak, Deborah Pino** and **Mehta, Sanjana** (2005) *Developing independent learning in the early years.* One report of the Cambridgeshire Independent Learning in the Foundation Stage project. Other papers available to download from www.educ.cam.ac.uk/cindle/index.html.

❖ **Whitebread, David** (2006) *Teaching thinking and the development of metacognitive abilities in the early years (children 3–8).* Summary at www.educ.cam.ac.uk/randd/proj5.html.

❖ **Wilson, George** (1999) *Thinking numbers: a discussion on mental mathematics 5–14.* Glasgow: Learning and Teaching Scotland. See www.ltscotland.org.uk.

8 Physical skills and healthy habits

Children and adolescents can potentially develop an impressive array of physical skills, especially when they have generous play opportunities. Childhood and adolescence is a crucial time to establish healthy habits of physical activity, diet and awareness of personal care. Key messages and opportunities depend on the daily life and learning environment that children experience and much depends on the actions, anxieties and attitudes of key adults. Children and young people in their turn develop beliefs about what is 'normal' in terms of dietary choices, physical exercise and an outlook on health.

> **The main sections of this chapter are:**
>
> ⋆ **Physical development and play.**
>
> ⋆ **Risk and opportunities to learn.**
>
> ⋆ **Personal care and habits for health.**

PHYSICAL DEVELOPMENT AND PLAY

Most 5–7 year olds will be able to use their bodies and limbs for a wide range of deliberate physical movements. Physical activity is affected a great deal by children's choices: do they prefer to use their running skills in a game of chase or do they most like to combine running with kicking a ball? What you see children doing is also shaped by the activities that are made easily available to them: the opportunities as well as the restrictions created by adults. Children apply their skills in different ways and by middle childhood the choices they make are as much, 'Do I want to . . .?' as 'Can I manage to . . .?' Experience has also taught them to wonder sometimes, 'Am I allowed to?' or 'Will they see us and stop us?'

Agility, speed and balance

Children use their physical skills in spontaneous games of their own devising – running, chasing and climbing. Children can move deliberately at different speeds, although some may already be showing a flair for a serious turn of speed. Unlike younger children, over-5s are much more able to change direction, at least with a bit of warning. However, some collisions with other people and objects will still happen. Children can be fearless, or cautious, jumpers and leapers. They can manage the one-legged movements like hopping, and 6–7 year olds may like and already manage the combination movements that are involved in games like hopscotch.

Games demonstrate children's impressive skills of coordination

Children are effective climbers and clamberers – on anything. They climb up slopes and hillocks, and run or roll down again, clamber up trees and use fixed play equipment and clamber nets. They can climb up steps to sliding equipment or use the same kind of movement on a ladder. By middle childhood many children are comfortable with balancing on low walls and gym balancing equipment. They steadily learn the balance, jump and steadying skills that are needed to move from one large object to another – in the built or natural environment. Some children will be more at ease with height than others, and you will notice older children and adolescents who are seriously ill at ease with height even if they have not had a scare.

On firm open spaces and surfaces children show how skilled they have become with the range of wheeled vehicles. At 5, 6 and 7 years old, children are adept with push, pull and pedal vehicles and can manoeuvre trolleys and barrows. If they have had the opportunity to learn, 7 year olds can be efficient riders of bicycles: two-wheelers without any trainer wheels.

At 5–6 years old, children can be steady and even move at a fair pace on equipment that demands good balance, like roller blades or ice skates. In areas with easy access to skiing, this age group can already have learned to ski. These are all examples that highlight the very wide range of potential skills that can be gained during childhood, but that much depends on

MAKE THE CONNECTION WITH . . . EQUIPMENT AND OPPORTUNITY

Learning to ride a bicycle or a scooter is often easier when children have a vehicle designed with a low centre of gravity. The youngest bicycle riders I have seen were 4 year olds in a nursery centre that had bought a style of low-slung 2-wheeler. Children's feet could reach the ground, so it was easy to feet-push the bike and set off in that fashion. This option removed the scary interim stage (I recall!) when you have to push off from a hand hold, precarious foot push or deal with the moment when a running adult lets go.

Children of 7 years old are also sometimes very speedy on foot-propelled scooters. Those of 5 and 6 years old now have a useful option, with two wheels at the back and one at the front, making the balance challenge more possible for a younger or less confident child.

You will observe that not all older boys and girls are equally adept at or keen on riding bicycles or scooters. For whatever reason, some never feel confident, nor able to gain the necessary balance. Ask around your adult circle – some friends or acquaintances may admit they never felt secure on a bicycle.

children's opportunities. Competence also depends on helpful coaching by adults who understand both the actual skills and how to help children through the stages of proficiency. These physical skills, along with other possibilities, can progress to impressive levels of ability if adolescents choose to stay with the practice. Swimming, diving, horse riding, gymnastics, judo or basic martial arts are just a few additional examples.

Children of 7 and 8 years old can be adept at skipping, either with their own length of rope or skipping within a long rope turned by someone at either end. A whole raft of physical skills and visual attentiveness are involved in skipping. When children hold their own rope, they need to coordinate the grasp of the rope and hand movements to keep the rope revolving at least fast enough. Skipping requires concentration in order to watch and move your feet in time with the rope. Skipping tends to be more associated with girls, at least beyond middle childhood, but boys and young male adolescents can feel it is acceptable to use skipping as exercise if it is presented, by male role models, as an effective form of sports training.

Hand-clapping games between a pair of children have a long history and are often accompanied by a song or chant. These kinds of games are far more likely to be played by girls than boys and the expert pairs move very fast – 7–8 year olds are capable of such games, although they need to watch and imitate someone – an older child or an adult – who is adept at the game. Children may learn through imitation, direct instruction or a combination of the two strands for learning. Like many outdoor, street and school playground games, some activities have a long history that can be disrupted if children are prevented from active play through middle childhood.

LOOK, LISTEN, NOTE, LEARN

Many creative activities like dance, singing and making music require sophisticated physical skills as well as those of communication. Children need plenty of opportunities for informal enjoyment. Some of the best early-years and playwork settings I have known had an atmosphere in which children often broke into song spontaneously and set up their own dance times.

Children also benefit from good quality coaching, given by adults who have creative skills and are keen to share that enthusiasm – with patience. Children and adolescents will work very hard under these circumstances and are rightly thrilled with their achievements.

I recall one music festival, organised by the schools in my area of south London, where a class of 9 and 10 year olds from a local primary school gave us a beat-perfect version of 'Can't help falling in love with you', set to a Caribbean rhythm and accompanied by their peers on the steel drums. They had learned with the teacher who conducted them and he looked just as proud as the boys and girls.

- What examples have you encountered that show children's potential in the creative arts?
- How do their physical skills work together with communication, concentration and practice?

Some children may already show a sharp ear for music and a sense of rhythm, but all children can manage the deliberate movements of dance and become attuned to the underlying beat of music, singing and dancing to different kinds of music. At 7–8 years of age, children can manage the more organised patterns of movement such as folk dancing from a range of cultural traditions. They need practice and a patient adult who coaches them in the different kinds of steps. You also need to be alert to those children who are unsure about their left and their right: a confusion that leads to panic and crashes. (When I was this age, a strong motivation not to turn the wrong way led me finally to crack the left–right problem.)

Older children and adolescents make their own choice about whether to continue with an activity like dance or the physical intricacies of playing a musical instrument. Informal opportunities may encourage continued involvement and the temptation to try something new. School clubs or what is on offer within a holiday playscheme or leisure services may be more attractive, and less expensive, than formal tuition.

Hand–eye coordination and use of tools

For some activities it makes no sense to distinguish large movements and fine coordination, since both kinds of movement are involved. Gardening, for example, can enthuse children and young people. This experience requires a combination of large-scale movements for digging, forking and wheel-barrowing, but planting out seedlings, pruning and picking fruit or vegetable crops all need finer movements of hand and finger and close visual attentiveness.

Children, unless they have specific physical disabilities, have gained all the relevant basic skills of hand and finger movements and can coordinate deliberate small-scale movements with the information from vision. Children who have some level of visual loss may already be experienced in using the sense of touch, as well as hearing, to inform their movements. In the same way as with energetic physical activities, children's potential to extend their fine physical skills depends a lot on what is available to them.

Children need the fine physical skills of hand and finger control to become confident in their handwriting. The availability of computer keyboards, which also require dexterity, has not removed the importance of being able to write with pen or pencil. However, children and young people use similar fine skills for projects in art, craft and design. They can use their physical skills on small-scale crafts or larger-scale building projects, for instance, in adventure playgrounds. The skills are not exclusively physical because such projects offer significant scope for creativity: children and young people make choices about what materials they use, how they use them and the nature of an end product.

There is a huge range of potential arts and crafts that spreads over different cultural traditions; some, like patchwork, can be found in different styles in many cultures. What children learn depends on availability of materials, time to explore and the impact of any attitudes already learned about gender – are some skills and activities more for girls than boys, or vice versa? Projects like large murals, gardening enterprises, patchwork in materials or paper, or any large-scale joint enterprise also gives scope for the skills of communication, discussion, negotiation and teamwork – or support towards constructive teamworking.

215

TAKE ANOTHER PERSPECTIVE

Attitudes about talent are as relevant for use of fine physical skills as for the larger movement and sports. Children and young people will give up if they gain the message that you have to be 'good' at something to persevere, or that you are either talented or you are not, and that is the end of the story. Adults need to show a positive role model. Everyone can paint or draw, can make music and join in music, can create something that satisfies through working with recycled materials, cloth, wood and so on.

- In much the same way as practitioners need to address their own 'maths gremlins', everyone needs to catch themselves before they say, 'I can't sing' or, 'I'm rubbish at drawing'.

- Are you inclined to dismiss yourself in this way?

Sharing skills and techniques

The word 'coaching' used to be mainly linked with sports (see page 226), but it has become more widely used to mean the process of transferring skills from an individual who is competent to someone who is less adept. The concept is useful as an alternative to 'teaching', since that word implies someone from the teaching profession and within a school or college situation.

In order to coach someone effectively you have to recapture what it was like not to know the actions and useful techniques for this skill. If you are new to a skill, then make sure you have gained basic techniques before introducing the opportunity to children or adolescents. An effective coach also needs patience and the willingness to break learning down into steps that are as fine as the less skilful person needs. Coaching is often undertaken by adults, but there is no reason why children or young people cannot learn to coach each other (see also peer mentoring on page 163).

Children and young people benefit from coaching that explains and shows how to use tools effectively and safely. It matters how you line up a sewing needle or hold a screwdriver. There are some choices that are equally effective, but some options will not work or will be dangerous. Children can and should learn how to handle everyday tools for cooking and woodworking. However, I have seen 4 year olds who understand how to use a saw or pliers with suitable care, and 11 year olds who are safe with a sewing machine.

Children and young people do not always listen to advice. So long as the consequence will not be dangerous, there is an advantage to learning from safe mistakes. For example, if children do not take care over measuring before they cut wood, their book case may collapse. Tension squares do matter for accurate knitting, otherwise a jacket may end up fitting someone twice your size – a hard lesson I learned in my adulthood.

WHAT DOES IT MEAN?

■ **Coaching**: the pattern of transfer of skills from an individual who is more competent in this area of expertise to someone who is less adept or confident.

LOOK, LISTEN, NOTE, LEARN

With the time to reflect, children become able to organise projects and make choices. Older children and young adolescents show that they can take responsibility for most of a creative endeavour, and often guide and coach younger children within the club or playscheme.

Children in adventure playgrounds, as well as the increasing number of outdoor or forest projects, spend significant amounts of time and energy on construction – building dens, taking constructions apart and rebuilding them to a different design. When children know they have a generous time scale, they run long-term projects. One summer at Cool Kids at St Josephs, the older children in the playscheme – 10 and 11 year olds – worked over the whole of one summer holiday on constructions made entirely from recycled materials. Another time they organised a talent show for the last day of the scheme, supporting younger children as the project unfolded. The adult playworkers were easily available for advice and discreet hints about managing the skills of the youngest children in the scheme.

■ These examples show the physical skills available to older children, given a chance to use them. Any longer-term project also shows how children develop skills of planning, communication, teamwork and negotiation.

■ What similar examples have you observed?

Increasingly, older children have the coordination to manage materials and tools and greater patience to see through more complex projects. Again, however, I have known 4 and 5 year olds persevere over time, with no need for adults to press them, as they remain utterly absorbed in large outdoor sculptures or big willow structures. This kind of successful enterprise is characterised by generous time and space with a 'workshop' approach which respects that a creative endeavour is not complete in a short time. We should be alert to older children who cannot sustain interest, who daub and go, or who have sadly learned that they should wait for an adult to tell them what to draw or make.

The importance of lively activity

Children use and hone their physical skills when they have plenty of genuine play opportunities, a great many of which are outdoors and which children themselves determine. Adults do not have to plan complex programmes to get children started on their physical abilities. In much the same way as for communication, specialist programmes for physical development are only needed when children have a disability or chronic health condition that directly affects their physical development or energy levels.

Children do not usually have to be persuaded to use their growing skills in energetic activities. Discussions and consultations with children generate long lists of what they like doing. I heard many examples from the children of Crabtree Infants School and the Kids City playschemes. They liked energetic play in their school grounds and the holiday playscheme (see page 48). They were also enthusiastic about activities that adults would recognise as promoting fine physical skills like painting and modelling, making large and smaller-scale constructions and cooking.

However, some children have their active play restricted, sometimes from an early age. Sally Goddard Blythe (2004) has explored the later problems that can arise when children have not been allowed the level of exercise in the early years that is crucial for healthy, physical development. She also makes the practical point that staying still is the hardest movement of all and one that children still find tough in middle childhood. Priscilla Alderson (2000) is one of a number of writers who have raised concerns about the impact on children of over-structured group experiences. She points to the possibility that some of the increase in diagnosis of ADHD (Attention Deficit Hyperactivity Disorder) in young children is due to unrealistic expectations that under-6s will sit still for long periods and manage without generous outdoor time for easy physical exploration.

Many of the skills described so far depend on easy access for children to an interesting and spacious outdoor environment. Some large movements and physical skills can be enjoyed and practised within a large indoor area, but the rich scope for children of spontaneous play and more lively games requires plenty of outdoor time. There is a high level of concern that a growing proportion of children and adolescents spend too much time indoors in sedentary activities: watching television or playing video games.

TAKE ANOTHER PERSPECTIVE

There are relatively few studies in the UK that focus on the impact on children of playing video games, especially given their prominence as a leisure activity. As Mark Griffiths (2006) points out, most of the research quoted has been undertaken in the USA. In his review, Griffiths concludes that the more negative consequences reported for game-playing, including physical effects like repetitive strain injuries or problems over toileting, are the result of excessive time spent without breaks on this activity.

The practical implication is that responsible adults need to ensure that video game playing does not dominate the waking hours of children and adolescents and that a close eye is kept on the content of games, including the level of violence. The significant exception is the risk to any games player who is photosensitive and may experience a seizure triggered by the high-intensity flickering patterns in many games.

A positive consequence of the physically repetitive movements is that video game playing is sometimes used as a form of occupational therapy for children and as a way to help them to distract themselves from pain.

▧ What kind of checks and ground rules do you have in place about the use of video games for children and adolescents for whom you are responsible?

RISK AND OPPORTUNITIES TO LEARN

This concern about a generation that sits indoors is partly a sweeping assumption that does not describe the leisure time of all children. However, a more sedentary lifestyle has been pushed by adult anxiety about letting children outdoors, resistance to taking children to available outdoor space and some deeply unwise decisions in early years and school outdoor areas in the name of safety.

Adult anxiety and managing risk

Of course, adults are responsible for keeping children safe enough and avoiding preventable accidents. However, a lively, enjoyable and therefore playful childhood will include bumps, bruises and some accidents. The aim is that any injuries remain minor, but trying for zero accidents will remove many of the necessary opportunities for developing physical skills over childhood and adolescence. Apart from taking a balanced approach to risk, adults also need to share practical skills with children about what to do when an accident happens. They are capable of learning basic first aid, such as how to clean a cut or graze, what to do if you get a nose bleed, how to take care if you hit your head and so on. Some children are already taking charge of aspects of their own safety, such as their asthma inhaler, because they live with chronic health conditions.

Since the 1990s an atmosphere has grown in the UK that has heightened adult anxiety (individuals, organisations and local authorities) about being blamed for accidents to children or young people. Tim Gill (2007) highlights the serious problems from the resulting approach of risk aversion: an attempt to block any kind of risk, however unlikely as a

Active games will get lively and physical

source of genuine danger. He describes the ways that the fears of practitioners and parents have already limited play and children's safe freedom of movement. Bans on some lively games, resources or access to parts of a playground are justified as required by the health and safety policy, when there is no such ruling. Excessive, and sometimes misplaced, adult anxiety also corrodes a positive relationship between children and their familiar adults.

Sensible risk management

Children are aware of problems in their school playground and want them resolved, but not through banning games. Sharon Rafferty (1997) describes how 4–12 year olds in a Strathclyde primary school were actively involved in ways to improve the schools grounds and their playtime. Staff and parents were already concerned and wanted to get children properly on board as the 'main players'. Children identified 16 concerns that divided into four main themes: that the current playground was boring; they wanted effective adult help with antisocial behaviour from some children; the physical condition of the playground was unacceptable; and the children judged some aspects to be dangerous. A fifth grouping was around sexist attitudes, specifically a complaint from the girls that they were not allowed to play football, apparently because the boys made it impossible. This finding surprised the adults, who presumably were more concerned about balls hitting people. Other consultations and informal discussions have revealed similar views.

The Health and Safety Executive (2006) set out principles of risk management which stressed that the process was about reducing genuine risks with serious consequences and enabling individuals to assume some responsibility for their own safety. The process was not about trying to create a risk-free society (impossible anyway), generating piles of paperwork, nor stopping recreational activities where risks could definitely be managed. Proper risk assessment does matter, but this process is not the same as imagining the worse that could happen, however unlikely, and using that prospect to restrict the experiences of children and young people.

The Play Safety Forum (2002) summarised well that risk management of play provision for children has common ground with general health and safety in workplaces. However, in play provision of all kinds there is a place for appropriate risk in ways that do not arise for health and safety at work. Children and young adolescents need a childhood in which they can enjoy an acceptable level of risk and challenge. The need for adventure is not really an issue in most workplaces. The key steps of appropriate risk assessment and then management during childhood and adolescence are as follows:

- Identify a hazard that might cause harm, such as watching the trains, taking children swimming, playing ball games or using woodwork tools.
- Assess the kind of harm that could result for children and young people, if they had access to this material, activity or location.
- What is the likelihood that harm could result (very low, medium, high) and how serious would that harm be, if it happened?
- What are the benefits of enabling children to have access to this resource: what is likely to happen if they are denied access?
- If there are benefits, how can the hazard be managed so that the risk is reduced to an acceptable level?

In all of the examples given in the first bullet point, there are real benefits for children of having these experiences. The potential harm of watching the trains or swimming is only significant if children are unsupervised. Even young children gain great pleasure and interest from watching trains go by, accompanied by an adult, and standing in a safe position – on a railway platform or waving from the top of a secured embankment. Children need to hear the safety messages about the serious dangers of direct access to any railway tracks. Proper risk management of the genuine dangers from water leads to teaching children how to swim, because older children and young people will be at far greater risk if they are weak swimmers when they are no longer accompanied by adults.

WHAT DOES IT MEAN?

- **Hazard**: anything that might cause harm, but will not necessarily lead to accidents, if managed appropriately.
- **Risk**: the chance that a given hazard could lead to harm for somebody. The likelihood could be anything from very low to very high.
- **Risk management**: attentive assessment of the level of risk from a given hazard, including the likelihood of harm occurring and the seriousness of that harm, if it does actually happen.
- **Risk aversion**: an avoidance of risk of any kind, however unlikely it is that harm will result.

Children learning to manage their own risk

When anxious adults try to control and remove every potential source of alleged danger, they create a situation in which children and young people can be placed at greater risk – now and in the future. Children may cooperate with the restrictions on more lively activities and accept a more sedentary lifestyle, with negative consequences for their health (see page 245). However, some children will not cooperate in what they view as foolish restrictions. They will pursue more interesting play out of sight of adults, which pushes legitimate play into secrecy. In the end, older children and young people will go out independently of their parents and any other adults. They may also get themselves into real danger, because they have not been enabled to learn to manage their own risks when they would be prepared to listen to adults (Lindon, 2003a).

A study by the Child Accident Prevention Trust (2002) considered the perspective of 11–14 year olds who lived in a relatively deprived area in the north of England. These adolescents had few organised leisure activities in their neighbourhood and some admitted spending time in locations they knew to be risky, like abandoned buildings and quarries. The young males were more likely to seek out activities they knew to be unsafe. Danger was part of the attraction, which they deliberately increased by daring each other to run across roads or sit on the railway tracks. This age group also reported regular unintentional injuries, arising from sporting activities, traffic accidents including falling off their bike and not wearing a helmet. However, these adolescents were still concerned about their own safety and took some steps to protect themselves through avoiding particular people and places and moving about in a group.

LOOK, LISTEN, NOTE, LEARN

- Reflect on how risk assessment and management is handled in your current workplace. Is there an atmosphere that inclines towards risk aversion – trying to create an impossible 100 per cent risk-free situation?

- Consider the steps for risk assessment given in this section and apply them to a safety concern that is current, or one that was not well resolved in the past.

- Recall that the main point for sensible risk assessment with children and young people is that they are enabled to enjoy a wide range of activities.

- Look at the rich source of play images within the online photo exhibition at www.freeplaynetwork.org.uk/playlink/exhibition/index.html. Consider how you could approach sensible risk assessment and management of the activities shown in some of the photos.

Looked-after children and adolescents are especially vulnerable and service managers understandably wish to avoid accidents in a residential home. However, foster and residential carers who spend their days with the children are usually very aware of the dangers created by a policy of risk aversion. Children and adolescents who do not have enough lively interest in the home, and from regular outings with adults, are more likely to head off into town, with or without permission. Then they risk getting themselves in more trouble than would arise from climbing trees or playing football in the garden.

Inclusive play

Allison John and Rob Wheway (2004), speaking about inclusion, say much that is applicable to all children and confirm the main points from the Yard project in Edinburgh (see page 49). They stress that an assessment of whether play provision is accessible for disabled children should never overlook that the purpose of the facility is enjoyable play. Opportunities should not be lost in a focus on treatment, adult definitions of worthwhile educational experiences or an over-anxious approach to safety because children are disabled.

WHAT DOES IT MEAN?

- **Inclusive play**: a commitment to enable disabled or chronically-ill children and young people to enjoy the full range of play opportunities, often within mainstream facilities open to all children. (The term 'inclusion' is sometimes used with a more general meaning: that services should not exclude children from any group.)

Physical disabilities and chronic ill health will affect, probably limit, children's possibilities in one way or another. A genuinely inclusive approach in schools, clubs, playschemes and public play spaces means that children with physical disabilities, or learning disabilities that affect their understanding of physical risk, are no more limited for activity and enjoyable games that is unavoidable. The previous section about risk is equally applicable to play provision that is inclusive of disabled children and young people. The Kids Playwork Inclusion Project (PIP) has been active in finding and promoting good practice. I learned a great deal (Lindon, 2003a) from the Kidsactive team (now part of Kids) who ran adventure playgrounds for disabled children and their siblings. The whole aim of risk assessment for children in their playgrounds was to find the way that physically or learning disabled children could get on the walkways and have some adventures.

It is foolish to pretend that disability or chronic ill health does not make a difference, but it should not be used as an excuse to avoid adult effort over equipment, adjusting the rules of games or proper risk assessment that leads to 'you can, so long as we . . .' and not inevitably to 'you can't'. Adults need to offer discreet support to children with chronic health conditions affecting their possibilities in exercise, or which mean that a responsible adult has to monitor their level of exercise. Older children and young people will need to take over this responsibility for their own well-being, but ideally within the positive framework created by adults with a 'can do' orientation.

Action for Leisure together with Contact A Family (2004) confirmed that disabled children and young people were interested in the same range of play and leisure opportunities as their peers. They are perfectly capable of explaining, in different ways, what they enjoy already and what facilities they really wish could be made available. The clear message from children and their families was that being made welcome was crucial. So the staff of any play- or leisure-scheme need to be aware of their outlook, assumptions and probably their anxieties about what inclusion actually means. Practitioners in general facilities do not need to be fully trained and informed about every possible condition – an impossible goal anyway.

This joint consultation confirmed that appropriate play and leisure facilities for disabled children and young people were not about creating new or specialist activities, but about enabling them to access what already exists. The children and young people wanted leisure activities to be with their friends and offer real opportunities to meet and make more friends. They wanted a social side to their leisure options and their wish list for activities was much the same as their non-disabled peers': different kinds of sports, getting out and about locally, playing with friends, playing at home and, increasingly for the adolescents, dancing and discos.

Helen Woolley et al. (2006) spent time in six Yorkshire primary schools and highlighted what worked well for disabled children as well as the potential barriers to enjoying a full playtime in the school playground. Children themselves focused on the importance of friends and some were adept at getting involved in play. Disabled children had more contact with an adult, often their specialist assistant, and sometimes their individual routines and special input cut into their playtime. Having an adult assigned to them seemed to work both ways: it could mean they had less contact with peers, but some children creatively used their adult as a help to get them into play or as a play companion. Some adults were more wary than others about risk for disabled children and adult caution sometimes restricted the child's play.

Physically active games and sports

Physical exercise supports emotional and mental well-being, because children – just like adults – can slump into a general lowness. Children need happy experiences that lay down the awareness that they felt better for getting active enough to be tired. Energetic activities work with good nutrition over childhood to build strong bones, muscle strength and lung capacity.

TAKE ANOTHER PERSPECTIVE

A consistent theme for friendly and informal coaching is that older or more adept players need to play so as to make it easy for the younger, or less experienced, player to connect with the ball. This objective is the precise opposite of competitive games between more evenly matched partners, when your entire aim is to make it as tough as possible for your opponent to reach and hit the ball.

Sensitive adults adjust the game, whether it is play with sports equipment or coaching children to play chess or draughts. Children do not usually like it if adults lose in an obvious way; it is more about ensuring that you do not win all the time. If you are a good coach, children and young people will soon be better matched to your skill and some will beat you with no help at all.

Building on skills: the coaching process

Children are able to build their skills when adults, or supportive young people who act as mentors, simplify games to build confidence, success and enthusiasm.

- Five to 8 year olds have a chance at cricket if you roll a ball at their bat along the ground. Both the ball and the bat need to stay low. The same adjustment helps with tennis when you ensure that you aim the ball for a child's racquet, avoiding the mad swivel of eyes and hands to try to connect.
- Of course, you need to coach children in safe use of equipment. But I have known learning start effectively with 4 year olds, who in one nursery school I visited were safely playing a game of simple hockey, keeping to the rule that 'we don't lift our sticks higher than this (waist height)'. Hockey can be easier for young children because you 'dribble' the soft ball with your stick.

- Netball or basketball can be made simpler, right down to early versions of the game where balls are thrown into a container that sits on the ground, not up in the air at all. In the second half of middle childhood boys and girls are more able and keen to play the 'proper' version of these games.
- I visited one centre which had a single tennis ball tied in the foot of stockings, fixed to a length of washing line secured between two trees. The children (aged 3–7 years) were able to use table tennis bats to swipe the balls, which stayed still while they took aim, and then the ball simply came back (without the speed that results from balls on elastic!).

The process of adjustment for 5–7 year olds was brought alive for me when I watched a practitioner in the Poplar Play holiday playscheme. The children experienced proper warm-up exercises and there was a visible difference between the eldest and youngest children in their balance and coordination but no difference in their enjoyment. They worked their way through games that used racquets, but in ways that the children could achieve reasonable success. For instance, they transferred a bean bag between them using the racquet and then batted a ball a short distance between children in a circle. The children wanted to play 'proper' tennis for a while and enjoyed that time, although they spent much of it running after the balls. (For a longer description of this observation see Lindon, 2003b.)

TAKE ANOTHER PERSPECTIVE

Children themselves need to be willing to deal with further problems and ideally have the ear of a supportive adult as they persevere.

My daughter Tanith and two friends, when they were 10 years old, were keen to take up on a series of sessions in cricket coaching that included children from several local primary schools. The sessions were mainly attended by boys and some were actively rude about the girls' skills and their wish to play cricket. The girls supported each other and knew they were not 'rubbish', because they played at their own school. They decided to show the ill-mannered boys how to behave and very deliberately ignored hissed rude comments, while making positive comments of their own, like 'good shot' for any impressive play. After a few sessions the sniping stopped.

I asked if the girls wanted me to talk with the cricket coach and was told not to say anything, because they had sorted it out themselves. So my only role was to say, 'Well done'.

Through middle childhood you will notice children's awareness of attitudes around physical activities. You cannot overlook opinions and values if you are to encourage involvement in activity and build some healthy habits for children. At 7–8 years of age, children can be very aware that some games are regarded as more for one sex than the other. Both girls and boys may be reluctant to cross the invisible gender line or be told to 'go away' by an existing group. Adults can help to blur or push through the barriers by ensuring that adult males and females act as role models to cross the line and by offering relevant coaching that specifically includes both girls and boys.

Interest, enthusiasm, talent?

Some older children show the beginnings of a real flair for some sports. It makes sense to grow any talent, but the objective of schools, out-of-school play facilities and sports and leisure services should be to sow the seed of enthusiasm for all children. Children's confidence depends on how games and skills are introduced. They will opt out, actually or in spirit, if the message is, 'you have to be good or there's no point', and useful exercise does not begin and end with competitive and/or team sports.

A proportion of children and young people will enjoy football, cricket, tennis or athletics and will continue this involvement into adulthood, without ever becoming a household name. However, all children and young people need to find enjoyable physical pursuits if they are to build up stamina and overall fitness. (It is possible to overdo physical exercise – see page 257.) To support a more general openness to vigorous exercise, you need to have enough activities in which children and young people can improve against their individual best.

- Primary school sports days are usually full of all kinds of physical challenges that children work around during the afternoon, often with older children supporting the younger pupils. There are some races but they are in the context of plenty of energetic games.
- A boy or girl who finds it tough to climb up a rope or a wall bar needs a learning situation in which adults, and peers who respond to the adult-led atmosphere, are pleased that they have personally managed to climb another half metre up the rope, never mind that some of their peers have been shinning up to the top for weeks.

Inspiration to try harder comes from challenges that stretch an individual; that seem feasible, but not utterly impossible. The supportive process of coaching means you view physical skills as a step-by-step process and make those steps as small as necessary for this child or adolescent.

- To be an effective role model for physical activity with under-11s, adults do not themselves have to be 'good' at sports. You need to show enthusiasm to play, be patient in explaining the rules of games (more than once) and work from simple to more complex in terms of the physical skills.

- You can create a balance towards cooperative games and stress how children are improving against their personal best so far. However, it is sensible to introduce some games where scoring will mean winners and losers.

- Address the experience of competition and deal with issues around winning and losing while you are part of the games, much like playing board games or strategy games like chess. You then have a chance to encourage graciousness in winning and manageable regret over losing.

- Ensure that you are sometimes on the losing side. If you play a wide range of games with older children and adolescents, you should not have to pretend to lose; it will happen naturally on some occasions.

LOOK, LISTEN, NOTE, LEARN

Children just want adults to play with them and be fair umpires in any games. Adolescents expect sports coaches and PE teachers to be skilled in the games or athletics they aim to teach. But even adolescents show tolerance in informal play services, so long as you know the rules of any game and are scrupulously fair about any contested decision.

On outdoor sports and adventure holidays I have known adolescents accept grown-ups in the party who were learning alongside them and who put up with good-natured wind-ups about their lack of skill. On one secondary school holiday (described to me) it was to be expected that the 13 and 14 year olds would realise one teacher was a skiing novice. However, he got serious points for effort, also for not being angry at the laughter when he lost his footing on the drag ski lift and provided an unintentional demonstration of exactly how not to do it.

- Share experiences with your colleagues or fellow students that highlight what helps from adults – either memories of your own adolescence, or your involvement as an adult.

A great deal also depends on the behaviour and enthusiasm of the adults – and these are not all PE teachers. Playworkers, youth workers, residential and foster carers are very important for many children and young people. I have known even very disaffected young people who became enthused about an activity, because the adult responsible for their care was keen and shared that personal enthusiasm.

Older and larger?

So long as adolescents have no disabilities or ill health that cramps their style, they are capable of all the skills described so far. However, adolescents, and children who look older than their chronological age, often find themselves barred from public play spaces, even sometimes from exciting-looking adventure playgrounds. They may have fewer informal outlets for enjoyable physical skills, such that most opportunities are within school life or require joining some kind of club.

Adolescents are very likely to be more aware of how they appear and of their perceived dignity than their younger selves. It may not seem inappropriate to run around unless there is a good reason, such as involvement in specific sports or possibly to avoid being late. Females may be especially cautious about showing a level of physical prowess and enthusiasm that seems to compromise their feminine attractiveness. Some situations may justify the physical exertion, such as energetic dancing or an organised exercise class. Consultations with young people usually avoid the word 'play' and ask about leisure activities or what adolescents like to do in their free time.

Some adolescents, in single- or mixed-sex groups, choose to be physically active as part of their shared leisure time. They may go swimming together, play impromptu cricket or football in a local park or go for rambling walks. Some have chosen to spend at least part of their leisure time in practice at a local sports, gym or swimming club. Finance is an issue, as well as what is available locally. Some young people and their families simply do not have the spare money to pay for coaching sessions or club membership, even at a subsidised rate. Attendance is easier if older children and adolescents can get themselves to sessions or clubs by walking or public transport. However, there are many parts of the UK where car transport is required. Families who drive young people are not all thoughtless devourers of energy; parent-chauffeurs are the only option where there is very limited public transport.

The need for adventures

Children and young people need interesting outdoor pursuits, adventure days and holidays. Despite the anxiety over risk assessment (see page 220), many schools and playwork facilities have continued to organise a range of opportunities. The forest school movement has gained popularity in the UK, along with other outdoor learning initiatives. Any outing needs sensible risk assessment. In many cases this process is simple information gathering, alertness during the trip and ensuring that children have personal safety skills appropriate to their age. Lively outdoor activities and adventure trips need more detailed safety planning, but such experiences should not be ended because of fear of something, anything, going wrong.

It is heartbreaking if children or young people are injured or die; nobody wants this outcome from an adventurous activity or residential holiday. A few tragedies in recent years have exposed a lack of thorough risk management or training for the adults in charge of a trip. Of course, it is right and proper that all practitioners of whatever profession should know what they are doing and/or be guided by a specialist in this activity or outdoor pursuit. However, proper attention to safety has meant that some groups caught by unexpected bad weather, even adolescents trapped without the adult of their party, have known how to act in an outdoor emergency and kept themselves safe until rescue arrived or the weather improved.

Part of risk assessment and management with older children and young people has to be practical advice, explained more than once, about how to keep themselves safe, not least if they are inadvertently separated from the group. It will also be appropriate on residential trips, in the UK or taking children abroad, that they have free time. The responsible adults have to be able to trust older children and adolescents to behave in a safe manner and not place themselves in avoidable danger. So teachers, and any other involved professionals, have the right to expect families to have taught basic safety to their sons and daughters.

TAKE ANOTHER PERSPECTIVE

A problem nowadays is that full public attention through the media is focused on those outings when something has gone dramatically wrong. Headlines are not created from, '15 year olds have mainly good time in Lake District. Everyone comes back in one piece.' This would be an accurate, but presumably boring, headline to describe a hill-walking holiday some years ago in which I was one of the adults with a co-educational secondary school trip.

It was an eventful week. I spent a lot of time on rearguard patrol, feeding Kendal Mint Cake to female students on a diet, who consequently lacked the energy to get up hills. A stomach bug struck down everyone in waves of vomiting, except for me and the two female teachers. One couple (adolescents) broke up during the week. The trip was enjoyable despite the problems, but of no interest beyond our immediate circle.

The trip was led by a teacher who was a very experienced hill walker and who paid close attention to safety, without spoiling the fun. She ensured that nobody boarded the coach in the first place unless they could produce a pair of fell walking boots. It was also known that she meant business over the rules of the trip. In a previous year, three male students had deliberately taken a different route down the hill. Their absence was swiftly noticed and when sorties failed to find them, mountain rescue was called. They were found unharmed and unrepentant in a local café. Their families were telephoned and all three students were put on the first train back home.

PERSONAL CARE AND HABITS FOR HEALTH

Children need to learn how to take care of themselves and to build a basis of healthy habits, strong enough to last when there are no more adult reminders. During middle childhood, adults still do a great deal for girls and boys, although adult responsibility becomes more that of providing the facilities for children to take over their own personal care.

Children and their personal care

Children are potentially able to become responsible for their own dressing, choice of clothes, alongside negotiation with parents when necessary, and at least get dirty clothes into a washing basket. Some children and young people are able to undertake simple hand washing themselves and/or use a washing machine. Over the first part of middle childhood, boys and girls are able to take on responsibility for their own personal hygiene: washing, bathing and cleaning their teeth – probably with some friendly reminders from adults.

Toilet training

Children of 5 and 6 years old should have been daytime toilet-trained for some time now. Children can still experience accidents over the primary school years, usually because they have waited too long to go to the toilet during or as the result of a stomach upset. Some children entering primary school are not yet toilet trained, because their early life has been chaotic and nobody has got around to the task. Children who cope with physical disabilities may take longer to become continent; some will never be able to manage this task. Learning disabilities may mean that a child takes longer to understand and take responsibility for this aspect of their personal care.

Being dry at night can take longer and bed wetting is a hidden problem for quite a few children and even adolescents. Apart from the stress at home, uncertainty about what will happen leads older children to wonder whether to go on any kind of overnight stay – school trips or sleepovers with friends. The organisation ERIC (Education and Resources for Improving Childhood Continence www.enuresis.org.uk) estimates that at 5 years of age, around one in ten children wet the bed. By 10 years of age it is estimated that still about one in 20 older children cannot be sure they will be dry overnight and that about one in 75 young people from 15–21 years old are still coping with this problem.

The aim is that disabled children and young people are enabled to take over as much of their personal care as is realistic. The exact nature of the disability will affect what tasks the child or young person can take on for themselves and at what pace. Learning disabilities are likely to slow down the process of learning, with the need to allow more time at each step along the way. Children who cope mainly with a physical disability may manage well with the support of specialised equipment, although more slowly than they would ideally wish. Personal issues such as choosing clothes can become more complex when children are in a wheelchair. As they will tell you, some styles of clothing ride up and fastenings become uncomfortable after a while.

Adults' own feelings and their continued adjustment are also a feature in the lives of children and young people with disabilities. Parents, or practitioners, may find it very difficult to hand over the details of everyday care when they are used to taking the responsibility. It can also be very tempting to step in when an older child or young person appears to struggle with a task. Yet taking over does not help in the long run and children need to remain the expert on whether they want some help.

TAKE ANOTHER PERSPECTIVE

Children have an impressive range of skills, but adults have to look carefully about the circumstances created in some schools. Discussions with children, and thoughtful staff, highlight these practical issues that need to be resolved.

- Children struggle to manage dressing and undressing for PE in school or putting on outdoor clothing, if not enough time has been allocated. Some primary schools still expect children to change in a school corridor. This public situation offends the sense of privacy felt by some children – let alone the concerns of families who place a high value on modesty.

- Adolescents express similar irritation over insufficient time for changing and the shower that is required after sports. They object to being nagged by the PE teacher to hurry up and then criticised by the next teacher, for whom they are inevitably late. Young males and females sometimes also feel that facilities do not give enough privacy at a stage when everyone feels self-conscious about their bodies.

- Five and 6 year olds feel intimidated by a large, noisy school canteen or lunch in the hall. Considerate teachers insist on a slow introduction of the youngest children to full school lunchtime, and also to assembly (which the youngest children find intimidating or boring).

- Consultations with school-aged children can surprise staff by the distress and annoyance caused by unsavoury toilets. Some facilities are poorly maintained, without basics like soap and drying facilities, and sometimes they are the location of harassment and bullying. The strength of feeling led the Schools Council UK in 2006 to run a campaign called 'Bog Standard – better toilets for pupils'.

If you work in a school, what steps have been taken in your setting to ensure that children are supported properly to use their skills of personal care?

For any readers – do you have memories from your own school days that connect with the points made here?

Encouraging healthy habits

It is unrealistic to expect children and young people to develop healthy habits without a clear adult lead over good nutrition and personal care. This responsibility is shared between children's own family and their school, after-school club or childminder. Residential and foster carers carry the same responsibility as parents in the family home.

Children need to develop the habit of regular visits to the dentist and optician. They are taken by their parent or other family carer until the time when adolescents and young adults make their own arrangements. But dentists and other health professionals cannot work magic and become frustrated at repairing damage that is avoidable, for instance dental decay. Health care monitoring over childhood is partly about measurements such as weight and height. However, weighing children or adolescents achieves nothing in isolation, either to counteract obesity or to address the risks for children and adolescents of being persistently under weight (see page 254).

Care of teeth

The first teeth appear in babyhood and by 5 years of age children will have their full set of 20 first teeth, sometimes called 'milk teeth'. Around 6 years of age the second set of teeth start, one by one, to push out the first ones. This process takes time: by 12–14 years of age most adolescents have the 28 teeth in their second and permanent set. The last four teeth to complete the usual set of 32 are the so-called 'wisdom teeth' at the very back of the top and bottom of the mouth. These do not push out existing teeth and tend to emerge over late adolescence and early adulthood, around 18–25 years of age. Some wisdom teeth remain in the gums and, unless they are causing a problem, dentists do not recommend their removal.

Dental decay is a serious problem for many children in the UK and is largely preventable, so long as adults start the process and guide children and young adolescents to continue with the healthy habits of cleaning their teeth and eating a sensible diet. Excessive confectionery and sweetened or fizzy drinks can cause cavities in the milk teeth, sometimes serious enough that children have to have teeth extracted. When the first teeth come out too early, the result can damage the structure of the second tooth that is still in development. Worse still, some of this second set of teeth can actually start to decay in the gums and have to be removed as a matter of emergency.

Diet and body chemistry

There are different ways to reach a diet that supports health and, so long as individuals do not have allergies, no genuine foods are 'good' or 'bad' in themselves. For example, fruit and vegetables are part of a healthy diet but neither children nor adults remain energetic if they eat nothing but these foods. Fruit juices are acidic and children who are allowed to drink large amounts, instead of water or milk, can develop tooth decay as a result. Teeth do not distinguish between 'good' and 'bad' sugars.

Problems arise from unbalanced diets, low in nutrition, and from high dependence on processed meals and drinks. The impact of diet on health results partly from what happens within the complex chemistry of the way the human body processes food and drink. The additional factor during childhood and adolescence is that nutritious food and drink has to fuel physical growth and build a strong body ready for adulthood.

Children and young people need to develop the habit of drinking non-fizzy drinks because the carbonation depends on phosphoric acid, which seems to interfere with the body's absorption of calcium. Fizziness also depends on carbon dioxide which increases the acidity in the body. In order to redress the balance, calcium is leeched from the bones. This double header is especially negative for children who are in the process of growing and strengthening their bones. Some levels of damage in the form of osteoporosis are now being found in 10 and 11 year olds who have been allowed to drink significant quantities of carbonated drinks.

Good nutrition depends on as much food as possible being cooked from scratch with fresh ingredients. This method is the only way to be as sure as possible about what has gone into the meal. Processed meals and 'fast food' or 'junk food' frequently contain significant amounts of fat and carbohydrates in the form of sugar – ingredients that are not always predictable from the nature of the meal. This combination seems to stimulate production of opioids, natural chemicals in the body that trigger the desire to eat more, while reducing the body's message of feeling full.

Processed food is also manufactured in ways to make it quick and easy to eat, reducing the time needed to chew – another way in which children, or anyone else, fails to experience that 'full up' sated feeling. Additionally, if children and young adolescents are allowed to snack without limits, they can fail to learn a pattern of feeling hungry, eating to feel nearly full and then stopping. Munching and drinking can become simply a habit of something to do, possibly also a form of comfort.

Poor eating habits in childhood seem to prime children's body chemistry with the desire to eat the less healthy options. It is genuinely hard for them to shift those habits later because food does not taste strong enough without added chemicals or hidden sugars that have made processed food and drink palatable. Eating significant amounts of fast food seems to exert a cumulative, almost addictive effect on the metabolism of children's bodies.

Drinking

Children and young people need to be encouraged to drink water as their main drink. Many schools have now recognised the negative effect of dehydration on children's ability to concentrate, and an increased adult responsibility to ensure that children drink enough in hot weather or after vigorous exercise. Easy access to plain water also helps to build the habit of quenching thirst in this way.

Manufacturers promote low-sugar drinks as more 'healthy' or even 'better' for teeth – the key question is 'compared with what else?' Also, without the taste created by some type of sugar, an artificial sweetener is necessary to create a product that people would be willing to drink. These chemicals are not nutritional and some have dubious effects in anything other than minimal amounts.

Nutritious food

Children and adolescents need to experience consistently good quality food, presented in an appetising way and organised around enjoyable, social mealtimes. They also need to be involved as much as possible in the knowledge and skills that contribute to healthy habits for food and drink. By middle childhood boys and girls can already be active in discussing menus, purchase and preparation of food and learning how to cook.

Any meals and snacks given to children in inspected provision like schools should provide a balanced and healthy range of foods. However, 25 years of neglect created an unacceptable situation for many schools in England and Wales. The Education Act 1980 removed the duty of local authorities to provide a suitable lunch at a fixed price and abolished minimum nutritional standards for the meal. The Local Government Act 1988 then introduced compulsory competitive tendering, which meant that the school meals contract went to the lowest bidder. Not surprisingly, the quality of most school lunches declined. Financial rather than health considerations also led to many snack and soft drinks machines that made a profit for the school and/or the company with the contract for lunches.

Some minimum standards were reintroduced in 2001, but the true state of most lunches was not exposed nationally until 2005 in the Channel 4 television programme *Jamie's School Dinners*. Jamie Oliver, already well known as a 'television chef', then started a national campaign (www.jamieoliver.com/schooldinners/) that spotlighted the ridiculous situation of firm, official guidance about health that ignored the poor quality food in many primary and secondary schools. The national campaign has helped to encourage more schools to address menus and training of kitchen staff, and to face the serious problem that some schools no longer have a proper kitchen.

LOOK, LISTEN, NOTE, LEARN

Prior to the publicity generated by Jamie Oliver, some individual schools had already improved their lunches for children. Jeanette Orrey, a school cook, changed the whole pattern of food for her primary school in Nottinghamshire, fully supported by her head teacher. It is worthwhile reading her description (2005) of the step-by-step changes she made and how she continued to invite opinions from the children. It is also the first book I have ever read that includes recipes to feed '4 adults and 96 children' (Jamie Oliver acknowledges Jeanette Orrey as a pioneer in his foreword to the book). The narrative lasts over several years of steady change. So, the account is a timely reminder that this kind of significant overhaul needs persistent effort and does not happen within just a few months.

▓ **What has happened in your local schools about the quality of lunches and snacks for children or adolescents?**

Enjoyment of food and cooking

Healthy habits are also supported when children and young people become involved in the actual cooking and food preparation that makes meals a genuinely shared experience. Some schools have brought back cooking as an activity with children. I have encountered early-years settings and after-school clubs that involve children as much as possible in proper cooking, preparing their own snacks and other aspects of eating like laying the table and tidying up afterwards. I have also encountered teams in residential homes who have gained control of their own food budget. Adults and adolescents have planned menus, bought food and cooked together in a family atmosphere. The consequence has been better quality meals and less wastage than when meals are produced with no input from children and young people. The active involvement is also a powerful link to practical life skills.

TAKE ANOTHER PERSPECTIVE

The National Children's Bureau's Healthy Care Programme was developed to support local authorities in England to implement the *Promoting the Health of Looked-After Children* guidance from the Department of Health (England and Wales). This programme looked in detail at the health and health care needs of an especially vulnerable group of children and young people.

One project explored the leisure activities that looked-after children said they wanted or showed they enjoyed, when given the opportunity. One successful example was a cooking club, where the adult aim was that children and young people learned life skills and information relevant to their health. But from the perspective of children and young people, the contact with friendly adults was just as important as the club agenda. The atmosphere made it easy for children and young people to talk when and how they wanted. The club worked to increase their confidence and provided a vital experience of a warm relationship with a caring adult.

LOOK, LISTEN, NOTE, LEARN

Children and adolescents benefit from an understanding of how to choose genuinely healthy options, including that indulgent treats are enjoyable occasionally. The problems arise when snacks, confectionery and processed food and drink dominate their daily diet. Children and adolescents need a healthy level of scepticism about how food and drink is labelled and marketed: the word 'healthy' on a packet is not necessarily true in any useful interpretation. Problems arise also because this younger generation is on the receiving end of aggressive marketing to persuade them to develop the habit for specific items and to nag their parents while they are the purchaser.

If you work with older children or adolescents, look together at the two reports below, from the consumer organisation Which? They provide an informative read for adults but are also written in a style that aims to catch the attention of young potential consumers.

- Which? (2006) *Childcatchers: the tricks used to push unhealthy food on your children.* See www.which.co.uk/files/application/pdf/060131childcatchers_rep-445-76882.pdf.
- Which? (2006) *Food Fables: exploding industry myths on responsible food marketing to kids.* See www.which.co.uk/files/application/pdf/FoodFables%20231106-445-100487.pdf.

If you want to find out more

❖ **Action for Leisure** and **Contact A Family West Midlands** (2004) *Come on in: developing inclusive play and leisure services.* See www.cafamily.org.uk/wmids/ComeOnIn.pdf..

❖ **Alderson, Priscilla** (2000) *Young children's rights.* London: Jessica Kingsley/Save the Children.

❖ **Blythe, Sally Goddard** (2004) *The well balanced child: movement and early learning.* Stroud: Hawthorne Press.

❖ **Child Accident Prevention Trust** (2002) *Taking chances: the lifestyles and leisure risk of young people.* Summary at www.capt.org.uk.

❖ **Freeplay Network** includes an online photo exhibition of images of play, briefing papers and links to other useful sites. See www.freeplaynetwork.org.uk/playlink/exhibition/index.html.

❖ **Healthy Care Programme** – projects and resources about the health and well-being of looked-after children and young people. See www.ncb.org.uk.

❖ **Gill, Tim** (2007) *No fear: growing up in a risk averse society.* London: Calouste Gulbenkian.

❖ **Griffiths, Mark** (2006) *Videogame playing in children and adolescents.* Highlight no 226. London: National Children's Bureau.

❖ **Health and Safety Executive** (2006) *Principles of sensible risk management* and other papers. See www.hse.gov.uk/risk.

❖ **John, Allison** and **Wheway, Rob** (2004) *Can play: will play: disabled children and access to outdoor playgrounds.* London: National Playing Fields Association. Available for download from www.npfa.co.uk/content/playforchildren/index.html.

❖ **Kids Playwork Inclusion Project (PIP).** See www.kids.org.uk.

❖ **Lindon, Jennie** (2003a) *Too safe for their own good? Helping children learn about risk and lifeskills.* London: National Children's Bureau.

❖ **Lindon, Jennie** (2003b) *What does it mean to be five? A practical guide to child development in the Foundation Stage.* Cheltenham: Step Forward Publishing.

❖ **NHS Direct Online Encyclopaedia.** See www.nhsdirect.nhs.uk.

❖ **Orrey, Jeanette** (2005) *The Dinner Lady: change the way your children eat for life.* London: Bantam Press.

❖ **Play Safety Forum** and **Children's Play Council** (2002) *Managing risk in play provision: a position statement.* London: National Children's Bureau. Available for download from www.ncb.org.uk/cpc/.

❖ **Rafferty, Sharon** (1997) *Giving children a voice – what next? A study from one primary school.* Spotlight 65, Scottish Council for Research in Education. See www.scre.ac.uk/spotlight/spotlight65.html.

❖ **Woolley, Helen** with **Armitage, Marc; Bishop, Julia; Curtis, Mavis** and **Ginsborg, Jane** (2006) *Inclusion of disabled children in primary school playgrounds.* London: National Children's Bureau. Summary at www.jrf.org.uk/knowledge/findings/socialpolicy/0016.asp.

9 Physical growth and development into young adulthood

Children and young people experience significant changes as their bodies grow and the process of puberty takes them into the beginnings of being an adult male or female. There are many physical changes, but development over these years also includes learning habits and attitudes that will shape current and future health or health risks. The events of puberty for boys and girls are as much emotional as physical in their effects. Young people negotiate the years across adolescence into early adulthood as they develop an awareness of their own body, deal with issues around sexual awareness, attraction and their own sexual identity and orientation.

> **The main sections of this chapter are:**
>
> ⁕ **Physical growth and change.**
>
> ⁕ **Sexual awareness and attraction.**
>
> ⁕ **Relationships, sex and young parenthood.**

PHYSICAL GROWTH AND CHANGE

Children go through perceptible changes in body shape and features, but the shifts are less striking than the changes from a helpless baby to wobbly toddler and then physically competent 3–4 year old. The sketch on page 244 gives an indication of how children's bodies change in terms of the proportions. At birth a baby's head accounts of about 25 per cent of the full body length. Compared with the rest of the body, a child's head grows the least, until the head is about 12 per cent of body length in adulthood. After the significant changes of early childhood, the next dramatic shift arrives with puberty and all the changes start towards being a mature female or male (see page 246).

Gaining a healthy level of weight

From 5–18 years, children and then young people are growing towards adulthood. Their bodies will do a great deal of this physical development regardless of external circumstances. However, growing bodies are affected by what is taken into the system and how bodies are used. Seriously imbalanced diets and inappropriate exercise – too little, too much, a significant imbalance – all leave their mark on physical development. Experiences of food and drink through childhood and adolescence also

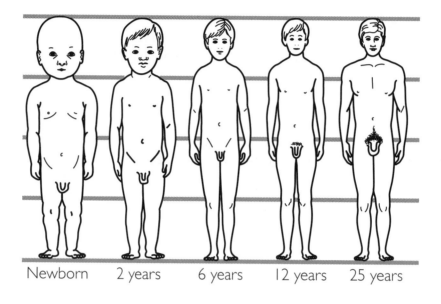

Newborn   2 years   6 years   12 years   25 years

Changes in body proportions over the years –
as shown from boyhood to a young adult male

leave observable traces in terms of the habits that are laid down as a view of normal, daily life for boys and girls (see page 237).

Children or young people who are significantly overweight can get caught in a vicious circle. They may find physical activity less easy, even if their peers do not tease them, and so it seems easier to avoid lively play. Lack of exercise makes them feel less energetic, and they may also eat for comfort, which worsens the situation. Older children and adolescents can become depressed, because they are so unhappy about their body image. Unless there is a sound medical reason, children and young adolescents should not be placed on a diet that reduces calories. They still have some growing upwards to complete and there is a good chance of adjusting their body shape with a more balanced diet, which may address portion size. Children and young people need practical help to change their eating and exercise habits towards a more healthy pattern.

A healthy weight range for adults is judged by calculating an individual's body mass index, which compares weight against height. (If you want to know more about the BMI try the Healthy Living section of http://info.cancerresearchuk.org/healthyliving/obesityandweight/bodymassindex/.) However, the same calculation is not used for children and young people. The weight of a child or adolescent is compared with the distribution of weight for their age and gender. Separate growth charts are used for girls and boys. An individual is usually judged to be underweight if they fall within the lowest 5 per cent of the distribution of weight for their age and overweight if they fall within the highest 5 per cent. Health professionals would want to look at the individual pattern over a period of time and take account of height.

The high level of concern about obesity in childhood has led to plans to weigh all children at the beginning and end of primary school in England and Wales. There are practical issues around the plan, not least who will do the weighing and how the information will be used to actually help children and families. However, it also matters how children are likely to feel as the owners of the bodies to be weighed and measured.

Stella Muttock and Jo Butcher (2005) undertook a consultation with 4–11 year olds, which contributed to Department of Health guidance on the initiative. The results remind adults that children are able to think about health issues:

- The children in the survey understood mostly why adults might want to weigh them, but expressed fair concerns about how this was to be done.
- They wanted to be viewed as able to take some responsibility for their own health, not as children to whom things would just be done by adults. Children wanted any measuring session to be an opportunity when they could ask their own questions of the health care professional.
- Children wanted weighing to be done in private, not in groups – or if there was a group element that boys and girls would be separate. The survey results also remind any adult that some 11 year olds will be in the middle or close to the end of puberty and even more sensitive to their bodily dignity than younger children.
- Children were aware and concerned about legitimate issues of privacy and confidentiality, such as who would see the information and how it would be shared.

Being seriously overweight complicates many health issues. Health services are already seeing the consequences for children and young people who have been allowed to become obese by parents or other adults who were responsible for monitoring and guiding daily diet. Before they reach adulthood, children and young people start to experience the consequences of obesity through strain on their joints, heart and lungs from carrying excessive weight and the lack of exercise that is often associated with the problem. Obesity increases the risk for young people of health problems that were previously associated with the middle and later years of adulthood. Health professionals in the UK are now seeing the pattern that was obvious from the 1990s in the USA, such as early onset of osteoarthritis, breathing problems, high blood pressure, type 2 diabetes and strokes.

There are also health risks for young people when they are seriously underweight or follow a pattern of excessive exercise – see page 254.

The transition into puberty

Puberty is the process that shifts boys and girls into physical adulthood. The entire process takes time and includes internal changes as well as the

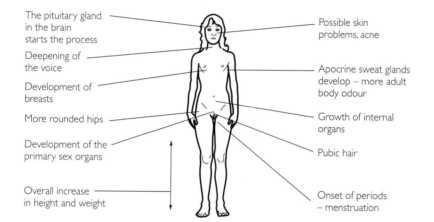

The pituitary gland in the brain starts the process

Deepening of the voice

Development of breasts

More rounded hips

Development of the primary sex organs

Overall increase in height and weight

Possible skin problems, acne

Apocrine sweat glands develop – more adult body odour

Growth of internal organs

Pubic hair

Onset of periods – menstruation

Changes in the body as a girl moves through puberty

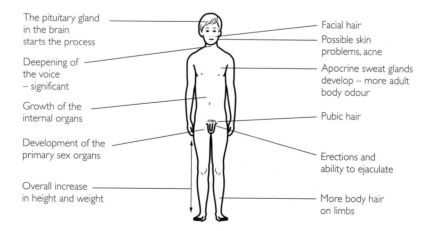

The pituitary gland in the brain starts the process

Deepening of the voice – significant

Growth of the internal organs

Development of the primary sex organs

Overall increase in height and weight

Facial hair

Possible skin problems, acne

Apocrine sweat glands develop – more adult body odour

Pubic hair

Erections and ability to ejaculate

More body hair on limbs

Changes in the body as a boy moves through puberty

more obvious external physical changes. The process is also emotional, affected by the new chemical balance in the bodies of young people, and by the wide range of emotions experienced about the move into alleged adulthood: young people's own feelings and those of peers or adults around them. The physical transition into adulthood is given shape by social and cultural messages communicated to older children and young people about what becoming a mature adult means for them.

There is a wide age range for the start and completion of all the changes that make up puberty, with markers that alert health care staff to an unusually early or delayed onset. On average, girls start the process and mature at an earlier age in years than their male peers. The age of the onset of puberty can be delayed for individuals by poor nutrition and hard physical activity – either because adolescents live in harsh social conditions or that situation is mimicked through extreme dieting and obsessive exercise.

There is a persistent belief that the average age for starting puberty is continuing to fall in the western world. Improved nutrition and less physical work led to a steady decline in the average age of puberty but it seems now to have halted. In their review of the data, Peter Smith and Helen Cowie (2003) conclude that the average age of puberty appears to have been 14–16 years in the western world during the 1860s. Estimates of an average age of 16–17 years are now generally thought to have been a misinterpretation of the available information. The average age of puberty declined to about 13 years by the 1960s. Since that period, there may have been a very slight average decline but not much. The belief that children are growing up, literally, much younger seems to arise from misleading messages given through how some older children, especially girls, are allowed to dress.

The process of puberty

The change from child into adult becomes obvious to outsiders once a boy or girl has passed through significant external bodily changes. However, the internal process of puberty is started earlier by a chemical signal from the hypothalamus, at the base of the brain, to activate the pituitary gland to which it is connected. The pituitary gland increases the production of growth hormones and so stimulates the growth of different kinds of body tissue. The same gland also releases specific hormones that influence the primary sex organs of children. A girl's ovaries are stimulated to produce the hormones estrogen (also spelled oestrogen) and progesterone, which in turn sets off the release of mature ova (eggs). In a boy's body the testes (testicles) and adrenal gland are stimulated to produce testosterone, which triggers the manufacture of sperm.

The growth spurt

The first external sign that puberty has started is usually a significant growth spurt of height and weight for both sexes, although girls tend to have their spurt earlier in the entire process than boys. Over this period it is even more important that adolescents have a well-balanced diet to fuel the growth. They may be very hungry and even individuals who previously had to be persuaded to eat, start to fill up their plates. Significant changes can happen over a few months – the reason why adolescents are often embarrassed by adults who announce accurately, 'Haven't you grown!' Over the entire growth spurt, an average adolescent can grow as much as 30 centimetres in height and put on 9–12 kilograms in weight.

It is usual that the limbs and trunk appear to grow out of balance with each other. Young adolescents, especially boys, tend to go through a period when they feel ill at ease with their own body. Their discomfort is explained by the fact that the final length of their legs is usually completed about half a year before their trunk. There is usually a further delay before they reach the final width of their chest and shoulders.

As girls turn into young women they cope with the changes in body shape brought about by the development of breasts and the expansion of their hips. Overall, young females develop more rounded body contours. Both sexes put on additional weight within the growth spurt, but young males have a much larger proportion of muscle to fat than is the case for girls. So most young women will not naturally fit a body image that is very angular (see page 254).

Both sexes find an increase in physical strength and endurance, although the changes now create a more obvious difference between the sexes. Girls who could previously hold their own against brothers or male play companions can now find they struggle to win or cope in physically lively games. Since male peers may literally not know their own strength, there is a risk that girls and young female adolescents can get hurt.

The growth spurt would be regarded as very early for girls at 8–9 years and for boys at 10 years. The average growth spurt occurs at around 11 years of age for girls and 12–13 for boys. But simple observation of the 9–14 years age group will show you that there is a significant variation. A 13 year old girl who had not started the growth spurt at all would be regarded as late, whereas the same would not be said of a boy until about 15 years of age. Skeletal growth usually stops at 16–17 years for young women, but can go on to around 21 years for young men.

> **LOOK, LISTEN, NOTE, LEARN**
>
> Take the opportunity to look at a class or year of children at the beginning of secondary school. They will be 11–12 years of age.
>
> ▪ The girls will vary from some individuals who are head and shoulders above their age peers and have the body shape of an adult female. They look much older than a pre-adolescent. On the other hand, some of the 12-year-old females still look girl-like.
>
> ▪ The male students are likely to include a higher proportion of individuals who still look like boys. However, there will be some 12 year olds who tower over the group and look like young men.

Development of the sex organs

The primary sex organs mature and increase in size as part of the process that makes reproduction possible.

In young males the testes produce sperm cells and the prostate produces semen, the fluid that carries the sperm. Their penis increases towards the final adult size and shape. Boys are then able to experience erections and ejaculation of the seminal fluid, sometimes when they are awake but also during sleep as a nocturnal emission, known to adolescents as a 'wet dream'. Many male adolescents also experience random erections, not necessarily as part of feeling aroused. The sperm in the seminal fluid are not mature immediately so young adolescents, who are sexually active, are unlikely to make their female partner pregnant. However, there is a wide variation: on average young men have mature sperm at 15 years of age, but that hides an age range of just over 11 to 17 years.

In young females the ovaries begin to release mature ova into the fallopian tubes. If the released egg is not fertilised then it is lost, along with blood and some of the lining of the womb as part of menstruation (periods). All the ova are already in a girl's body but are not mature, whereas a boy's body does not produce sperm until the changes of puberty. The menarche – the term to describe the start of a young woman's periods – comes relatively late in the whole sequence of female puberty. Girls sometimes have a clear discharge, noticeable on their underwear, some time before they start to menstruate. The first periods are often irregular until the pattern settles down for this individual. Some females then have a very predictable pattern for menstruation, but some continue with irregular timing. The first periods do not usually include a mature ovum (egg).

Girls who are relatively early in starting puberty will have started to menstruate while still in primary school. Later developers may be well into the secondary school years before they start to menstruate. Periods do not usually start until after the growth spurt and when a girl has started to develop breasts. If she is still waiting on this change at the age of 15, development would be judged as delayed. At 16 years old the lack of menstruation would be seen as late, and worth checking. After their periods have started, females then reach a final development of their breasts and pubic hair.

Female adolescents, just like their male peers, need reliable information and a friendly adult, most likely of the same sex, who can reassure them when they are genuinely still within the wide normal range for puberty. Girls sometimes are not aware, or have forgotten information heard long ago, that periods are the last major step in puberty and not the first. Boys can be taken aback by random erections or wet dreams and are not necessarily any happier than their female peers about getting more body hair.

Other bodily changes

All the major internal organs, like the heart and lungs, also grow in size during puberty. The brain is the only organ that does not increase in actual size, but puberty is a busy time for reorganisation in the human brain (see page 293). Other significant changes follow, some of which bother or surprise adolescents.

- Both sexes develop more body hair, including pubic and underarm hair. This development takes time and there tend to be temporary halts in the growth, and then more hair develops. Boys are usually more hairy overall than girls and develop facial hair.

- Cultural traditions vary for both sexes. It is important in some cultures or faiths that males grow a beard. In other social and cultural groups facial hair is a matter of personal choice or may even be unwelcome. Some cultures emphasise the importance of removal of body hair by women and this tradition is strong for many social groups in the UK.

- Late in puberty, both sexes experience a deepening of the voice but the change is more noticeable in boys. The larynx expands and the vocal cords lengthen. Some young males also experience sudden changes in the pitch of their voice until the development is complete.

- A change in body chemistry brings a more adult body odour as the apocrine glands develop in the later part of puberty. Children prior to puberty do not have an unpleasant body odour, unless they or their clothes are not washed at reasonable intervals. However, male and female adolescents need to pay closer attention to personal body hygiene, especially after physical exercise, and to the regular changing of their clothes.

Skin problems

During puberty most adolescents have some problems with their skin erupting with acne. Even the most fortunate have to deal with a few spots over the years, but a proportion of adolescents have more serious outbreaks.

All the glands in the body become more active during puberty including the oil glands that are located just under the surface of the skin. When oil and bacteria become trapped in an oil gland, it infects the surrounding area. The first sign of trouble is an area of inflammation or a spot. The spot can become a cyst or a boil if the infection is located below the immediate skin surface. Acne appears where the oil glands are most numerous: often on the face, especially around the hairline, on the neck, shoulders and back.

Regular washing of the hair and face and good hygiene stops the problem getting worse, but acne is not caused simply by adolescents' refusal to wash their face and neck. A healthy diet helps but, again, there is not a simple cause and effect relationship between food and skin problems. Adolescents need to find over-the-counter preparations that work for them; few if any bring about the magical transformation promised in advertisements. Persistent and extensive problems need a visit to the family doctor. Some types of acne do not disappear towards the end of adolescence and remain a life-long trouble.

Early and late developers

All adolescents have feelings about going through their own puberty, because the process is emotional as much as physical. Adolescents may also be aware within their own family that their parents, or other family members, have strong feelings about the process. Some parents struggle to come to terms with visible evidence that their son or daughter is growing into a young adult. In some social and cultural groups, puberty is the time that serious restrictions come to be placed on young people, especially females, affecting their independent movement and contact with the opposite sex.

The normal process of puberty can happen over a wide age range. Consequently, some girls and boys are significantly early or very late developers in comparison with their peers. Both sexes worry increasingly when they are later than their friends. Adolescents may feel patronised because they still look like a child and the confidence of boys seems

251

especially to be shaken when most of their peers are taller than them. There is a mix of feelings in both sexes about being very early in terms of maturation.

The experience of early developers

All early developers are likely to be mistaken by unfamiliar people as older than their actual years. This adult error is not always a disadvantage, but the results can be annoying if very young adolescents get told off for not 'acting your age' or are assigned additional chores and unwanted responsibility.

Older children and very young adolescents may find they are told to leave a public play facility 'because it's only for children'. Playworkers in particular need to be sensitive to the feelings of 11 and 12 year olds who are too long or wide for the equipment – not obese, just their personal adult size. Mature, 11-year-old girls may forget themselves and go to take their top off in hot weather or continue to hang upside down with the consequent flashing of underwear. They are not being provocative; they are still emotionally more like a child.

On balance, early maturing boys tend to be pleased to be ahead of their peers. They may be at an advantage socially because the growth spurt literally gives them a head start and strength in more challenging sports and physical activities. Success can bring status with their peer group. So long as adults do not react negatively, it can be a pleasant experience to look some teachers in the eye, maybe even be taller than some adults. The downside for the male early developers is that it takes time to know what will happen as their peers reach their final size. Some adolescents, who have enjoyed being the tallest for some years, have a shock when their peers catch up and maybe pass them in size. Their social status may come under threat, although emotionally secure adolescents make the adjustment.

Girls who mature earlier are often pleased to feel more grown up than their peers, but some feel ill at ease because they are taller and bigger than other girls. Early maturing 11–12 year olds also seem to be at a higher risk of becoming convinced they are 'fat' and trying to diet. It may be some time before their peers catch up and it becomes obvious that the early developer is of average size for a mature female, or even petite, now that everyone else has grown to full size.

In some studies, early puberty for females has been linked with an increase in risky behaviour, including under-age sexual activity. A possible explanation is that female adolescents who look older than their years mix with a social group who are actually older and includes older male adolescents who are sexually active. This pattern is not, of course, inevitable and much depends on family support and setting boundaries. Any young female adolescent who looks older is likely to have to deal with the interest of young men, who may genuinely believe they are talking with an older adolescent.

SEXUAL AWARENESS AND ATTRACTION

The biological boundary between childhood and adulthood is the process of puberty. After the changes of puberty, a young person is sexually mature, but can be below the age of legal consent for sexual activity – 16 years in England, Wales and Scotland, but 17 years in Northern Ireland. Ages are set with the assumption that younger adolescents do not have the emotional maturity to make the decision to engage in full sexual activity. There is a related concern that they are not ready to care for the baby that can result from unprotected heterosexual activity.

Attractiveness and body image

Part of the unease felt by most members of both sexes through the changes of puberty rests upon whether they are attractive – both in general for their peers and to specific individuals whom they would like

Young people spend some time as a couple

to attract. Adolescents are aware of how they measure up against their own sex, as well as the opposite sex – the focus of attention for heterosexual adolescents. Young males and females compare themselves against same sex peers in their judgements about body shape, dress, hairstyle, toiletries and cosmetics. Fashion styles for young people are only partly determined by styles that dominate in high street shops or magazines. Entire patterns of dress are influenced by the social sub-culture to which adolescents have committed themselves.

Older children and young people become aware of the body shapes that are regarded as most acceptable within their social and cultural group. As with most images, only a proportion of the population will ever meet an exacting standard. Currently in the UK, young women usually aspire to be under- rather than overweight, despite the fact that few heterosexual males seem to find extreme thinness at all alluring. Young males are now also alert to an ideal shape, usually involving visible muscle tone.

Risks of being seriously underweight

The health risks of being significantly overweight are discussed from page 245. An opposite extreme of unhealthy habits of nutrition arises when children or young people become so anxious about being overweight that they fail to eat enough for their daily requirements. Until they have reached their full adult size, children and young people need nutrition that fuels the growth of their bodies as well as eating enough to have the energy for daily life and some bursts of physical activity.

Media images of fashion models and a proportion of successful female film stars, especially in the USA, are thin to the point of emaciation. Some adult women are naturally on the slim side, but this shape is different from what has been called the 'lollipop look': stick thin legs and arms and a head that looks out of proportion for their body. Mature females, living in a country with sufficient food, do not have this shape, unless they are seriously ill or living in a state of self-imposed starvation.

When an adult female body is starved, it loses muscle tone, including the rounded shape of breasts and the buttocks. So the appearance of some 'celebrities' is achieved only by hours of very specific physical training and cosmetic surgery. The increased danger for young females, who take this shape as their goal, is that they derail healthy physical development. Some weight loss diets are seriously unbalanced, for instance, lacking enough calcium for adolescents to build necessary bone strength. About 50 per cent of a female's final bone strength is determined by 14–15 years old and is built especially within two years either side of the onset of menstruation. Severe dieting, with or without vigorous exercise, also stops menstruation, because the body shuts down less vital processes in an effort of self-protection.

Eating disorders

Many young women are aware of their weight but some become enmeshed in dieting to the extent that it becomes the eating disorder of anorexia. Some additionally develop bulimia, when they use self-induced vomiting or heavy doses of laxative as a way to deal with having eaten too much – either in their view or as the result of binge eating. A pattern of obsessive eating and purging creates additional problems of undermining the body's ability to digest and eliminate what is not needed. Regular, self-induced vomiting can also bring up stomach acids that attack the surface of the teeth.

There are additional dangers when young women are supported in semi-starvation by friends, because there is less challenge that this pattern (rather like over-eating and acceptance of obesity) is presented as an appropriate lifestyle choice. A complex pattern of disordered behaviour and compulsions then builds around an obsession with controlling food intake and use of anything, like cigarettes or caffeine, that is believed to act as an appetite depressant. Support through internet technology is now also established with the so-called pro-ana and pro-mia websites that actively support the disturbed patterns of anorexia and bulimia. These sites have images of rail-thin female celebrities with messages praising them up for being beautiful in the 'thinspiration galleries'.

Many more females than males have become enmeshed in the complex health problems that accompany eating disorders like anorexia and bulimia. However, some male adolescents and adults develop eating disorders and there is some concern that young men are overlooked, partly because of the assumption that it is a female disorder. Information sometimes focuses only on the consequences for females, like the disappearance of periods and possible long-term damage to fertility. For more information look at the website of the Eating Disorders Association, www.edauk.com.

Body image and males

Some young men slide into an eating disorder through wanting to be super-fit for sport. They increase their amount and level of exercise to an obsessive level and adjust their food intake in a way that unbalances their nutritional needs. Male adolescents need to eat enough to fuel their growth spurt and they need additional calories if they engage in vigorous sports activity. So a young male could be eating what looks like sufficient food, yet still not be getting enough calories and might even lose weight.

For a long time, pressure towards an ideal body shape disproportionately affected girls and young women, but a percentage of boys and men have always been less than content with how they look. From the 1950s, Charles Atlas claimed to be able to transform the 'seven-stone weakling' through his body-building programme. The advertisements originated in the USA but were prevalent in the UK from much the same period. Young males take time to reach their final adult shape and some 16–18 year olds still look like overgrown boys. They feel they are underweight and compare themselves unfavourably with fully grown male sports stars or actors.

LOOK, LISTEN, NOTE, LEARN

There has been an increase in recent years of media images that inform young males that they should have a muscular shape. Male readers will be aware of this situation. So if you are a female, then take some time to look along the row of magazines for men that have males on the cover, rather than scantily clad females or shiny vehicles. Some magazines are aimed at gay men but some, for instance about men's health, are aimed at males regardless of sexual orientation.

Young men sometimes feel they have to manage the 'six pack' shape for the male abdomen. This body outline, so called because of a vague similarity to the rolling contours of cans of beer or lager, is not easily achievable without hard physical training. Since males, like females, come in all shapes and sizes, the 'six pack' is no more achievable as an ideal for all males than the female equivalent. Getting close to the high level of toning of muscle outlines that accompanies this ideal is not possible without specific physical exercise over time, through weight training or vigorous physical activity like working on a building site.

The sense of pressure has tempted some adolescent and adult males to take a chemical short cut with anabolic steroids to build strength, muscles and bulk. The drugs are sometimes also used by young men as part of body building in a strategy of self-defence. The side effects of steroids can show relatively quickly and some damage to major organs is not reversible. Psychological effects include more aggressive behaviour and sometimes delusions. Steroid use disrupts the normal hormonal balance and, because it can stop the production of testosterone, the drugs may stop the growth spurt in younger adolescents. Steroids also make testicles

MAKE THE CONNECTION WITH . . . TECHNOLOGY AND LIES

It is important that young people are enabled to see through the misleading images that can bedevil a sense of comfort in their own body. One route is to stimulate their technological awareness to recognise that many images of media role models are not accurate portrayals of what that person looks like in the harsh light of day.

The photographic techniques of airbrushing, use of lighting and angles always allowed a blurring of reality, but digital techniques now mean that the image of a real person can be dramatically different from their appearance face-to-face. Images of actresses and singers have been changed to enhance facial features, remove less welcome body features and lengthen legs to change the proportions of someone's body.

shrink and breasts develop, although these effects may be reversible so long as the drug use ceases. Steroid use is a growing problem for sports, so some websites cover the risks. I found useful information on www.itftennis.com/juniors/usefultips/antidoping/steroids.asp.

Excessive exercise

The human body is well designed to take most things in moderation. Physical activity is important but can be harmful if taken to excess. Adolescents, and adults, with eating disorders sometimes use very frequent and prolonged exercise as a way of trying to burn calories or purge from a food binge. Extreme patterns of exercise increase the chance of injuries to anyone and people with eating disorders are already in a fragile state of health.

However, the human body chemistry delivers another potential problem through the effect of endorphins. These chemicals are opioids, released from the pituitary gland as the result of vigorous physical exercise. They provide a 'buzz' or positive emotion, which is a useful boost to motivation when you do not feel like going for a swim or a run. You still go because you know from experience you will feel better for the exercise. Many young people or adults who reach a pattern of excessive exercise have unresolved emotional problems and the endorphin buzz temporarily masks their distress. But the effects wear off and so exercise comes to dominate daily life to a greater and greater extent, in an addictive pattern. This problem can be hard to identify, partly because distressed young people may be secretive about how much exercise they do, but also because of the general message that exercise is 'healthy'.

RELATIONSHIPS, SEX AND YOUNG PARENTHOOD

Friendships continue to be important for adolescents, but many seek a more intense relationship through being a couple with someone else.

Sexual awareness and attraction

During childhood, girls and boys operate to a large extent in single sex social groups for play and social activities. Over early and mid-adolescence they tend to come back together again, unless their families require them not to mix with the opposite sex. Adolescents become very aware of peers, or people outside their age group, to whom they feel sexually attracted. Depending on the social norms of their group, individual adolescents start to pair off, even if the period of going out together is sometimes brief. Couples do not necessarily operate independently from their existing friendship group but some adjustment and negotiation is usually needed if they have so far had different friends.

Over the years of adolescence, some couples move towards full sexual activity. When this development starts before the legal age of consent, the situation can place the young male in a vulnerable position, even if he also is too young in the eyes of the law. Some families are less concerned than others, or the responsible adults feel they have lost the struggle to set boundaries for the adolescents. Some social, cultural and faith groups are especially committed to a message that any kind of sexual activity outside marriage is unacceptable. Across time and place this ruling has been usually applied with far greater strictness to females than to males.

Sexual orientation

Part of the shifts over puberty is that adolescents have an increased sexual awareness and attraction to others. The personal route for some young people through this transition includes a steady recognition that their sexual orientation is not heterosexual and they may spend some time working out whether they are gay or lesbian, or bisexual. Experiences over the years of adolescence lead a young person to an understanding about whether they are attracted exclusively or mainly to the opposite or their own sex.

UK society is more open than in previous decades, but there is still considerable support, even pressure, for taking the heterosexual option. Studies of bullying in school show that homophobic taunts and rumour-mongering are often part of verbal or physical bullying. The pattern can become established regardless of whether a young person genuinely has a gay or lesbian sexual orientation. Offensive ways of describing non-heterosexuals are often used as general purpose insults. Adolescents may hope their family will accept any choice that they make, but some young

WHAT DOES IT MEAN?

- **Sexual awareness**: an increased sensitivity to others in terms of their attractiveness, or not, and potential for emotional and physical involvement.
- **Sexual orientation**: the main focus for an individual's feelings of sexual attraction, which may be to the opposite sex (heterosexual), the same sex (gay or lesbian), or to attractive individuals of either sex (bisexual).
- **Gender dysphoria**: the conviction of being trapped in the body of the wrong sex.

people realise their parents would rather they were heterosexual. Some families are part of social, cultural or faith groups that support uncompromising rejection, even violence, against non-heterosexuals.

Sexual orientation seems to have elements of a continuum within the population and some young adults come to realise that they are not exclusively heterosexual or homosexual. Bisexuals are occasionally accused of being in denial about their gay or lesbian sexual identity. On the contrary, it does seem that sexual orientation is a flexible matter for some adults.

Sexual identity

Young people during puberty have to adjust to being an adult version of their sex. Despite being uneasy with some of the changes, most adolescents make the transition into becoming an adult male or female without any significant problems. A small proportion of young people, however, are very distressed, feeling trapped within a body of the wrong sex. This condition is known as gender dysphoria or gender identity disorder.

Individuals who were unhappy through childhood about being a boy or a girl often coped by opting for a style of dress, toys and books that were a better fit for their feelings. However, the physical changes of puberty transform their child's body into a visibly mature female or male form. This development can be devastating when a young person sees all the 'wrong' sexual characteristics. A sense of desperation and hopelessness can overcome young people in this situation, worsened by fear about the possible negative consequences of confiding in family or friends.

There is no clear single cause for why some individuals feel utterly at odds with their biological sexual identity. It is possible that some chemical changes before birth rewired basic masculine or feminine patterns. However, some explanations focus more on experiences in early childhood that lead a child to become convinced that they must be the opposite sex, because their behaviour and inclinations do not fit the clear expectations of key adults around them. As George Stewart explains (2006), adolescents and adults with issues over their gender identity can have any sexual orientation. The sex to which they feel attracted is a separate issue from the sex which they believe themselves to be, and may seek medical help, including surgery, to achieve.

Sex and relationships education

Families have a responsibility to prepare their sons and daughters for the events of puberty and the facts of adult sexual life. Some parents are considerably more comfortable about this role than others. Schools also have a responsibility and they address the issue through different approaches, including sex education – sometimes called sex and relationships education (SRE). Guidance across the UK highlights that good practice within schools is to go beyond the biological details of reproduction and place this aspect of education alongside health and the personal and social strand of the primary and secondary school curriculum. However, there is considerable variation in what is actually made available in schools. You can find more details about programmes from the Sex Education Forum (www.ncb.org.uk/sef) and Learning and Teaching Scotland (www.ltscotland.org.uk).

Some adolescents are sexually active and a proportion have their first full sexual experience younger than the legal age for consent. The aim of SRE programmes is to cover relevant information and understanding well before this time, and some start in primary schools. The content of SRE programmes varies and those in faith schools are very likely to take a moral stance against sex outside marriage. However, the main aim of any SRE programme, in mainstream school or delivered through other settings, is to place possible sexual activity within the context of considerate relationships and applicable to both sexes. Practical information is provided about contraception, pregnancy, the risks of sexually transmitted diseases (STDs) and the rights of adolescents to access health services on all these issues.

Studies and consultations regularly show that children and young people welcome SRE in school or other non-family settings, but they still want to have conversations with their parents or carers in a parental role.

▨ Children and young people are keen to have decent information but also a chance to talk in an open way, with confidences respected. Both sexes often welcome mixed groups for part of SRE and say they like to hear the other 'side'. But they also usually want an option to have single sex group discussions as well.

- Young people are aware that many adults have sex, including their parents, but they usually require that the adult professional who runs the SRE remains relatively impersonal and avoids an embarrassing (to the adolescents) enthusiasm about the joys of sexual activity.
- Boys and young men often feel that SRE focuses a lot more on females and on the biological factors. Young males want to talk about issues from the male perspective and that includes relationships as well as sex.
- Gill Lenderyou and Caroline Ray (1997) point out that, even more than young females, males can be reluctant to admit ignorance.
- Studies that reflect the views of young adults who are gay, lesbian or bisexual describe their concerns that the approach to SRE in school often does not reflect their experience. They may be wary, especially without confidence in the support of the teacher, or other group leader, or take an active and personal approach to open discussion.

Responsible SRE programmes address the fact that it is possible to decline as well as agree to sexual activity: the issues are not exclusively about avoiding pregnancy and infection from STDs. This focus for discussion does not have to rest on a total abstinence option. Despite many social changes in UK society, the double standard still operates: young women who are sexually active outside a couple relationship are more likely to be judged harshly than their male peers. Youth workers like Shaun Bailey (2005) highlight the importance of empowering young women to say 'no', and to understand, however socially unjust it may seem, the serious negative consequences for them of easily saying 'yes' to the pressure from young men in their neighbourhood.

Not all children and adolescents attend mainstream schools. Families who choose to home educate need to organise this aspect of learning like any other. However, some children and young people are in special schools or have, for some reason, experienced intermittent schooling. It is expected that SRE will also be made available for young people with disabilities, adjusted as necessary to enable understanding. Some programmes have been organised for pupil referral units or taken into residential homes to create suitable opportunities for looked-after adolescents. When childhood has been disrupted, adolescents' schooling has frequently also been sporadic. Hansa Patel-Kanwal and Gill Lenderyou (1998) describe how vulnerable adolescents can appear very streetwise and may already be putting themselves at risk because of sexual activity. However, they often have significant gaps in their practical knowledge and an SRE input needs especially to address the relationships side of the issue.

Partnership with families

Guidance for schools recognises that some families have strong views, often arising from their faith and/or cultural background, about what, how and whether their children and young people are taught about SRE in school. Families have a right to withdraw their sons and daughters from some aspects of SRE, but schools always try to reach a compromise by which children and adolescents can experience the full curriculum. Whatever the religious or other values held by a family, school can be the place where young people are informed about their legal rights, for instance, on contraception or abortion. Young people can choose not to take either of those options on the basis of belief, but they have a right as citizens to know about the law.

Parents of disabled young people are sometimes, not always, wary about SRE for their son or daughter. It can be an additional and tough adjustment to realise that young people with physical or learning disabilities, who will continue to need a great deal of care, are nevertheless growing into full adulthood. Even if they continue to live in some kind of sheltered accommodation, disabled young people may well develop important relationships that involve sexual activity.

Giving advice and information

Health and other professionals are bound by rules of confidentiality in their helping relationship with over-16/17s, who for most legal purposes count as adults. The situation can be less clear, and open to different interpretations, when adolescents are younger than the legal age of consent. Teachers, health professionals, youth workers or residential workers can be in the situation of offering, or being asked for information and advice on sexual matters by young adolescents.

The concept of 'Gillick competence' applies to decisions over sexual matters as much as to other aspects to personal health. In 1985, Victoria Gillick legally challenged the right of her local health authority to provide medical treatment, specifically contraception, to a female under 16 years of age without her parents' knowledge and consent. The House of Lords ruling on Gillick versus West Norfolk and Wisbech Area Health Authority established that the appropriate level of parental control depended on a child's maturity. The legal precedent was established that the rights of parents to make the decision, on this matter or any other health decision, ended when children had sufficient understanding and intelligence to grasp fully the implications of their choices.

The practical implication of the Gillick ruling has been that health professionals are not obligated to inform parents that their daughter or son has asked about contraception or any other sexual health matter. However, there are concerns about the position of the professional when young adolescents seek very specific advice that moves more towards counselling about options and/or towards support to follow through actions. Carolyn Hamilton (2006), the Director of the Children's Legal Centre, describes the reasons for uncertainty. The advice from the CLC is that any practitioners should be very careful about moving into a situation in which they are effectively assuming a level of parental responsibility.

Young parenthood

Since the 1990s the government has been concerned to achieve significant reduction in the level of 'teenage pregnancy', with the usual meaning of under-18s becoming parents. The motivation has been strongly financial: if young parents are not supported by their families, then there can be significant social costs through state benefits. Suzanne Cater and Lester Coleman (2006) report that the cost to the government of under-18s pregnancy is around £63 million pounds per year.

A problem of social exclusion

Young parents, especially adolescent mothers, are very likely to end their education, with social consequences for their employment prospects in the future. The usual stresses of parenthood can be accentuated for young parents, especially those without family support or positive adult role models. In terms of statistics, the children of adolescent parents have less positive outcomes, because the families are more likely to have a very limited income. The children are more likely (statistically again) to struggle at school, perhaps to fail and to be drawn into trouble – minor or major. Much of the explanation of this cause and effect revolves around the social circumstances of many young parents, rather than early parenthood itself.

In 2006 the government issued another set of targets for local authorities in England and Wales, insisting that they reduce high local levels of teenage pregnancy. Previous statistical targets have often not been met and tend to be revised quietly before another official re-launch. Part of the failure to meet targets of reduction seems to be an inability to affect, and possibly to understand, different motivations behind young parenthood. The overall UK rate of adolescent pregnancy is the highest in Western Europe but there is marked variation between different areas of the country. Half of the total number of under-18s conceptions arise in only one-fifth of the census wards.

Knowledge and life choices

Discussion around reducing rates of teenage pregnancy tends to home in on SRE in school and easy access to family planning services. These issues are relevant, but experienced professionals in the area point out that not all adolescent pregnancy is a consequence of ignorance or carelessness. Research papers and reviews on the website of the Teenage Pregnancy Unit, such as the report by Catherine Dennison (2004), show that there are rarely, if ever, simple patterns of cause and effect.

Some basic issues are:

- Adolescents need to know the practical details of how pregnancy can follow from sexual activity and effective ways to prevent that result. Even adolescents who sound very knowledgeable, sometimes still believe inaccurate information that has misled previous generations, including the traditional mistake of 'it won't happen to me'.

- But accurate information and access to contraception is not the beginning and the end of the issue. Young people need to be motivated to use that knowledge, in the heat of the moment, as well as from more deliberate planning. They also need to be alert to the combination effects of alcohol, drugs and the prospect of sex (see page 322).

- However, young people, especially young women, also need a strong rationale not to get pregnant and start parenthood. Some young people see no reason whatsoever to delay this marker into adulthood. They look around their neighbourhood and see no prospects and/or they hope that a baby will fill an emotional void for them.

TAKE ANOTHER PERSPECTIVE

A considerable number of young people do not become parents during their adolescence. It is just as useful to explore what leads young people to postpone parenthood as it is to understand what, in addition to failures in contraception, leads to becoming a young mother or father. Studies tend to focus on adolescent parents, rather than their peers. But the 'reverse' of those findings, linked with anecdotal evidence from conversations, suggests that the 'non-parents' feel they have other options.

- Adolescents talk of choices that they believe are possible for them to action and would be far more difficult to follow if they were responsible for a baby or young child.

- They have at least some notion of what care of a baby or young child entails and that it is simply not possible to avoid disruption of their previous lifestyle. Useful SRE programmes often include realistic experience of the normal demands of an infant, sometimes through the insight from being responsible for a 'virtual baby'. (See www.bbc.co.uk/videonation/articles/b/beds_virtualbaby.shtml.)

- Adolescents may wish to travel, complete their further education and training. Some plan to become established in a career before having children. Some are specific about being involved with a partner who is a serious long-term prospect: someone with whom they actively want children.

What do you think?

'Planned' early parenthood

Suzanne Cater and Lester Coleman (2006) interviewed 50 young people, living in areas of high poverty and disadvantage, who described their pregnancy as in some way 'planned'. All the young people were described as 'white' by ethnic group and most of the sample were young women. This report highlighted that some adolescents view pregnancy as a pathway into mature adulthood and therefore out of childhood. The findings are consistent with other reviews and studies that invite the opinions of adolescents.

Some young people have what they regard as good reasons to enter young parenthood. These reasons influence their decision not to bother with contraception or to refuse an abortion, if the option is offered.

- An unsettled, unhappy or violent home life is the impetus for some young people to create an alternative and, they hope, better family with their own baby. Some young parents aim to lavish love on a baby in ways that they have not experienced and some hope for unconditional love in return.
- A disrupted or unhappy school experience, for instance, from persistent and unresolved bullying, can discourage young people from seeing any point in continuing with their studies. Pregnancy is an effective exit route from school for disaffected young women.
- Using parenthood as the path into adulthood works positively for some young people, who report a sense of personal worth and the value of having someone who needs them to make the effort.

265

■ There is some indication that young mothers, with suitable family or other back up (there is less information about young men), feel that having a baby gave them the motivation to study, perhaps to improve fragile literacy or numeracy skills. They are keen to improve themselves for the prospects of their baby or young children.

■ Without family, or other effective social care, some young parents find it all much more difficult than they thought. This finding should not surprise people since older, and presumably more knowledgeable, parents can be shocked by the neediness of young babies.

■ Some young parents also argue that it makes sense to have your children when you are a young adult and then you are still young enough to have a lively adult life when they have grown up. Many of them saw local role models in older adolescents: being a teenage parent was a 'normal' option.

In summary, studies of young people, especially in areas where they have few positive prospects, show that early pregnancy is sometimes viewed as a fairly rational choice and one that was much more within their control than other options for trying to improve their personal life. The high rate of pregnancy among looked-after young women rests upon many of the issues outlined above. Additionally, an experience of disrupted schooling can also mean that the young women have serious gaps in their knowledge about sex, pregnancy and the reality of parenthood.

Young fathers

Studies of young parents, like that of Charlie Lewis and Jo Warin (2001), reflect how young fathers can find themselves inevitably in a different position from young mothers. The idea of careless young men running away from the responsibility of paternity is true for some, but certainly not for all young fathers. The continued involvement of young men with their baby or child depends on their own motivation but also a great deal on the young woman and her family. Young fathers are sometimes denied involvement that they would like to develop.

In some neighbourhoods with long-term unemployment, social changes around family life have created a pattern in which men, young or older, are regarded as a waste of space beyond their necessary involvement in conception. Parenthood can provide a sense of purpose for young men. Being denied a possible role as a father can operate as a serious, further rejection of male self-worth in a situation where they are unlikely to gain self-esteem through the route of paid employment. Projects have been developed with looked-after young males, or those in young offenders' institutions or in prison. Even in these especially vulnerable groups, there are always individuals who want to be active fathers to their children.

If you want to find out more

❖ **Bailey, Shaun** (2005) *No man's land: how Britain's inner city youth are being failed.* London: Centre for Young Policy Studies. See www.cps.org.uk.

❖ **Burgess, Adrienne** (2005) *Fathers' impact on children.* Fathers Direct. See www.fathersdirect.com/index.php?id=0&cID=479.

❖ **Cater, Suzanne** and **Coleman, Lester** (2006*) 'Planned' teenage pregnancy: views and experiences of young people from poor and disadvantaged backgrounds.* Bristol: Policy Press. Summary at www.jrf.org.uk/knowledge/findings/socialpolicy/0336.asp.

❖ **Dennison, Catherine** (2004) *Teenage pregnancy: an overview of the research evidence.* Wetherby: Health Development Agency. See www.dfes.gov.uk/teenagepregnancy/dsp_content.cfm?pageid=36.

❖ **Family Planning Association** (fpa) 50 Featherstone Street, London EC1Y 8QU. Tel: 020 7608 5240; www.fpa.org.uk - works to improve sexual health for everyone in the UK. A range of resources are available on the website.

❖ **Gender Identity Research and Education Society** Melverly, The Warren, Ashstead, Surrey KT21 2SP. Tel: 01372 801554; www.gires.org.uk. Information about uncertain gender identity.

❖ **Hamilton, Carolyn** (2006, 6th edition) *Working with young people: legal responsibility and liability.* Colchester: Children's Legal Centre.

❖ **Lenderyou, Gill** and **Ray Caroline** (eds) (1997) *Let's hear it for the boys! Supporting sex and relationships education for boys and young men.* London: National Children's Bureau.

❖ **Lewis, Charlie** and **Warin, Jo** (2001) *What good are Dads?* Fathers Direct. See www.fathersdirect.com/index.php?id=3&cID=111.

❖ **Martinez, Anna** (2006) *Sex and relationships education: the role of schools.* Highlight no. 229, London: National Children's Bureau.

❖ **Muttock, Stella** and **Butcher, Jo** (2005) *A report for the Children's Commissioners Office on NCB's consultation with primary school children on measuring children's height and weight in school.* See https://www.childrenscommissioner.org/documents/finalreport1hwcom missionersoffice.pdf.

❖ **Patel-Kanwal, Hansa** and **Lenderyou, Gill Frances** (1998) *Let's talk about sex and relationships: a policy and practice framework for working* *with children and young people in public care.* London: National Children's Bureau.

❖ **Royal College of Nursing** (2006) *The role of the school nurse in providing emergency contraception services in educational settings.* (An RCN Position Statement that also has useful background information for non-health professionals.) See www.rcn.org.uk/publications/#r.

❖ **Ruck, Tat** (2006) *Case studies: working with teenage parents and parents-to-be.* Basic Skills Agency, part of the *Raising Expectations* series, some of which can be downloaded from www.basic-skills.co.uk.

❖ **Scottish Executive** (2001) *Sex education in Scottish schools: a guide for parents and carers.* See www.scotland.gov.uk/library3/education/a5parents.pdf. Other papers on this topic can be found on this site or through Learning and Teaching Scotland www.ltscotland.org.uk.

❖ **Sex Education Forum** (2005) *Sexual orientation, sexual identities and homophobia in school.* Forum Factsheet 33; www.ncb.org.uk/sef. The website has a range of Factsheets and Spotlight briefing papers that can be downloaded.

❖ **Smith, Peter K.** and **Cowie, Helen** (2003) *Understanding children's development.* Oxford: Blackwell.

❖ **Stewart, George** (2006) *Understanding gender dysphoria.* Mind. See www.mind.org.uk/Information/Booklets.

❖ **Teenage Pregnancy Unit** offers research papers and reviews to download from www.dfes.gov.uk/teenagepregnancy/dsp_content.cfm?pageid=36.

10 Taking care: from self-reliance towards independence

Older children and young people can become confident to take care of themselves, so long as they are given time and support to learn practical life skills. By late childhood, boys and girls can be well able to manage many aspects of their personal care and daily life. As the years of adolescence pass, young people can and should become ever more competent. However, skills and practical knowledge do not simply appear with the passage of months and years. So much rests on experience: what children and young people are guided, helped and trusted to do.

The main sections of this chapter are:

⁂ **Taking care of self and others.**

⁂ **Decisions, opinions and responsibilities.**

⁂ **Keeping safe.**

TAKING CARE OF SELF AND OTHERS

Children learn to operate in a more independent way in different parts of their life through having someone upon whom they can depend for help while they are still learning. Families in different cultures value the move away from dependence by children on adults. However, all cultural traditions do not regard growing out of childhood as a severing of ties. For some, maturity is marked by taking on more adult responsibilities within the family and becoming part of a mature family network of interdependence.

Ready for an independent life?

A great deal of discussion about the process of growing up is grounded in the perspective of 'old' adults. In preparation for this chapter, I asked

---

WHAT DOES IT MEAN?

- **Self reliance**: the development of children's and young people's ability to depend on their own practical skills and knowledge.
- **Independence**: the point at which young people can run their daily life without intervention from adults. Being independent co-exists with willingness to seek advice from other people.
- **Interdependence**: a view of maturity that values a network of support that goes in both directions between generations.

young adults in their early 20s what skills they judged should be in place before young people leave home to go to university. The insights from this informal exploration confirmed much of what is highlighted in more formal studies, initiatives for young people about to leave care and advice books for parents (see the resources on page 299).

The consistent message from experts still within their early adulthood was that young people, without practical life skills, have more difficulty with the adjustment to university life. These skills should be built over time with older children and young adolescents; there should not be a desperate panic in the final run up to going to university. A useful image given to me was that ill-equipped young people approach the university experience more like a short holiday in which nothing needs to be organised. Since university stretches over 3–4 years, there is time for disorganisation to lead to serious crisis.

The strong view was that adolescents needed to know how to look after themselves: to shop and cook, how to work basic domestic appliances, keep things reasonably clean and yourself reasonably healthy. Young people who have left home need to be able to organise themselves, for study but also to manage money through working within a budget. They also made the point that a large number of students become ill, with ordinary problems like flu, within the first term. The view was that some illness was down to young people pushing out the boundaries, now there was no parent telling them not to do something.

Everyone who contributed ideas also stressed that an active social life was an enjoyable part of university life; these young people had not spent all their time in the library. They also described that, however well prepared you feel, leaving home for university or independent ventures like gap year travelling, will most likely feel daunting at some point. Young people need to realise that other people will feel much the same and be ready to access help from friends or support services at university.

Learning practical domestic skills

Older children, who have been helped by patient adults, can be competent to take care of their daily personal needs but can also be active in meeting those needs, such as preparing snacks and helping with meals. By early adolescence, girls and boys are perfectly capable of having learned to prepare and cook a wide range of light meals. Some older children are already very competent and justifiably proud of what they can manage. The problem is that many have not been taught the skills and how to be safe in a kitchen.

Children and young people resist giving up a more dependent state, if greater self-reliance is presented in terms of 'ought's and 'should's or bald commands to 'Grow up!' The key points of a positive approach are that you move steadily from taking full responsibility for children's everyday lives, to sharing specific tasks and then to handing over specific responsibilities to children and young people. The whole process should take time and begins with young children.

■ You need to be prepared to go more slowly with everyday tasks. What is obvious to you about how and why is not necessarily at all obvious to children or young people and certainly not the first time round. You should be patient with confusions and mistakes, including quite messy ones with skills like cooking or household DIY.

■ Helpful adults are ready to make a task simpler at the outset. You often need to recapture what it was like not to know how to do this skill. Reflect a bit on 'what do I know that this child may not?' and, 'are there important techniques that I need to give these young people before I let them try?'

■ Children and young people are far more likely to accept domestic responsibilities at home, or in a residential care home, if their efforts are met with warm encouragement and thanks – as far removed as possible from, 'you should be doing it anyway!'

Willing involvement in tidy-up time

■ Young people cannot become competent without practice, so adults need to find ways to encourage them to get that practice, and to be pleased with the young people as their skill improves, whether the focus is tidying their bedroom or behaving safely as a pedestrian.

Support for children and young people needs to be a joint effort between their own family and initiatives over the years of formal schooling. There is very good reason to reverse the trend that has led few schools to offer proper lessons in cookery. Some practical life skills programmes, like Life Routes (www.makeaconnection.org.uk), have been especially aimed at young people who are already disaffected. Preferably children's involvement starts at a younger age.

Children can be very competent in being an active helper in terms of the daily routines of home, school and after-school club. They undertake a range of simple domestic jobs, either by request or because these are the agreed chores for a child in the family or club. Children may be responsible for laying the table for a meal, doing some work in a garden or vegetable patch or contributing to the care of a pet, at home or in

---

LOOK, LISTEN, NOTE, LEARN

One of the groups of primary school-aged children, who shared their views within their Kids City summer play-scheme, was especially keen to tell me what they could do. The discussion started with the children's enthusiasm for cooking activities at play-scheme. But the contributions, of boys and girls, then flowed onto wanting to tell me how they helped within their family home.

Of course, I have no knowledge of how much the children actually did at home, but there is good reason to suppose that they helped at least sometimes with the domestic tasks they were able to describe: cleaning, doing some work in the garden, cooking and some shopping, tidying up, using the vacuum cleaner – a range of basic jobs about the home, including help when their mum was tired or unwell.

The other striking point about this open discussion was that the children talked in such a positive way. The tone was all about pride in what they did and certainly not complaints about being given unwelcome chores.

■ Children do not always moan about helping in domestic tasks. In what ways have you heard or seen children and adolescents who are happy, even keen, to help out in the regular routines of the day?

**MAKE THE CONNECTION WITH . . .
MAKING IT EASY TO BE HELPFUL**

Adults help by allowing enough time within the schedule for the day and setting up being helpful for children, and later young people, as part of being a working and active member of the school or club community. Sensible adults are ready to problem-solve, often with the children, to find a better way of organising a regular routine.

During my visit to Crabtree Infants School it was the children themselves who explained to me 'the new way' they had of tidying up at the end of the lunch break. It was understood that the class of children who went into lunch first were the tidy-up team for that day. The classes rotated on who went first into lunch, so the tidying up task naturally passed between the classes and then back again.

One member of staff explained further, in conversation, that the new system had arisen because tidying up had become disorganised and there had been a high risk of nagging reluctant children or that one or two adults did most of the task. The new system seemed fair to the children and they had days when they did not have to tidy up at all. The system of a warning bell, at which children froze like 'statues' before soon shifting into tidy-up, worked fine and did not need to be changed.

school. Children can be trustworthy over tidying up and dealing with simple spillages. Of course, 'being able to' does not always translate into 'wanting to'. Children and young people may be reluctant to use their tidying skills, especially in the territory of their own bedroom.

Taking care of others

By middle childhood, boys and girls can be trustworthy in taking limited responsibility, in the short term, for younger or less-able children. Practitioners often under-estimate the extent of responsibility taken by older siblings within the family. In larger families, daily life is often not possible unless the older siblings watch out for younger ones and sometimes take temporary responsibility for them, for instance, in walking to and from school with a younger brother or sister. The same pattern applies in some families where there are only a couple of children but the parents have a very busy life and delegate a lot of responsibility to the eldest child. Practitioners need to acknowledge that older children, not just adolescents, can be trusted to take care of siblings and are often proud to do so. However, you may judge it is time to talk with parents if the responsibility brings serious complications in daily life for the older child, or if you are concerned about the safety of either sibling.

273

TAKE ANOTHER PERSPECTIVE

The legal situation is blurry over children who take serious responsibility for other children or for adults.

- The law across the UK does not specify an age at which children can be left alone in a family home. However, parents can be held responsible for actual or potential harm to children under the circumstances in which they were left without an adult.

- It is not possible legally to hand over responsibility for children to anyone younger than 16 years of age. It is a family choice to pay a young evening sitter and some 14 or 15 year olds are trustworthy. But parents remain responsible for the well-being of children in their absence. Under-16s can also be held responsible for harm they have knowingly caused to a child.

- The law does not give a minimum age to be responsible for the care of adults, although child protection/safeguarding legislation recognises young carers as 'in need' of family support services.

In a friendly and safe environment, with adults ready to take the final responsibility, children are ready and able to take some care of their peers (see also peer support on page 162). The practical issue is often to ensure that keen helpers do not insist on aiding a younger child, one new to the setting or a child with disabilities, when those children want to do it for themselves. A practical tip for adults to model for children is to ask, 'Can I help?' or 'Would you like me to ...' rather than taking over without asking.

Young carers
A considerable number of older children and adolescents are responsible for taking care of their parent(s). Known as 'young carers', these children and young people are responsible on a daily basis for ensuring the well-being of a parent whose physical or mental ill health leaves them unable to take care of themselves. The situation of young carers started to emerge from the late 1980s. Of course, many children and adolescents had been coping as the main carer in their family prior to this date. Their situation had remained hidden, partly because professionals seemed to find it hard to believe that non-adults could possibly be carrying this weight of responsibility. Additionally, young carers and their parents are often very anxious that the social care response will be to 'solve' the problem by breaking up their family.

Most young carers are adolescents, but some older children are carrying similar levels of family responsibility. The 2001 census estimated that there were about 175,000 young carers in the UK, but the general view of professionals involved in the area is that the figure is an under-estimate. This section draws on resources listed on page 298, but I also appreciate the input of the Princess Royal Hammersmith and Fulham Young Carers Group and their support workers, who brought alive the issues of being a young carer.

As well as carrying the responsibility of caring, these young carers were also adolescents. They had informed views about being in their teenage years and the experience of transition into secondary school, which I added to my other sources. They were involved in negotiations with their parent(s) about going out in the evening and when they should be home. They, too, sometimes did not tell their parents everything, on the grounds that grown-ups only worry if you are too honest with them. However, the big difference for these young carers, in contrast with their peers, was that their leisure time was never completely free time. They knew that their parents worried about them being out in the evening in London, but these young people were always slightly anxious about their parent and whether she or he was alright at home over the hours that they were out with their friends.

Young carers have multiple roles. They can carry serious responsibility for their parents – over personal care, medication and communicating with a range of involved professionals. Being a young carer creates additional layers to dealing with adolescence.

- Young carers are also attending school and teachers do not always know, or want to appreciate, the level of domestic responsibility carried by these older children and adolescents. Even when teachers are made aware, not everyone is prepared to make allowances for an adolescent who has a huge struggle to arrive on time each day and to complete their homework.
- Young carers often feel protective of their parent(s) and need to stand up for their family if people are off-hand or unpleasant. On the other hand, even their friends at school may not know about their family situation. Young carers may choose not to tell friends and are uncertain of the reaction. Something needs to be said if young carers want friends to visit them at home and exchange the kind of visits that children and young people like to arrange between their homes.
- One advantage of joining a young carers group seemed to be that it could make the telling easier. Adolescents meet fellow young carers who face a similar decision. It is possible to talk face-to-face, as well

as online with supportive websites (see for instance the award-winning www.bubblycrew.org.uk). Sometimes the practical way through was via young carers mentioning the group to friends, which led to questions that the young carers were ready to answer.

▨ However, a young carers group and the backup of website communication is not exclusively about being a young carer. These adolescents want to talk with each other and friendly support workers about anything that interests or concerns them. So a proportion of group conversations and snack table chat revolves around ordinary adolescent interests and worries.

Nevertheless, young carers can end up having separate sections to their daily life, maybe choosing to divide up family from school and social life. Young carers' lives are significantly different from their peers' and the details of daily life are structured around their caring responsibilities:

▨ A real plus of a special group for young carers is the social contact and an extended circle of friends, who understand their family role. Local young carers groups offer different facilities, sometimes including a study group. This opportunity is appreciated since some young carers find it difficult, even impossible, to complete homework at home.

▨ Being at the young carers group, or school, can be welcome as a break from family tasks. But the sense of responsibility never goes away and it is hard for young carers not to worry about whether everything is alright back at home.

▨ This responsibility is seen as life-long; it is a forever responsibility until young carers' parent(s) die and this perspective is how many carers realistically see their life. Their peers may look towards growing up as a chance to break loose from family, but many young carers do not see that aspect, and they have already taken on serious responsibilities that their peers will not experience until full adulthood.

▨ Some adolescents sometimes worry about their parents, but for young carers, worry is a continuous part of their life, with the sense of being responsible for making things as alright as possible for their parent and often also for younger siblings.

Looked-after young people

Looked-after children frequently experience a considerable number of changes in their living conditions. The shift towards adult independent life can be tough for young people in residential homes, because they often have to transfer around mid-adolescence to a different setting, established for this slightly older age range. Some then have to move again into independent living units or supported lodgings. Looked-after young people who live with foster carers may be able to stay with the same family throughout these years. Some foster carers continue to offer a parental role to young adults well beyond the age at which there is any official fostering arrangement.

Foster and residential carers have to provide supportive parenting that helps children and young people build up practical life skills over the years. I have known practitioners who have made great efforts, but they are limited by their obligations to the next wave of residents and sometimes by the view that professional carers have to feel detached in ways that would not be acceptable for a birth parent. The majority of young people leave care at 16 or 17 years of age to move into independent living. Studies like that of Ravinder Barn et al. (2005) describe the variable levels of support in what sometimes becomes a fast-track exit.

Some projects offer a mentoring service to young people at various stages of leaving care, as described by Jasmine Clayden and Mike Stein (2005). Mentors are sometimes adults but can be peers who have already left care. Overall, this consistent support does seem to ease the process of what can be a difficult and intimidating process. Without continued support, care leavers can be isolated, lonely and at high risk of various exit routes of their own, including homelessness, pregnancy and crime.

DECISIONS, OPINIONS AND RESPONSIBILITIES

Children's growing ability to make their own choices is helped by adults who see decision-making in a rounded way, as a skill that is learned. Children and young people need:

- *helpful adults* – in the family, school or out-of-school provision – who are ready to guide children and young people, so that they understand the possible consequences of different options, whether over how to spend their weekly allowance or choice between school subjects;
- *times when they are allowed to experience the consequences of their own choices*, in ways that are neither disastrous nor unsafe. Kindly adults support children and young people to live with results of unwise decisions without announcing, 'I told you so!';
- *good quality information* for some decisions and time to consider their realistic choices, along with plenty of experience when they are consulted over general decisions for school, the local community and their own family.

Ability to manage money

Children and young people need the life skill of being able to manage money. Younger children need to learn literally how money works and the details of coinage and paper money. Those basic mathematical skills can be in place by middle childhood. However, children need practical experiences to understand that money is not magic – especially when linked with the 'credit' figure on a plastic card. Within family life, parents are wise to start children with weekly pocket money and not to keep funding additions. Young adolescents learn to operate a clothes allowance and young people at sixth form college can work with a weekly allowance to cover their usual costs. Children and young people in school, club or a residential home can be involved in decisions about what to buy within a given budget, whether it is for food or equipment.

Young people have stressed to me (see also page 270) that adolescents really need to know how to handle money before they get hold of their student loan at university. Serious difficulties arise when young people have no grasp of budgeting. Money that should last an entire term would be spent in a few weeks, often on socialising, and then young people would head into overdraft and other forms of debt. The Connexions service has useful material to download about managing finances (www.connexions-direct.com).

LOOK, LISTEN, NOTE, LEARN

Once young people pass the age of 18, they are bombarded with offers of credit cards and other means to buy now and pay later. However, in 2006 the magic of plastic was pressed down to a younger age range when the magazine *Bliss* launched pre-payment Splash cards, with the company Bluecorner. The concept was that parents put money onto the card, which their son or daughter then spent. The card was launched with advertisements that said, 'Shop 'til you drop with your very own exclusive Bliss Platinum Card'.

■ Look out for similar cards that have been launched, usually with a minimum age of 13 years. How do the cards work and how are they pitched to young adolescents?

Part-time jobs

Adolescents are often keen to earn their own money, although some young people share their earnings when the family income needs a boost. In terms of formal paid work, young adolescents can work part-time from the age of 13 in jobs classified as 'light work' (definitions vary between local authorities) and on an occasional basis. There are legal limitations on hours worked within term and school holiday periods and the national minimum wage does not currently (2006) apply to anyone under 16. The Children's Legal Centre has a Q&A page for readers who need further details. See www.childrenslegalcentre.com.

In some areas there are few opportunities for young adolescents to earn money. Kids City undertook a consultation with adolescents, who were clear that they wanted to earn money to pay for leisure activities that they chose. A project was run with 12–14 year olds who explored a range of schemes for earning money: baby-sitting, making snacks for playworkers, washing cars and retouching murals in school playgrounds.

The Kids City team offered some direct help, but the adolescents were active in setting up ground rules for how everyone had to behave and finding a realistic work–play balance in each week. Playworkers let the adolescents experience the consequences of low standards in their service. For instance, they soon discovered that poorly made sandwiches were rejected and that it was worth talking with their potential customers to create a product that was welcome. Money earned went into a group pot and the adolescents decided how this would be spent on enjoyable activities over the same summer: an experience that led to a greater understanding of budgeting. With thanks to Jackie Nunns, who explained the details of this project. Kids City also runs Teenscene, a sheltered workplace scheme for 14–19 year olds that supports young people in gaining general skills important for paid work and employs them as assistant playworkers on holiday playschemes. See www.kidscity.org.uk.

Leaving school

More young people than in previous generations now continue to further education at university. However, many adolescents still leave school for paid employment – either as the pattern of their future adult life, or as an interim option before exploring further education and training. Depending on their previous experience, the requirements of being an employee can be a shock to young people. They have left behind teachers who told them what to do and now have a boss or someone more senior in the hierarchy.

Starting a job

Secondary schools offer work experience to young people towards the end of their compulsory school years. In England, the Connexions service has organised this opportunity and their website (www.connexions-direct.com) offers practical hints about the move into more sustained employment. Anyone supporting young people needs to help them unravel some of the

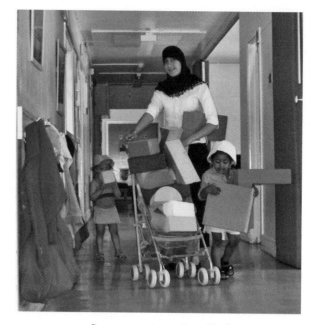

Some young people will choose to work with children

mystery around the basic dos and don'ts of job applications, creating a professional-looking CV, conducting yourself at an interview and the boundaries of behaviour expected from any employee, even a young one. Liz Maudslay (2002) points out that disabled young people and their families are not always aware that legislation against disability discrimination also applies to higher education, providing work placements and all the usual needs of being a student.

Of course, all young people do not follow the same track as they emerge from their years of statutory education. School exclusion creates a serious interruption and is usually the end result of a series of problems for a student, their family and the school. However, the unpleasant experience can be what Cecile Wright et al. (2005) call a 'critical moment' that led some adolescents to be determined to get themselves back on track and accept help for study.

The pattern for young people is variable and researchers such as Gill Jones (2002) challenge the assumption that young people all experience an extended youth with dependence on their families. She reviewed studies in the Joseph Rowntree Foundation's Young People in Transition programme and concluded that there is a growing polarisation between the experience of young people who are able to stay in further education and those who leave school at 16 or 17. In the summer time, newspapers regularly have features about young people who take a gap year and the advantages, or not, of travel and voluntary work. Taking this kind of break is not an option for many young people.

MAKE THE CONNECTION WITH . . . POSSIBLE CHANGES

The 'fast-track' transition into adulthood is followed by many adolescents who leave school, with limited qualifications, into a job market that has lost many of the unskilled occupations or craft apprenticeships that previously took these school leavers. Concern about high rates of youth unemployment appears to be the main motivation behind the government's plan, announced in early 2007, to raise the end point of statutory education to 18 years by 2013. The options for young people will be to continue at school or college in an academic or vocational course or to enter employment with a guaranteed minimum level of training, such as an apprenticeship. The only exceptions proposed are for young carers and adolescent mothers.

Follow up what has happened since the announcement, starting from relevant websites given in the resources section from page 331.

- In what ways have realistic training opportunities been expanded for young people who will otherwise be unqualified and unskilled?

- Has anyone done the 'joined-up thinking' that disaffected young women may be more tempted to use pregnancy as an exit strategy (see page 263)?

- Is it another financial decision that leaves young carers without the presumed advantages of further education – would it just cost too much to cover their responsibilities (see page 274)?

- Has the government continued with the punitive idea of withdrawing the driving licences of 17 year olds who have legitimately passed their test yet decline to continue in their education?

Participation and consultation

Public policy now strongly encourages the participation of children and young people in decisions that directly affect them, including local plans for children's services and community developments. However, there is limited information about the extent to which children and young people are directly involved in decision-making in the personal arena of their family life. Anecdotal evidence, including my own conversations with many children and young people over the years, suggests that some parents are active in bringing their children into family decision-making (see also page 156).

There has been a significant increase in viewing children and young people as individuals who have expertise on their life and informed views that should be heard. It is important that an enabling role by adults does not bring an undertone of patronage and permission-giving. The significant development of consultation with children and young people sometimes comes with the phrase 'giving children a voice'. Yet, as Priscilla Aldersen (2000) has pointed out, children and young people already have a voice – the issue is whether their views are heard and offered respect.

The concept of participation is to ensure that children and young people are properly involved in decisions and changes. Informal discussion or more organised consultation would often be part of the process. Sensible practice holds the balance of rights and responsibilities for the younger generation; the process does mean conspiring in a culture of demand. A regular option for participation in school life is now through a school council. Children and young people on councils show an informed understanding that there are limits to what is possible – financial and otherwise. You can find out more from the website of School Councils UK; www.schoolcouncils.org/.

WHAT DOES IT MEAN?

- **Participation**: an active role for children and young people in decision-making that affects their life.
- **Consultation**: a process of inviting the views of children and young people.

As Mark Gladwin (2004) explains, there is no single, 'correct' model of consultation. He describes various ways of inviting the views of children and young people. The main point is that adults – parents or practitioners of any profession – should be honest with children and young people; any consultation has to be authentic. Such exercises tend to backfire when they are 'mere window dressing', undertaken to look good or satisfy a funding body.

Roger Hart (1992) developed the concept of a Ladder of Participation to explain and describe qualitatively different ways that children and young people could be offered participation in decision-making. The 'lower' rungs of Hart's ladder show ways that children and young people can be manipulated, for example, when they are not fully informed by adults or when adults take ideas without acknowledgement. Dishonesty also colours

MAKE THE CONNECTION WITH ...
GENUINE CONSULTATION

In 2001 the Labour government undertook a survey through the DfES, published as *Building a strategy for children and young people* (2002). The survey questions asked about seven different aspects to daily life, including health, education and other relevant areas. The children and young people repeatedly put 'play, leisure and recreation' as a top priority. Yet this aspect was lost when seven were reduced to five outcomes in *Every Child Matters*.

The word 'enjoyment' was merged with 'achievement' to make a single outcome of 'Enjoy and achieve'. Of the five bullet points under this heading, four related to school achievement. Children's strongly expressed views about the importance of play were shunted into 'achieve personal and social development and enjoy recreation.' In 2006 Hull local authority decided to reinstate six outcomes in their children's services plan, so as to respect the difference between 'Enjoy' and 'Achieve'.

the experience when children or young people are effectively used as props at an event or reported consultation to give the false impression of participation. Older children and adolescents are sharp observers and become disaffected, as well as disheartened, if their skills and time are misused.

The 'higher' rungs of Hart's ladder are not necessarily 'better' and it would be an irresponsible adult who left younger or less-experienced children to organise some projects entirely by themselves. However, the concepts presented by the ladder are an effective support for adult reflection. Mark Gladwin describes the important shift away from 'bogus participation':

- *Informed choice* – where adults determine what is on offer but children are fully informed and have a genuine choice whether to take part.
- *Consultation* – the boundaries are still set by adults, but children and young people can express preferences and real effort is made to provide what they would like.
- *Participation* – children are able to initiate and carry out projects of their own, with help from adults if wanted. There is a real power sharing between children and adults.

Children and young people are content to become involved in different kinds of decision-making, so long as the boundaries are clear and adults are straight with them. There is now plenty of material about ways to involve children (see the resources on page 298). Julia Flutter and Jean Ruddock (2004), for example, make the case for consultation in primary and secondary school and offer practical guidance on techniques like interviewing. Sharon Rafferty (1997) describes how 4–12 year olds in a Strathclyde primary school were keen to improve their playground (see also page 221). This report showed, like the work of Learning Through Landscapes (www.ltl.org.uk), that in involving children, they have well-informed opinions about their school grounds.

However, consultation does not necessarily flow without incident. Sharon Rafferty describes that the reclamation of an unused area of the school grounds was particularly successful. The children were fired by a sense of ownership, as the 'waste ground' became known as 'our wild area'. They developed a Green Forum that moved into a very public arena when they, with growing community support, fought the local council who wanted to sell the land for housing. However, as Rafferty describes, the children's vocal community action then 'became an embarrassment to the school once it was in conflict with the voice of the local authority' (1997, page 9) and a stark gap was shown between avowed policy and actual council practice.

Dealing with professionals

Young people have already experienced relationships with non-family adults through school. Children and young people educated at home do not necessarily have all their schooling in the family and those who are completely home-educated are still most likely to have encountered non-family adults at facilities like the library and leisure services. Parents, or other adults, are part of the exchange when children meet health professionals such as a doctor or dentist. However, older children and young people need and are able steadily to take over this communication as the person whose eyes, teeth or anything else are the current focus of attention.

Relationships with teachers

Children and young people are sharp observers of adult behaviour – within their experience of schooling as well as their own family. Informal conversation, as well as more organised consultation in primary and secondary school, highlights that children and young people watch, listen and judge adults.

Friendly relations between staff and pupils were appreciated but older children and adolescents realised that teachers had to take a responsible adult role. A key issue was how teachers dealt with a legitimate challenge, such as pupils who had specialist knowledge, in some cases greater than that of the teacher. I have listened to views that a good teacher is not threatened by knowledge and should be able even to cope with being corrected on fact. A history teacher was positively recalled for showing respect to one adolescent who was more widely read on a particular topic. In contrast, a science teacher was recalled for a dismissive response to an adolescent who knew considerably more about arachnids and snakes than the adult.

Adolescents in secondary school want to feel that they are not treated simply as large children. A significant issue for young people who continued in the sixth form of their secondary school was that the staff made a serious effort to create a different kind of relationship. A great deal came down to teacher attitudes, as shown in their behaviour. One young man recalled being shouted at in public by the teacher in charge of sixth form to tuck his shirt into his trousers. Since this example was typical of the teacher's approach, relations went from bad to worse within that sixth form.

TAKE ANOTHER PERSPECTIVE

Young adults in their 20s offer a fresh view on their years in school. They are old enough to have time for reflection and not yet into the period when some adults shape their memory to complain about 'young people today'. Young adults with whom I have spoken recalled teachers as individuals, not an undifferentiated mass, and commented on the details of how they behaved. They also showed understanding that teaching was a tough job.

- What can you recall of your own years in secondary school or sixth form college? What would you add to the points expressed in this section?

Active involvement in their own health
Children and young people need steadily to take over responsibility for their own health and this shift includes the relationship with different health professionals and services. Children are already aware of some health issues and do not want adults simply to tell them or impose health checks without consideration of children's views (see page 245 about weighing all children).

Many adolescents are motivated to find out about health issues that they feel are important to them. They can be responsive to information campaigns to let them know about health risks they will need to be able to recognise and manage, such as the signs of meningitis or glandular fever. Young people may ask trusted adults but they also use the internet. The website www.teenagehealthfreak.org, run by Ann Macpherson, receives around 200,000 emails a year, about a quarter asking for information about sexual health. The website www.youthhealthtalk.org provides a forum for young people to discuss their experiences of health problems including cancer, diabetes and sexually transmitted diseases.

Older children and adolescents are clear about what helps and what does not. Nicola Madge (2006) drew from consultations with 12–19 year olds, an online survey and literature review. The main points were that this age group wanted clear information and many young people did not know what kind of services might be available. They were particularly uncertain about sexual health services and provision for mental heath. The survey confirmed points that have also arisen in other consultations and points. General issues and concerns have included the following:

- Young people want information well judged for their age and to have it provided discreetly. They are sometimes especially concerned about confidentiality around sexual health. But their uncertainty about whether their parents will be told about medical consultations is a more general question.

- Adolescents appreciate having some idea of what is likely to happen and how, if they approach health care services. Part of adult support for growing up has to be guiding children and young people, who initially have very little idea of how services work. Practical issues start with how you get an appointment with your doctor, do you have to tell the receptionist why you want one, and other issues that are far from obvious at the outset.

- Adolescents in urban areas can have more option to phone for their own appointment and take themselves to the family doctor or a clinic. Young people in smaller, more rural communities express two main concerns. One worry is whether they can trust the GP and/or the receptionist, both of whom know their parents very well. The other practical issue in rural areas or small towns is that there is very limited or no public transport, so adolescents need their parents to drive them to a GP's appointment or clinic. This situation naturally provokes the query of 'Are you ill?'

- Adolescents do not appreciate being told off by health professionals and cease to listen, or attend, under those circumstances. Any kind of health education or service needs to recognise that some level of risky behaviour is within the norm for adolescents. Health education and care will not work to control young people, any more than it does with adults.

A drop-in health service can help sometimes, although really to work, this may need to be located in a secondary school and within school hours. Even if the facility is developed in response to sex education and sexual health issues, it makes sense to have a more general drop-in health facility, so there is no chance of users being labelled by their peers or anyone else. It is not enough that services are, in theory, confidential. Young people need to be told, with honesty, that their confidences are kept to the professional, and if circumstances arise when this would not be so. Health professionals are themselves sometimes confused over this boundary (see page 262).

TAKE ANOTHER PERSPECTIVE

Look over these pages on health services. Can you identify common themes linking the expressed views of children and young people with the likely feelings of adults?

How do you prefer to be treated during contact with health professionals?

Transition into adult health services

Many young people can continue, if they wish, with the family doctor, dentist or optician. However, specialist health services are often sub-divided into child and adult sections, sometimes also with an adolescent sub-section. The pattern varies considerably between medical specialisms, local organisation and financial allocation. This situation is especially significant for children and young people who live with disability and/or chronic illness. Studies describe that the transition is sometimes handled with careful consideration and step-by-step movement across to adult services. Yet some young people experience sudden and uncommunicative re-assignment to unfamiliar specialists, even when they are still in mid-adolescence. Adolescents are often not ready for adult services but they feel patronised by a system that makes no distinction between children and the 12–18 age range.

Young people who have a disability or a chronic health condition, often view themselves, accurately, as experts on their condition and certainly how it affects them. They want specialist services to treat them with respect and they may be daunted at the prospect of losing contact with the paediatrician or health care team who have supported them for many years. Adolescents are also dealing with the reality of taking on full responsibility for their condition, such as asthma, diabetes, epilepsy, a serious heart condition, HIV/AIDS, sickle cell anaemia or cystic fibrosis.

- Older children and young adolescents may still be coming to terms with the details of their health condition: what it is, what it means to them and how they might talk about it with other people. There may be a delay over their actually knowing the nature of their condition. Elizabeth Lewis (2001) points out that some families do not tell children, even young adolescents, that they are HIV positive.

- It is normal for adolescents to take risks, to choose not to take the healthy option that has so far been guided by their family. Adolescents with serious, even life-threatening, conditions share these feelings. They are tempted not to take care, fail to take their medication or want to enjoy a lively social life that could endanger their health.

- In many cases adolescents have been living with their condition for many years. There can be a 'wear out' factor along with a new realisation that the medical regime is forever. Children who accepted guidance from their parents over a healthy and necessary diet may turn seriously un-cooperative as adolescents. Jessica Datta (2003) describes the perspective of adolescents who live with diabetes, but many of the points are applicable to other health conditions.

- Some adolescents are more self-conscious, or fed up, than others and do not want new friends, perhaps at college, to know about their condition. Adolescents can be at serious risk if new friends are ignorant about the signs of an impending sickle cell crisis, what to do if their friend has a seizure or the consequences of serious imbalance for diabetes.

- The hormonal changes of puberty can affect some health conditions such as diabetes. Adolescents need to be more attentive to their condition, not less, and more assiduous about going to medical appointments – all during a period when direct responsibility for their own well-being is shifting from a parent to the young person. Parents themselves may be very anxious about this handover process.

- Young people often want contact with peers who share and therefore understand their condition. Support groups can make a significant difference. Teen Spirit, part of Body and Soul, offers that support to adolescents who are HIV positive or have a family member with the condition (www.bodyandsoulcharity.org/).

Looked-after young people with profound disabilities or chronic health conditions are very unlikely to be able to stay in the same specialist residential home. The most likely event is that they will be moved into adult services. Residential care workers, experienced with children and young people, are often very concerned about a significant change in atmosphere in the adult homes. Practice varies, of course, but they worry about a lack of awareness of disabled young people's need for play and more playful activities.

KEEPING SAFE

In different ways children and young people need to learn about keeping themselves safe as they move around more independently of adults. They need an understanding of personal safety and feel able to assess and manage their own risk for different parts of their life. Helping children and young people to be safe rests upon steady coaching in practical life skills from early childhood (see page 271). Helpful experiences have to include a steady letting go in which children and young people are trusted to apply all the practice that adults offered over previous months, and often years.

TAKE ANOTHER PERSPECTIVE

The current generation of adults have become very uneasy about letting children travel with greater independence. So it is useful to focus on what is possible in terms of the physical, communication and intellectual skills of 8–10 year olds.

Explore in discussion with colleagues or fellow students the kind of trips that you made without an adult at 8, 10, 14 and 16 years of age.

- Where did you go and were you with peers?

- How did you travel – on foot, bicycle, public transport?

- Looking back now, in what ways had your family or other adults prepared you to go out on your own?

Moving about without adults

By middle childhood children can be competent to make local trips without an adult – on foot, bicycle and simple public transport. By 8–10 years old children should have learned sufficient skills of personal safety, should be able to memorise local routes and plan to get themselves to and from local shops, a nearby play park or leisure facility. Older children need the practical skills for simple travel, including what to do if they are faced with practical problems, like getting lost or split up from friends during a trip.

Some families are more comfortable to let over-10s complete these kinds of trip without an adult companion, but it is important that basic skills of personal and road safety and ability to organise simple outings are in place by early adolescence, otherwise young people are very likely to insist on greater independence, yet lack the key skills and may be unwilling now to listen to adult advice. The practical issues of independent travel can be difficult in more rural areas and where there is very limited public transport – one reason why some young people aim to pass their driving test at the first opportunity.

Adult anxieties

The main worries felt by adults living in realistically safe neighbourhoods are the dangers posed by traffic and strangers who are paedophiles.

- Children need skills of personal safety, including the confidence to move away from adults whose behaviour makes them uneasy and to shout at any who persist. Personal safety skills need to rest upon an understanding that adults have the responsibility to behave appropriately and experiences that have enabled children to know how responsible adults should behave (see Lindon, 2003a and 2003b).

- There is no evidence that children nowadays are any more at risk, statistically, from being harmed by strangers than any previous generation. The very few instances of abduction, injury or murder by strangers receive saturation coverage by the media, precisely because they are so unusual. In some instances, it has emerged that the harm was perpetrated by someone known to children and not by a stranger at all.

Safeguarding children and young people is important, but their social interaction and skills of independence are stunted if personal safety is narrowed to 'stranger danger'. In terms of abuse and neglect, children and young people are statistically most at risk from adults they already know, especially within their own family circle. It is also counter-productive, even dangerous, for the younger generation to be trained to regard everyone unknown as a potential paedophile. They will have to access 'strangers' for help and information when they travel. It is equally risky if the many safe adults are anxious about offering help and protection, because the 'strangers', especially males, are fearful of being accused of abusive intentions.

High-risk neighbourhoods

Some families live in neighbourhoods where there are realistic dangers from adults or young people who are seriously the worse for drink or drugs or who are ready to be violent at the slightest apparent provocation. Peter Seaman et al. (2006) interviewed parents, children and young people from disadvantaged neighbourhoods in Glasgow. The patterns they found are similar to information from other high-risk communities.

- Most families were very concerned about the well-being of their children and regretfully did restrict their movements for safety. There were many 'ordinary parents' working hard to protect their children in areas which could easily be dismissed as 'sink estates'.

- Children showed a high level of understanding about why their parents might stop them doing something. However, by adolescence many of the young people believed they could take care of themselves and did not tell their families about activities that they believed would only worry them. Young people had started to assess the risk themselves and make their own decisions about where to go and what to do in their leisure time.

- Older children and young people could explain their range of strategies for avoiding trouble and keeping safe in a neighbourhood that had many sources of risk. A major strategy was that peers stayed together as a form of protection. They were aware that these steps that they took to keep safe had the unfortunate side-effect of making some adults see them as a local risk, because they were moving around as a group of young people.

Adrienne Katz (2001) raises similar issues from a survey of 10–16 year olds who were concerned about their own safety and ability to protect themselves. Adolescents in unsafe neighbourhoods, even those who have no wish to be violent, feel obligated to carry a weapon as the only means of defence that they can see. Some peer groups operate as gangs that actively threaten other adolescents and some young people, especially young males, may join the gang as the only form of safety they can identify.

Independent travel and road safety

Most strangers who injure children are behind the wheel of a vehicle and most of them have made strenuous efforts to avoid the child pedestrian or cyclist. Children and young people definitely need to learn the skills of road safety: behaving safely as a pedestrian, a cyclist and then as a driver in their own right.

- There is a place for road safety codes, but adults need to recall that children younger than 8 or 9 years of age understand principles from plenty of practice and not the other way around.

- Traffic codes often tell children to 'find a safe place to cross', but children younger than 10 years are still uncertain about what makes a crossing point safe or dangerous.

- They often believe that moving quickly across a road is what makes them safe, but children are often poor judges of the speed and distance away of a moving vehicle.

- Studies have found that practice with computer simulation or pretend road layouts can help, supported by a series of conversations. But there is no substitute for continued practice with adults so children build direct experience of what is, and is not, a safe way to cross a road.

Schools and after-school clubs can work with parents to ensure children have plenty of safe practice. The key point with primary school-aged children is to make the rules explicit and, of course, to obey safety rules yourself. I heard from the team of Balham after-school club about the safety rules that apply to everyone during the daily walk from the pick up at two primary schools and back to the club building. All the children learn swiftly about the points at which the roads are crossed and that everyone, adults too, stops talking while they are actually crossing the road. The children understand that they still need to pay attention – listen and look – even when they are crossing on a proper crossing and the lights are in their favour.

MAKE THE CONNECTION WITH . . . WHAT MAKES SENSE TO CHILDREN

Readers could explore, ideally with colleagues or fellow students, some of the supporting materials for helping children and young people become safe on the roads for different forms of travel.

- Look at some of the advice – online, through leaflets and posters – and consider how well it is likely to match the understanding of children and young people at various periods over childhood and adolescence.

- You could start with these two websites: www.thinkroadsafety.gov.uk and www.road-safety.org.uk.

- Reflect on what worked for you in your own younger years.

- Ask older children and young people about what they think helps them to be safe as a pedestrian or cyclist.

Driving a vehicle

In the UK young people cannot legally drive a car on the public roads until they are 17 years of age. They can learn to drive low power motorbikes at 16 years of age. However, it is very clear that some young people are physically capable and have learned to drive a car before this age boundary. Some young adolescents learn to drive on private land or farm tracks. This activity is legal because they are not on public roads and the decision is legitimately taken by their parents.

Some youth projects with adolescents create safe circumstances for them to drive off public roads. The realistic objective is that it is far better to enable the young people to use their skills in ways that do not put the local population at risk, because the adolescents steal other people's cars and drive them dangerously. In such projects there is a good chance that enthusiastic, non-judgemental youth workers instil greater safety into the driving as well as sharing mechanical skills for taking care of vehicles.

The skills for driving a vehicle combine physical ability, coordination and the ability to make judgements. Young drivers crash with greater frequency than older drivers and this risk is not always explained by the effect of alcohol or the power of the car. Research into the pattern of traffic accidents with young drivers has highlighted that they sometimes struggle with the swift judgements that have to be made, even by careful younger drivers.

The human brain continues to mature and change beyond adolescence. The part of our brain that deals with weighing up risks, making judgements from diverse information and controlling impulsive behaviour is not fully mature until about the mid-20s. The dorsal, lateral pre-frontal cortex is the part of the brain that brings knowledge, priorities, awareness of long-term consequences – everything that is needed to reach a rounded decision. This kind of thinking, linked with the ability to resist doing something really risky, is crucial for drivers to control the buzz of wanting to go for that gap or overtake that annoying fellow driver. Undoubtedly, some 'old' adults are unsafe drivers in this way and some young adults do not take risks in their driving.

Safety online

There has been a significant growth in the use of personal computers by children and adolescents. In 2002 the estimates were that one in two children could access the internet at home and four out five had used it at school or elsewhere. However, there remains a lot of variability regarding ease of access. Being online is a fact of life for many children and adolescents and this huge social change has raised concerns about their safety when they use the internet. Sonia Livingstone has led some practical research and many studies can be found on the site www.children-go-online.net.

Many older children and adolescents have become the internet experts in their family and parents can feel left behind in terms of knowledge. Their uncertainty makes them less confident to discuss ground rules for use of computers in general and safe behaviour on the internet in particular. However, children and young people still have many gaps in their knowledge, despite being regularly described by the media as 'the digital generation'. Children and young people are active in determining how they use the internet and use the facility alongside other forms of communication and social interaction. However, their technical knowledge needs to be matched with general knowledge about how other people use the power of the internet. Children and adolescents need suitable wariness, without becoming unnecessarily anxious or cynical. This section summarises advice and practical issues, which readers can extend by using the resources listed on page 298 and practical magazines like *Computing Which?*.

Commercial naivety

Discussion and media concern about risks from the internet have tended to focus on the risks from paedophile activity and online grooming. Children and young people definitely need to be guided to safe behaviour online for this reason. However, they also need a healthy scepticism based on the knowledge that companies regard children as legitimate targets for marketing online (see also page 15).

Children and young people can be confused through information overload on the internet. They are not necessarily aware of the commercial motives behind some internet sites and the consequence of providing their email and mobile phone addresses. Children and adolescents are encouraged to text or email in response to advertisements, surveys and 'special offers'. Those companies have obtained details for texting back and it is possible to make technological communication in ways that appear very personal.

Taking care in a public forum

The technological possibilities of the internet have affected channels of communication (page 174) and making friends (page 52). Wise adult guidance applies for the virtual world as for the face-to-face world of communication. The support needs to come from children and young people's parents, but is a shared responsibility with teachers, club and youth workers.

It is unwise to allow children or young people to spend hours online. They need to spend time in face-to-face friendships and it is unhealthy to spend ages indoors, sitting in front of a screen. Families, and practitioners in residential homes, need to negotiate and hold to boundaries about how long children and adolescents spend on the computer, whether online or not. There is very good reason to insist on having the computer in a public area of a family or residential home and not in the bedroom of a child or young adolescent. Of course, children and adolescents do not always keep to the house rules – about anything, not just computer usage – but house rules cannot be revisited and emphasised if they are not established in the first place.

There are many internet chatrooms and they do not all work in the same way:

- Some are more like online message boards – the online support groups tend to work this way. Replies may be relatively swift but there will be a delay. However, some chatroom exchanges take only as long as typing a message, sending, receiving and typing a reply.

- Some chatrooms let users complete a profile. Children and young people need to be taught never to include personal details that could identify them and where they live. This wariness can be sensibly linked to the premise that they never provide personal details to unknown people through any channel of communication – mobile phone, landline or at the door.

- There is the option sometimes to step 'out' of a chatroom and have a private online conversation. Some advice suggests that children and young people should be discouraged from taking this option. Other experts with whom I have talked take the view that a prohibition is unlikely to be followed and young internet users should be guided on how to take this option in safety.

- It is wise to ensure that children and young adolescents only access chatrooms that have a moderator: a real person who can go online to check the conversations. But, given the huge flow of information, the moderator is more likely to check automated data like whether a user has had personal blocks set up against them or to follow up emailed complaints from users.

- Moderation of a chatroom does not take the place of responsible adults who remain alert to computer use in the non-virtual world. A moderator may intervene online, but children still need personal safety rules that nobody has the right to make you feel uncomfortable, you can refuse to reply and you can leave the chatroom.

- Children and young people should be told not to lie about their own age (they usually claim to be older) to anyone they talk to online. They could lose automatic protection from the moderator on a site.

Online chatting can be a form of let's pretend – enjoyable but with potential risks. Everyone met in a chatroom is a stranger, however familiar they become online over time. People are not always what they seem and there is greater scope for misleading and outright lies, when there is no objective check on what is said or of photos allegedly of this person.

- Many people in the chatrooms are who they say they are, or as close as makes no danger. However, there are genuine risks of grooming by paedophiles, another reason why the computer should be in a communal area of a family home, residential home, school or play setting.

- If online friends make a move to see each other in real time, then children and young people need to have been coached to tell adults. They should not go alone to meet a stranger and should be accompanied to a public place by an adult or a fellow older adolescent.

- Webcams – video cameras linked to the internet – are exciting and can enable full communication between people who know each other. Children and young people need to be reminded that the images are effectively public. Personal safety online has to include extreme wariness about somebody who is unknown other than online and who is pressing for inappropriate behaviour through the webcam.

- However, friends may encourage each other towards behaviour online that is regretted later. Even under-18s must not post provocative images of themselves online – in law nobody, even the young person themselves, should create indecent images and make them public.

Personal blogs and websites work like a diary kept online. They can be read by anyone with internet access, unless the blog is password protected. The blog concept is that people – adults too – are writing for other people to access. Children and young people need to understand not to put personal details and images on the blog. However, they often overlook that their blog, and their contribution to chatrooms, are in the public arena.

- Offensive remarks about other people, whether peers or adults, or allegations of wrong doing could be judged as libel; off-hand remarks take on a life of their own.

- In the USA, some employers and college admissions tutors now enter the name of applicants in one of the major search engines in order to check out online profiles and any other evidence of a 'cyber persona'. Some young adults have come to regret boasting in their blog or online profile about risky behaviour or entering highly offensive remarks about other people.

Quality of materials online

There is a huge amount of information on the World Wide Web. I have been very pleased to use its resources in research for this book. However, some sections of the net are an open sewer. In most surveys, many children and young people claim to have seen online pornography, often by accident. It is also possible to inadvertently access some unpleasant internet sites while undertaking legitimate research for school projects.

The blocking software that can be loaded onto any computer is rather hit or miss: it can prevent access to good materials and fail to block off offensive sites. Software may also be adeptly bypassed by children and young people who are considerably more computer literate than the adults around them. So, even good software of this kind is not a substitute for discussions about safety online. Adults need to share the interests of children and young people and invite them to share what they have accessed.

Children and young people can access a huge amount of information on the World Wide Web. In terms of their general knowledge and project work, they also need to be guided in ways to judge the reliability of information and the importance of checking sources. This guidance is part of helping them with proper study skills: how to judge whether to trust a source, the importance of giving proper references from the internet as much as from books. Children and young people also need clear guidelines about how to integrate their research and that plagiarism can be an issue with the internet, just as much as with books and articles.

MAKE THE CONNECTION WITH . . . ADULT COMPUTER LITERACY

Studies and surveys regularly show that many adults – parents and practitioners – do not know enough to guide children in online safety. One strategy is to ask older children or adolescents with whom you work to design a short familiarisation programme. Explain that you want to understand better what they find easy in using the internet.

Another strategy is to explore resources like the Internet Safety Zone – www.internetsafetyzone.co.uk. Set up by the Cyberspace Research Unit at the University of Central Lancashire, the Internet Safety Content Agent (ISCA) project aims to raise internet safety awareness and education across the UK, primarily to teachers, parents, carers and young people.

If you want to find out more

❖ **Aldersen, Priscilla** (1995) *Listening to children: children, ethics and social research.* London: Barnardo's.

❖ **Alderson, Priscilla** (2000) *Young children's rights.* London: Jessica Kingsley/Save the Children.

❖ **Barn, Ravinder; Andrew, Linda** and **Mantovani, Nadia** (2005) *Life after care: the experiences of young people from different ethnic groups.* York: Joseph Rowntree Foundation.

❖ **Bibby, Andrew** and **Becker, Saul** (2000) *Young carers in their own words.* London: Calouste Gulbenkian Foundation (from Turnaround Publisher Services, 020 8829 3000).

❖ **Clayden, Jasmine** and **Stein, Mike** (2005) *Mentoring young people leaving care: 'Someone for me'.* York: The Joseph Rowntree Foundation.

❖ **Connexions** offers advice about subject choices within secondary education, continued study, getting a job and practical skills like managing money – materials to download and links from www.connexions-direct.com.

❖ **Create Scotland** – a resource about the process of consulting with young people. See www.create-scotland.co.uk/advice/consultingyoung.

❖ **Datta, Jessica** (2003) *Moving up with diabetes: the transfer from paediatric to adult care.* London: National Children's Bureau.

❖ **Ely, Amanda** (2006) *Children and young people living with HIV/AIDS.* Highlight no. 228, London: National Children's Bureau.

❖ **Fajerman, Lina** and **Treseder, Phil** (2003) *Children are service users too: a guide to consulting children and young people.* London: Save the Children. Other projects described on the website www.savethechildren.org.uk.

❖ **Flutter, Julia** and **Ruddock, Jean** (2004) *Consulting pupils: what's in it for schools?* London: RoutledgeFalmer.

❖ **Gladwin, Mark** (2004) *Consulting children about play.* London: Children's Play Information Service. See www.ncb.org.uk/library/cpis.

❖ **Hamilton, Carolyn** (2006, 6th edition) *Working with young people: legal responsibility and liability.* Colchester: Children's Legal Centre.

❖ Hart, Roger (1992) *Children's participation: from tokenism to citizenship*. Florence: UNICEF.

❖ Jones, Gill (2002) *The youth divide: diverging paths to adulthood*. York: York Publishing Services.

❖ Katz, Adrienne (2001) *Fitting in or fighting*. East Molesey: Young Voice. See www.young-voice.org.

❖ Lewis, Elizabeth (2001) *Afraid to say: the needs and views of young people living with HIV/AIDS*. London: National Children's Bureau.

❖ Lindon, Jennie (2003a) *Too safe for their own good? Helping children learn about risk and life skills*. London: National Children's Bureau.

❖ Lindon, Jennie (2003b) *Child protection*. London: Hodder and Stoughton.

❖ Livingstone, Sonia (2002) *Children's use of the internet: a review of the research literature*. See www.ncb.org.uk/publications.free.asp. Other reports available on www.children-go-online.net (the National Children's Bureau website was under development when this book went to press).

❖ Livingstone, Sonia (2006) 'Reflections on the games families play', *The Psychologist* 19(10). Available for download from www.bps.org.uk/publications/thepsychologist/search-the-psychologist-online.cfm.

❖ Madge, Nicola (2006) *Young people talking about their health and health services*. Spotlight Briefing London: National Children's Bureau.

❖ Maudslay, Liz (2002) *Special Education Needs and Disability Act 2001: Post-16 duties*. Highlight no. 192, London: National Children's Bureau. See also the website of National Bureau for Students with Disabilities; www.skill.org.uk.

❖ Paterson, Claire (2006) *Grow up! The 101 essential things every child needs to know before leaving home*. London: Rochdale International Ltd.

❖ Participation Charter available from the Participation Unit of the National Children's Bureau. Tel: 020 7843 1909, more information at Participation Works; www.participationworks.org.uk.

❖ **Rafferty, Sharon** (1997) *Giving children a voice – what next? A study from one primary school.* Spotlight no. 65, Scottish Council for Research in Education. See www.scre.ac.uk/spotlight/spotlight65.html.

❖ **Scottish Schools Ethos Network** – a source of examples of consultation in schools. See www.ethosnet.co.uk/resources_casestudies.htm.

❖ **Seaman, Peter; Turner, Katrina; Hill, Malcolm; Stafford, Anne** and **Walker, Moira** (2006) *Parenting and children's resilience in disadvantaged communities.* London: National Children's Bureau. Summary at www.jrf.org.uk/knowledge/findings/socialpolicy/0096.asp.

❖ **Shah, Robina** and **Hatton, Chris** (1999) *Caring alone: young carers in South Asian communities.* Barkingside: Barnardo's.

❖ **Various authors** (1999) 'Children's road safety'. Special issue of *The Psychologist* 12(80). Available for download from www.bps.org.uk/publications/thepsychologist/search-the-psychologist-online.cfm.

❖ **Wood, Sophie** (2006) *Children, young people and life skills.* Spotlight Briefing, October. London: National Children's Bureau. See www.ncb.org.uk.

❖ **Wood, Sophie** and **Blake, Simon** (2006) *Spotlight: promoting emotional and social development.* Issue 8, October. London: National Children's Bureau. See www.ncb.org.uk.

❖ **Wright, Cecile; Standen, Penny; John, Gus; German, Gerry** and **Patel, Tina** (2005) *School exclusion and transition into adulthood in African-Caribbean communities.* York: Joseph Rowntree Foundation.

❖ **USA Today** *Is 16 too young to drive a car?* 2 March 2005. See www.usatoday.com/news.

❖ **Young carers** – useful information from these websites: Help the Hospices has www.timetocare.org.uk with a young carers section; the Princess Royal Trust has www.youngcarers.net; also the national children's charities of www.nch.org.uk and www.childrenssociety.org.uk/youngcarers.

11 Vulnerability in childhood and adolescence

Children and young people are potentially vulnerable as they negotiate the years towards adulthood. They gain a safe independence by being able to depend upon adults, and in different ways their peers, over the years of childhood and adolescence. Children and young people can be very resilient, so long as circumstances do not overwhelm their ability to cope and their sources of support. When pressures become too difficult for children and young people, daily life can undermine their well-being. There is also concern that they become socially excluded from opportunities within UK society.

The main sections of this chapter are:

⋆ **Mental and emotional health.**

⋆ **The risks from social exclusion.**

⋆ **Serious threats to health and well-being.**

MENTAL AND EMOTIONAL HEALTH

There has been increasing discussion around the mental health and possible level of mental health problems for children and young people. Practitioners need to reflect on these ideas, especially since you are likely to encounter media descriptions of surveys or new reports claiming a serious level of mental health issues for many children and young people.

The concept of mental health

The wording may initially seem puzzling to some readers. The term 'mental health' has strong associations for many people with the flipside of 'mental illness'. This phrase is often defined as patterns of disturbed and disturbing behaviour from adults, whose view and interpretation of the world is significantly different from 'normal' people. However, the phrase 'mental health' has a great deal in common with discussions of emotional well-being (see page 63).

What is a mental health problem?

A wide range of difficulties are usually included within the working definition of mental health problems as applied to children and young people. Some examples include:

▪ Emotional stress and distress that may show itself in significant anxiety, phobias or deep sadness, all of which may show themselves

301

> ## WHAT DOES IT MEAN?
>
> - **Mental health**: a state in which children and young people have the ability to develop fully in all aspects of their development, cope as an individual and in social interaction with others.
> - **Mental health problems**: a disturbance in the ability of a child or young person to function in one or more areas of their development and behaviour.
> - **Mental health disorders**: a mental health problem that is severe or persistent to the point that the difficulty significantly affects the ability of a child or young person to cope with daily life.

through physical symptoms. There is disagreement among psychologists as to whether childhood depression is genuinely on the increase – partly because there is a lack of agreement on a definition of clinical depression for children (discussions in *The Psychologist*, including November 2006, pages 646–7).

- Patterns of behaviour that are persistently disruptive in their effect and beyond the boundary of what should be regarded as 'normal' occasional non-cooperation or disobedience from children and young people. Warning signs include children who are persistently very aggressive or destructive.

- A broad range of developmental delays that affect how a child or young person communicates with others, makes relationships, is able to concentrate or take on their own personal care.

- Problems that affect physical health, and so emotional well-being, such as disorders that affect eating or sleeping.

- Deep distress and related patterns of behaviour that arise from traumatic experiences.

- Psychological disorders that significantly affect daily life, such as schizophrenia or bipolar disorder (manic depression).

Ways of helping

There is no suggestion that every kind and level of mental health problem requires the intervention of specialist practitioners and services. Some troubles will be eased by practitioners who work with children, adolescents and their families on a regular basis in school, in out-of-school provision, in different kinds of community centre, play and leisure facilities. The British Medical Association (2006) estimated that about one in ten children aged from 1–15 years live with a mental health disorder that would benefit from specialist services. A key recommendation of the BMA is that children and young adolescents should have access to flexible services tailored to meet their needs. Some local health trusts have established services for 16–18 year olds, who can be scared by experiences in adult mental health provision.

MAKE THE CONNECTION WITH ... YOUR PROFESSIONAL ROLE

Specialist services should be connected through professional knowledge and local networks to 'ordinary' services. It is important that you know what is available for children and young people whose struggles are beyond your ability or the time available to support them within your service. Appropriate knowledge includes online resources, for example, the kind of support available from websites like Young Minds (see page 329).

What look like minor troubles to inattentive adults can worry children or adolescents and disrupt their ability to get on with daily life. An effective system of full support needs to recognise when problems are about to cross the boundary from ordinary problems into out-of-the-ordinary struggles. Children and young people should not have to cross over that line, however blurry it may appear sometimes, to merit being offered help.

Never assume that somebody else must have shared useful life skills with a child or adolescent. Be ready to draw on practical advice, for example Sarah McNamara's (2005) useful guide about helping young people deal with stress.

A limit to resilience

Children and young people are generally at higher risk of developing mental health problems when their social circumstances increase the stresses of ordinary daily life and reduce the ease of accessing simple help from adults.

- Children and young people are a greater risk when they live with their family on a low income, partly it would seem because being poor brings other social disadvantages with the financial stress.
- The increased risk for looked-after children and young people is partly from the family disruption that led them into care, but being in care long-term is far too often associated with further changes and disruptions for healthy continuity in childhood.
- Children with asylum seeker status are another highly vulnerable group. Some are with their families but some arrive in the UK as

unaccompanied children and young people. This group automatically has looked-after status, but it is not always clear which authority will take responsibility. Severe problems arise from the disruptive and sometimes traumatic conditions that led children into becoming refugees and seeking asylum seeker status. But again, the social conditions that follow are rarely conducive to emotional well-being.

- It has been increasingly recognised that domestic violence is a serious risk factor for children and young people. They live with the emotional stress of being in a home where parents are constantly in dispute. Adult behaviour may also put children at direct risk of physical harm.

- Belonging to a minority ethnic group is often given as a risk factor for increased vulnerability. Any social intervention needs to acknowledge that a considerable number of families manage perfectly well to support their children. However, families from minority ethnic groups have an increased chance, statistically, of being affected by risk factors such as deprivation, discrimination and reduced educational and employment opportunities.

TAKE ANOTHER PERSPECTIVE

Children can be adrift in families who do not appear vulnerable to outsiders, because they are financially secure and live in advantaged neighbourhoods. All children and young people need time and commitment from key adults, specifically their parents. There is justifiable concern about the well-being of children and adolescents in families that are described as 'cash rich – time poor'. The concept of resilience should not be used to mean that children tolerate random change and adults who ignore their feelings and perspective. Nor will children and young people wait forever to be fitted into their parents' busy schedule.

When the concept of 'quality time' was first developed, it was part of advice to parents, often mothers in employment, to make the most of reasonable stretches of time with their children and adolescents. The phrase is now often used to justify extremely busy adult schedules into which children are fitted for very short amounts of time, pre-determined by the adults.

Robert Brooks and Sam Goldstein (2001 and 2003) describe the concept of genuine resilience and the practical applications to families, but the ideas are equally relevant to practitioners. Look also at the discussion about vulnerability and resilience on page 5.

Looked-after children and young people

Children and adolescents who are the responsibility of the local authority – looked-after children – are even more vulnerable to mental health problems than their peers. Difficulties arise from the circumstances that have led them to leave their birth family and enter care. Some children and young people stay in care for only a temporary period and return to their family, who are supported by services. Other children and young people remain looked-after for many years, and reviews, for example by Roger Clough (2006), have established the central importance of the relationships they make with their carers.

A report by the Mental Health Foundation (2002) described the greater risk created by continued instability because children and young people can experience far too many changes of placement in foster or residential care. The practical result is that some are not registered with a doctor in the local health clinic and referral to child and adolescent mental health services is usually through a GP. Services usually have a waiting list and some children and young people are moved to another area before their name comes to the top of the list and the whole process starts again.

Looked-after children and young people are supposed to have a social worker, who ensures that their health needs are met properly. However, in some areas there is a turnover of social workers, who do not in any case see the child or young person as often as their foster or residential carer. The situation can be improved when residential and foster carers are empowered to act as a concerned parent.

Feeling worried

Children and young people may feel very distressed as the result of single problems that permeate many aspects of their daily life. For example, a serious falling out with close friends can mean loneliness in the school playground as well as potential disruption to social life outside school. Children and young people can feel overwhelmed if they face a number of troubles simultaneously, for example, when the argument with close friends coincides with tension at home between their parents and a looming decision about their next school stage.

Specialist organisations like Young Minds judge that severe worry, which could fairly be called depression, is a growing problem for children and young people. The main explanations offered include high pressure on children within their school years, sometimes starting with attempts to fast-track them at an even younger age. There is concern about unrealistic expectations of a younger generation that is frequently criticised for

Even mainly happy children will sometimes feel worried

ordinary adolescent liveliness and yet often expected to manage the transition into adulthood with insufficient practical support.

In the *Leading lads* report, Adrienne Katz (1999) summarised the top ten worries from their survey of male adolescents: schoolwork and exams; money; their looks; relationships outside the family; conflict at home; worries about getting a job; failure at sport; feeling powerless; worries about sexual performance; and being followed or attacked. These were ordinary worries from young people who did not seem, by their answers to some key questions, to be utterly overwhelmed, nor depressed. But ordinary problems can prey on the mind if there is no easy outlet.

A great deal of what children and young people want is straightforward and costs only time and attention. They need to feel that they have someone to turn to who will take their concerns seriously. By 7–8 years of age many children understand, and may say clearly to a parent or teacher, that there is no easy answer to what is troubling them. They want what adults also appreciate: that someone listens to what they want to say, makes a real effort to understand what troubles them and avoids jumping to conclusions, interpretations and quick-and-easy solutions.

Children and young people often complain that adults, teachers or parents, do not listen or tend to belittle their problems. A positive experience of support and empathy on the current problem is likely to help children and young people with confidence and ideas about how to resolve problems in the future. Children and young people may support one another as friends and some peer support and anti-bullying schemes in schools have shown how children and young people can be effective counsellor/advocate figures (see page 165).

Worries that threaten well-being

Most young people feel low at some time but a minority do not emerge even with consistent and friendly support. Their harmful psychological state, perhaps persistent depression, deepens and may lead them into very risky behaviour, such as use of alcohol or drugs to medicate the problem, or a pattern of self-harm or attempts at suicide.

Admittedly, it can be tough sometimes to distinguish normal range non-communicative, cranky adolescent behaviour from signs of a serious level of distress and disturbance. The flipside is also true: practitioners who are responsible for vulnerable children and young people, for instance looked-after children, need to recall the normal 'job description' for being an adolescent. Young people, whose experience has not put them at heightened risk, can be confrontational with loved parents and will test the boundaries by failing to return by the agreed deadline for an evening out.

- Many adolescents at some time dramatically retreat to their bedroom, slamming the door while shouting, 'Everyone hates me and you are all so unfair!' However, it is a different level of worry if they scarcely emerge from their room and have apparently lost any interest in leisure or social activities that they used to enjoy, with friends or key adults.
- Part of the 'job description' for caring adults – parents and anyone else in a parenting role, such as residential and foster carers – is to wake up slumbering young people, to get them off to school or other commitments. But, it is not usual for adolescents to have persistently disturbed sleep patterns, continued difficulty in sleeping or refusal to leave their bed.
- Caring adults are responsible for ensuring that young people learn, and use, the skills needed to take care of their personal hygiene: body and changing their clothes. This adult responsibility can take serious time and effort in mid-adolescence. It should worry adults if they are responsible for individual young people who have lost all interest in their appearance and seem to want to remain grubby and smelly.
- Children and young people have emotional ups and downs, and a lengthy down may be linked with persistent struggles in a significant part of daily life, like school. Adults should be alert when a state of

307

depression does not lift over time, but continues with an all-pervading sadness, despite all the efforts of caring adults.

- All children and adolescents worry sometimes, but it is cause for concern when anxieties or fears have noticeably changed a child's or young person's social life. Feelings of hopelessness and helplessness that persist should not be ignored. It is not within the normal range of behaviour for children or adolescents to say, especially more than once, that they wish they were dead or that life is not worth living.

The response of self-harm

Young people can appear very dramatic on occasion, but it is not simply drama if they threaten to hurt themselves. Some young people turn to self-harm in response to persistent distress and many go to some lengths to keep their behaviour secret from family and friends. Given these circumstances, it makes no sense that, when a pattern of self-harm becomes known, young people find themselves accused of attention-seeking behaviour by professionals in health, education or social care. The secrecy also makes it difficult to reach accurate statements about the prevalence of this problem.

A Mental Health Foundation report (2006) suggests that about one in 15 young people in the country have harmed themselves, which would indicate there would be around two young people in any given secondary school class. There is no 'typical' profile of someone who self-harms. Studies (see www.selfharm.org.uk) that invite the views of young people show that a wide range of pressures can lead individuals to cope through self-harm: bullying or abuse, family problems, stress over studies, unresolved issues over sexual orientation, bereavement, in fact any source of emotional disruption.

Self-harm mainly seems to happen within the 11–25 year-old-age range. Some young people who self-harm continue well into adult life. It seems that more females than males take the personal self-harm route, but it is possible that desperate young males engage in deliberately high-risk behaviour, for instance, while in control of a vehicle. The circumstances lead to injuries, in some cases deaths, that are classified as accidental. Some children as young as 7–8 years old show a recognisable pattern. Anecdotal reports from practitioners who work with 8–12 year olds suggest that children from this age group are increasingly turning to forms of self-harm. It is possible that deliberate self-hurting by younger children is misinterpreted by adults as accidental injury.

Self-harm seems to be a coping mechanism for young people who feel overwhelmed by their troubles and unable to envisage or find effective support. Self-harm, which can be cutting limbs but includes other forms of deliberate self-injury, provides temporary relief: an outlet for powerful feelings of anger, hurt or pain. The actions are also within the young person's direct control. The reasoning underpinning feeling and actions is that self-inflicted pain is preferable to pain imposed by events outside the young person's immediate control.

Effective help for adolescents is complicated by the self-perpetuating nature of self-harm. An addictive cycle can be established, which continues unless the underlying pain is addressed and an individual commits to alternative ways of dealing with the emotional turmoil. Offering help to young people who self-harm is usually a long-term and complex process, only possible when they start to face the distress that started the self-harming cycle. Young people need support to find a behaviour that they can deliberately follow as an active alternative to self-harm. Some individuals respond well to writing down their thoughts or substituting vigorous physical exercise. However, some young people say they need to experience some pain, at least as an interim step, but flicking an elastic band at their hand or leg enables them to resist cutting.

Reliable support groups and online self-help websites can be valuable but adults need to be wary about the risks from open searching on the internet (see page 297). Face-to-face and online 'help' for self-harm, can be support to continue in this pattern, with reasons why the rest of the population does not understand the validity of your obsession. There are parallels with dangerous 'support' for young people with eating disorders (see page 256).

Suicide

Killing oneself is a very final statement of self-harm and there is serious concern about the well-being of a proportion of young people who feel so hopeless about their situation that they take their own life. Brigid McConville (2001) reported an increasing number of calls to ChildLine from children and young people with suicidal thoughts or who have taken some action with pills. There was a 14 per cent increase from 2003–4 in young callers with suicidal thoughts and plans, and then another 14 per cent increase over 2004–5. ChildLine knows that all callers cannot get through, they do not have enough lines and people. They estimate in general that 4,000 young callers try to talk to one of their counsellors each day and only 2,300 can get through. The ChildLine report highlights diversity in the experiences that callers describe. Some were suicidal because of a single, utterly distressing event; other young callers felt weighed down by complex problems and a sequence of painful losses.

Brigid McConville describes how secure children and young people have sources of support that keep them going through hard times. The years of childhood and adolescence are bound to include some disruption and much depends on the support available from family and friends. Young callers to ChildLine who contemplated suicide, or had already made at least one attempt, had steadily lost sources of possible help: their family was unsafe or unsupportive, school was a source of misery and their friendship network was very thin. Some callers appeared very dependent on one source of self-esteem in their life, such as success at school, or knew that this source was the most valued by their parents. A threat to this source of well-being could create a high level of anxiety, with no emotional safety net.

It is important that practitioners and parents do not over-react; most young people do not attempt suicide. However, it is crucial to take any threats seriously when young people's conversation or actions imply that life is no longer worth living.

- It seems that attempts at suicide are rarely impulsive actions, appearing with no warning at all. Distressed young people have sometimes already tried to deal with their problems by routes that have actually made matters worse: using drugs, alcohol or sexually risky behaviour. A history of problems, classified by adults as antisocial behaviour, sometimes predates adolescent suicide.

- On the other hand, some young people are very high achievers and face desperation, either because they can no longer meet exacting standards, or because they dread the prospect of never being able to coast; to stop striving. Of course, ambition and being a perfectionist is not inevitably linked with suicide. The additional risk factor seems to be when the outlook has isolated young people from a social network.

- It seems that many adolescent attempts at suicide are carefully considered. So adults need to take notice of young people who talk in a specific way about dying or who give away many of their important possessions, rather like a living will.

- Young people are at a higher risk when they have made previous suicide attempts and when a close friend or family member has killed themselves. It is crucial that young people are encouraged and enabled to talk in confidence if they have experienced a suicide within their family or close friendship network.

- Young people may be serious about their sense of despair but sometimes struggle with a true sense of the finality of death. Some adolescents appear to want more of a 'disappearance' or to punish family or others: a message of 'they'll be sorry when I'm dead'. Such emotions can be heightened by adolescent preoccupation with music, art or writing that focuses on death, possibly glamourising self-harm as well as suicide. This pattern has existed in previous younger generations.

There are sex differences in the pattern of suicide. Young men are consistently more at risk of dying from suicide than young women and one reason seems to be that they struggle more to ask for or to find help (see page 70). So even their family or close friends do not necessarily realise the level of their desperation. The other reason seems to be that young men who attempt suicide are more likely to choose 'no-way back' methods such as shooting, hanging themselves or jumping off a building. Some commentators suggest that a macho culture encourages young men even to be concerned about making a 'success' of killing themselves. Young women are more likely to use drug overdoses, a method that leaves a window for being discovered and brought back from near death.

Some sub-groups have a disproportionately high risk of suicide, for example, young people in prison or a young offenders' institution. The proportion of young men in prison outnumbers young women. It is also possible that suicidal young men are labelled as aggressive, rather than depressed, because their distress sometimes emerges through anti-social patterns of behaviour. Health care professionals estimate that many are coping with undiagnosed depression and there seems a real possibility that deep sadness emerges as anger for some young males (see page 70). Statistics are far from certain, but suicidal young women seem more likely to behave in ways that make other people think they could be very distressed and/or depressed. In a nutshell, desperate young women tend to look like they could hurt themselves, whereas young men look more like they could hurt somebody else.

THE RISKS FROM SOCIAL EXCLUSION

Childhood and adolescence will not pass without incident. A proportion of children will be very distressed by serious disruption in their lives and hurt imposed by other people. Part of safe growing up is for children and young people to be confident that they have back-up, from familiar adults who care about them, and increasingly from their siblings and close friends. Some children and young people, for various reasons, do not have that back-up, and may additionally face circumstances that make them more vulnerable than their peers. These children and adolescents are at risk of being socially excluded from the opportunities they have a right to expect as young citizens. Social exclusion brings financial costs to any society. The focus of this section, however, is much more on the price that children and young people pay for a situation that is not of their making.

Young people need to be able to take care of themselves

WHAT DOES IT MEAN?

- **Social exclusion**: the circumstances that combine to exclude children, young people and their families from services and the opportunities that should result from being a citizen of the UK.
- **Social inclusion**: practice that aims to address and change circumstances that operate to exclude individual children and young people and their families.

Family life under stress

Children and young people are put at greater risk by continuing family problems, especially in neighbourhoods that are characterised by poverty and limited prospects. There has been increasing enthusiasm from government and support services for parenting programmes and classes. Unfortunately, such initiatives have often been officially pitched as part of action against alleged antisocial behaviour from the younger generation. Newspaper and television media have often heightened this image with headlines about 'bad' parents and being 'made' to attend such classes.

It is hard to evaluate the impact of parenting programmes because, as Helen Barrett (2003) shows in her comprehensive review, there is such variety in the content, timing and approach of such programmes. Stephen Scott et al. (2006) looked at the impact of the Primary Age Learning Study (PALS), which blends support for parents to help their children with reading alongside practical advice about dealing with children's behaviour. The team report a high level of interest from parents across a range of ethnic groups who all lived in an area classified as disadvantaged. Parents continued to attend, not necessarily all the sessions, but made the effort despite having stressful lives. Many seemed to be especially attracted by the prospect of advice about helping their child with reading.

Some families in seriously disadvantaged neighbourhoods put huge effort into keeping their children safely on track for adulthood (see page 291). However, many do not manage this task and studies of areas of high poverty show that early experiences of disadvantage for children often continued in a debilitating cycle. Colin Webster et al. (2004) followed up a sample of mainly white working-class young people in Teesside. The impoverished position of many young people – limited educational and then employment prospects – made even modest ambitions hard to achieve. The attraction of a criminal route, often linked with drug dependence, had become a vicious circle for some young people. However, some had managed to use services to break their drug habit and, so long as they had also cut off contact with that social network, their prospects were more positive than the team had anticipated.

Some neighbourhoods are hostile for local families who strive to raise their children in safety. There have always been some communities in which criminal activity appeared to be a more attractive prospect than paid employment. Young people, especially young men, who attempt to keep on the right side of the law, can find themselves marginalised and directly threatened. Gavin Hales and his colleagues (2006) have studied the way in which weapons, including guns, have become a part of daily life in some city neighbourhoods. A successful local drug culture entices older children and adolescents with the prospect of easy money, and violence is linked with being shown unconditional respect.

Children who raise themselves

A proportion of children and young people are especially vulnerable because they lack a secure family background and an experience of being parented. There are many ways to organise and run a safe family for children and adolescents, but a non-negotiable aspect is that adults are available and take a responsible grown-up role. Children and young people who hit the headlines for genuinely cruel and violent behaviour are scary. What is mostly overlooked by anyone, other than highly involved youth workers or therapists, is that the children and young people themselves are frequently also very scared. They are frightened of other people who may be stronger then them and scared of the power of their own out-of-control emotions.

- These children and young people have not been guided by adults to consider other people, nor to believe that they cannot always have what they want right now. They have learned neither the skills nor good reasons to regulate their own emotions.

- They often have a very limited emotional toolbox and anger is at the forefront. This emotion is brought to bear over what appear to outsiders to be unimportant disagreements. Indeed, less stressed adolescents might be able to walk away from such minor conflicts, but for these individuals everything is important: winning is crucial and respect is gained by never losing.

- They are called 'feral' or 'street children' and this description, shorn of the punitive underpinning that accompanies the words, is an accurate description of their plight. Such children and adolescents have often effectively raised themselves and sometimes also their younger siblings.

- For whatever reason, their parents have not managed to be the adults in their children's life and sometimes very young girls and boys have had to depend on their own resources. They find support and protection from their peers, often through gang membership.

- Children and adolescents in this situation are not necessarily well served by all the professionals and services designed to safeguard them. However, if they enter the looked-after system, many practitioners in foster and residential care work unbelievably hard to build the missing foundations for emotionally healthy adulthood.

Camila Batmanghelidjh (2006) offers a moving description of the total desperation behind the highly disruptive, and sometimes self-harming, behaviour of children and young people who spend time at her Kids Company in south London. She is honest about behaviour that is highly challenging to adults and about the fact that such children can induce fear and anger in the very adults who wish to help. Her descriptions have much in common with accounts of the exhausting work of residential and foster carers who are committed to turning around the lives of children who are old before their time. Some children and adolescents have been comprehensively let down by their families – neglected and/or directly abused – and failed by social and medical services. Some have never really had a family life as such and took to the streets from a young age, as the only option they could find to escape from dangers within the home.

Shaun Bailey (2005) writes from his perspective as a youth worker in north London. Bailey shows a passionate commitment to standing up for young people. Yet his account is strongly underpinned by values: that parents have a primary responsibility to provide a safe family life, to spend plenty of time with their children, and to provide a positive role model. Shaun Bailey's stance is that women and mothers cannot be expected to do everything; that men and fathers should be closely involved. His argument is that boys and young male adolescents desperately need good examples from adult males, led by their own fathers, otherwise boys will be impressed, especially in high-risk neighbourhoods, by the fast track of criminal activity and a violent working definition of what counts for respect. He is equally outspoken about the need to challenge attitudes that treat women as disposable possessions and for young women themselves to realise that sex does not mean affection, let alone love and respect.

Camila Batmanghelidjh and Shaun Bailey do not excuse the behaviour of children or young people whose lives are seriously unsafe, whose experiences have made them 'feral', but their approach is a challenge to a simplistic approach of blame. They also make the practical point that punitive responses and threats are ineffective against children and young people whose lives have been dominated by violence and ill-treatment. Neither of these practitioners argues for lifting all the consequences of wrong doing. Both of them make a strong case that punitive strategies do not turn around very disaffected and damaged children and adolescents. See the discussion about ASBOs on page 13.

In discussing what does work – and what requires immense effort from adults – Camila Batmanghelidjh focuses on a therapeutic approach and Shaun Bailey on community-based youth work. They describe the complex patterns that give rise to highly challenging behaviour from children and young people whose childhood has been nothing less than traumatic. What they see in their work is very similar to the patterns shown by some, not all, looked-after children and young people, who are now the responsibility of the local authority.

- Children and young adolescents, who feel they are powerless in their own lives, find ways to exercise power by hurting peers or adults, with words, physical threat and attack. They are often deeply troubled and no longer care about their own well-being, safety or survival. This outlook makes them genuinely dangerous to other people, because they have a limited sense of self-preservation: they do not think they are worthy of care.

- Years of having to protect themselves and being realistically scared of danger, mean that children and young people can be hyper-vigilant. In contrast with peers who have experienced safe childhoods, these young people are swift to anger and slower to calm. They have very limited ability to empathise with other people, because they have received so little understanding themselves. Look back at the discussion about cortisol and brain development on page 64.

■ These children and young people desperately need parenting but this kind of input has to develop alongside what Camila Batmanghelidjh calls a therapeutic task of 'de-shaming'. This term describes the way in which neglected children can feel responsible for what they did in order to survive and sometimes to care for siblings, like theft and prostitution.

■ When they have been shamed by their experiences, children can find it hard to accept help and may alienate adults who struggle with the child's coldness or apparent lack of appreciation for help. Older children get to the point of being unable to accept affection and genuine care; they do not believe they are likable. They cannot believe emotional warmth from adults is real or will last.

■ Looked-after children are also often consumed with distress that their own parent(s) will not give them the affection that is being offered by a foster carer or other committed non-family adult. They often reject the care, again and again, and unless the carer's stamina, and own support systems, last longer than the continual rejection, the child or adolescent is further confirmed in their own feelings that they are unloved and unlovable.

■ They need the boundaries created by an adult who acts as a parent, but the children's experience means they struggle to tolerate any limits or ground rules. Responsible youth workers, foster or residential care workers need immense emotional strength to hold on to what will work in the end.

■ Camila Batmanghelidjh describes, what I have also heard in different words from foster and residential carers, that emotionally damaged children and adolescents often have disturbances in body boundaries. They may hold themselves rigidly apart or be excessively attention-seeking, often invading people's personal space in ways uncomfortable to the adult or peer. Physical contact, including sometimes keeping children safe through appropriate means of restraint, has to be established along with ground rules about bodily respect that children have not experienced so far.

Children who run away from home

Young people under the age of 16 cannot legally live on an independent basis in the UK: they have to be the direct responsibility of an adult. Some children and young people escape an unhappy or abusive home life by leaving. The Children's Society estimates that every year about 100,000 under-16s run away from their family home or substitute care. Young people of 16 and 17 years old can also be at risk if they run away, and they are still within the child protection system for most of the UK (Scotland counts 17 year olds as adults). Children and young people are usually counted as runaways when they have left home without agreement and have stayed away for a time that is significant for their age and abilities. It is important always to take running away seriously, but the patterns are very varied:

- Runaways are not the same as homeless young people. Some runaways become homeless and some homeless young people started as runaways.

- Children and adolescents sometimes run away over minor disagreements, which nevertheless need resolving. However, some adolescents have run from serious troubles and have been effectively forced out of their home by the rejecting behaviour of parents or their partners.

- Looked-after children and young people are significantly over-represented in the statistics on runaways and the greater majority run from residential units rather than foster care. Older children and young people run for many different reasons and the looked-after children may have run before they entered the care system.

- Some have a personal history of running as a way to deal with troubles at home, some run back to family, friends and where they recall being happier, and some run to the 'bright lights' of a city. There is not a close relationship between level of risk and how far children or young people run. They could be in the immediate neighbourhood but have gone to the home of a known abuser. Children who run further away may be safe with friends or acquaintances.

- Most runaways do not appear to go far and many return to their family or care home of their own accord. At this point it is crucial that adults deal with the issues around why the children or young people ran, and do not focus on punishment for unacceptable behaviour.

- In foster or residential care it is crucial that running away is always noticed and never allowed to become 'just an occupational hazard'. It is appropriate to treat leaving and staying away without permission as a potential child protection issue. But also children and young people need to know that they are swiftly missed and familiar adults are genuinely worried for their well-being.

Running away can put children and young people at serious risk as the result of where and with whom they stay, either on the streets or to get

317

off the street. Some children and young people slide into being sexually exploited as a way to eat and get a roof over their head. Of course, some children and young people are trapped in a sexually abusive relationship within their own home. Indeed, some children are running away from abuse or neglect from people they know. Sara Scott and Paula Skidmore (2006) describe the supportive work undertaken by Barnardo's and the variety in the pattern of exploitation.

- A consistent factor in the lives of most exploited children and young people is the lack of reliable and consistent support from adults – either in their own family or from continued instability within the care system.

- Sexual exploitation of children and young adolescents can develop from abusive relationships in which adults or older adolescents take advantage of the emotional neediness and trust of a younger person.

- Some exploitation moves into abuse through prostitution when the younger or more vulnerable person is coerced into selling themselves for money, drugs or material possessions.

- Some young women reach this route through what appears initially to be a couple relationship with an older man. The 'boyfriend' grooms the young woman towards earning for him through prostitution, often by presenting the acts as necessary to help him with financial or other serious difficulties.

- Young people are at much greater risk when they mix with a social network in which this pattern of activity is seen as normal.

You can find out more information about this complex area by accessing reports and briefing papers on the websites of national charities such as www.barnardos.org.uk and www.nspcc.org.uk.

Young people in closed institutions

There is great concern about children and young people who can become effectively invisible despite living in institutions that have a formal responsibility for their well-being. Especially vulnerable groups include children and young people living within a closed community, including different forms of secure accommodation. Children and young people with asylum seeker status can end up in detention centres when they have done no wrong as individuals; it is their right to be in the UK that has been challenged.

Even when adolescents have committed a crime, they have the right to a duty of care from professionals and to be treated appropriately for their age. Young people do not lose their inclusion within child protection/safeguarding legislation because they are currently in a young offenders' institution. Children over the age of criminal responsibility are detained because they have committed a crime, but these are not always highly serious or violent crimes. Lord Carlile QC reported in 2006 from an inquiry he led for the Howard League for Penal Reform (available on www.howardleague.org) and made a series of significant recommendations. Risks arise because young offenders are not necessarily treated in age-appropriate ways within the criminal justice system and are subject to unacceptable levels of physical restraint, solitary confinement and forcible strip searching. Significant levels of self-harm and suicide show the desperation of young people behind bars.

A greater awareness of the risks led the Youth Justice Board for England and Wales to develop a new strategy for what is called the 'secure estate': young offenders' institutions, privately run secure training centres and local authority secure accommodation. Children and young people in secure settings have not all committed any crime but they are judged to be a serious danger to themselves and/or other people. Looked-after children and young people are over-represented in the numbers of young offenders, as well as in the adult prison population. Di Hart (2006) describes how already very vulnerable young people can fall between professional boundaries. Many lose contact with their social worker because the criminal justice system is judged to have taken over, but the duty of care is not effectively passed back when young people are released.

There has also been serious concern about the welfare of under-18s in the armed services. A feature in *Children Now* (April 2006) reported that about a third of new recruits are 16 and 17 year olds and that, after the college stage of training, they are regarded as fully adult by the army. Nicholas Blake QC reported on an enquiry into the deaths of four young men at Deepcut army barracks in Surrey (www.deepcutreview.org.uk). He described a culture of intimidation in the past and a failure in the duty of care towards young people. A high proportion of recruits are young people leaving the care system or those who have limited family back-up. They are in need of even greater attention to their welfare, but the exact legal responsibility of the services has been uncertain.

SERIOUS THREATS TO HEALTH AND WELL-BEING

Most adolescents engage in a certain amount of risky behaviour; it is a time of life when young people of both sexes push out the boundaries. However, some patterns of behaviour, especially those that normalise high use of alcohol, nicotine or illegal drugs, can seriously raise the bar on risks to well-being.

Drugs and alcohol in the family

Concerned public discussion about children, adolescents, alcohol and
drugs usually focuses on their own use of potentially dangerous
substances. However, a forgotten number of children cope with family life
that is disrupted, even broken, because of their parents' alcohol
consumption or use of illegal drugs.

A limited number of specialist services across the UK focus on the
impact of problem drinking by parents on family life. A noticeable
proportion – some sources estimate up to about 25 per cent – of children
on local child protection registers have reached that position because their
parents' use of drugs and/or alcohol has put children at significant risk.
Local services often need to be more effective in working together. For
instance, professionals involved with addicted adults should always be
alert to whether individuals, who can scarcely take care of themselves, are
responsible for the well-being of children or young adolescents. The same
principle of practice applies to adult mental health services.

The level of the problem is hard to know with any accuracy. It is
estimated that about one million children and adolescents live with parents
whose use of alcohol directly creates problems in family life. Numbers of
children affected by drug addiction are based on self-reporting by parents
and data from those who have sought help. The figures of 2–3 per cent of
under-16s in England and Wales and 4–6 per cent in Scotland are
therefore likely to be under-estimates of the extent of the problem for
children and young people. Adults who are addicted to alcohol or drugs
cannot be effective parents all the time, although some make significant
efforts. Children are likely to be neglected and may also experience
physical or emotional ill treatment. An unknown number of grandparents
have taken on primary responsibility for their grandchildren, because the
parents are unable to cope as the result of their addictions.

The impact on children and adolescents

Studies that focus on the children's perspective most usually show that
they are more aware of the problems, and at a much younger age, than
their parents, or involved professionals, are willing to believe. Sarah Gorin
(2004) reviewed the research available on family life when children and
adolescents lived with domestic violence, substance abuse by their parents
and other serious parental health problems.

- Children had sometimes become aware of their parent's problem with
  alcohol as young as 3–4 years of age. But 9–10 years old was the
  average age given by children (in research interviews) at which they
  had realised that the family problem was alcoholism. They were aware

prior to that age that their parent was variable in their behaviour, but had not understood the reason and/or assumed their own experience was normal family life.

- Some parents were trying very hard to deal with their drug addiction, or to keep quarrels with their partner away from the children. Most parents interviewed believed they were more successful in keeping these secrets from their children than was actually the case.

- Children were often observant and knowledgeable about their parent's addictive behaviour. They were often very worried but did not know how to seek help, even if any was available. Additionally, children and adolescents were often scared that telling teachers or other professionals would cause the break up of their family life, rather than bring effective help.

- Older children and adolescents often reported that they found support from their close friends. Talking with their peers was sometimes preferable because the conversation remained within their control. There is, however, the practical consequence that children and young people are sometimes then very worried about the well-being of their friend. They may be torn between that anxiety and their promise to keep a confidence.

- Communication could also be more straightforward with peers. Professionals sometimes used words and phrases (like 'domestic violence' or 'substance abuse') that meant nothing to a child or adolescent. There was also the feeling that professionals did not respect the detailed knowledge of children who had no choice but to live with the problems day by day.

Many of the children and adolescents interviewed in a range of studies have become young carers: taking on the role of parent for their siblings and for their own parent. Many of them expressed strong affection for their parents and on the one hand did not resent having to support family life to such a high degree. On the other hand, they wanted help that would lift the burden, help their parents with the addiction and show respect for their own caring role.

Another aspect for drug use within the family is the extent to which children are affected when older siblings have a drug problem. Marina Barnard (2005) describes the serious risks to children from the behaviour of an addicted brother or sister. Parents who struggle to deal with the drug problem of one child, initially without outside help, are less available to other children. Family life is disrupted by the continuing anxiety and by actions of young addicts such as stealing from family members. The presence of drugs increases the risk that siblings may try them and some young people deliberately introduced their siblings to drugs.

Substance abuse by children and adolescents

Advice and information about these areas is often presented separately, but risky patterns of behaviour by young people often combine different kinds of substance abuse, along with lowering of inhibitions that can lead to other dangers. For example, seriously drunk young people are more likely to endanger themselves and others through traffic accidents: while driving a vehicle but also by wandering as a pedestrian into the path of a car or bus. Young people sometimes overlook that cannabis affects their judgement and coordination and so creates risks similar to driving while under the influence of alcohol.

Jeanie Lynch and Simon Blake (2004) point out that alcohol and/or use of drugs and risky sexual behaviour are not necessarily separate risk issues in the lives of young people. They describe the dangers of a social life, and friendship network, that regards being completely drunk as an essential part of a good night out and normalises not being able to remember the events of an evening. Lester Coleman and Suzanne Cater (2005) report a similar awareness from 14–17 year olds of the genuine risks that follow from risky drinking.

- A generous amount of alcohol, whether combined with illegal drugs or not, has the effect of lowering inhibitions and greatly increases risk-taking behaviour, including unprotected sex. Social norms within a group of adolescents (just like adults) can support using drunkenness as an excuse for unacceptable behaviour.

- Adolescents, young men as well as young women, describe using drink to boost their confidence in social situations. But young people of both sexes sometimes express regret about first sexual experiences that happened as a result of and under the influence of alcohol or drugs.

- Some young people describe using alcohol as a means to escape personal problems and distress. They were aware that the relief was short term but felt they had few other alternatives. Limited options also emerged as an issue for adolescents who had few social activities on offer that did not revolve around alcohol.

- Alcohol in small amounts can have the pleasant effect of lowering inhibitions and relaxing young people. However, alcohol consumed in large quantities affects coordination, judgement and mood; consuming more than six units within six hours is classified as 'binge drinking'. Short-term effects of a hangover are unpleasant, but young people who drink heavily are at risk of non-reversible damage to vital organs like their liver. Males and females metabolise alcohol in slightly different ways and the negative health consequences tend to affect females more swiftly than males.

Reports and briefing papers from the Drug Education Forum (www.drugeducationforum.com) describe the risk factors that make it more likely that young people will try illegal drugs, including a chaotic home life, failure at school and a friendship network that supports all kinds of deviant behaviour. However, support and information for children and young people has increasingly recognised that it is not helpful to approach education (school or through youth work) about illegal drugs as separate from dealing with the legal drugs of nicotine and alcohol.

MAKE THE CONNECTION WITH . . . EVIDENCE-BASED POLICY?

It is appropriate to be concerned about the impact of drugs – legal and illegal – on the health and prospects of young people. However, policy-makers have to consider the full consequences of any initiative that claims to address the problem.

Random drug-testing of pupils in school is relatively common in the United States. In 2004 the Prime Minister, Tony Blair, and the Leader of the Opposition, Michael Howard, both expressed public support for a similar programme in the UK. However, Neil McKeganey (2005) reviewed available studies and concluded that there is limited evidence that such an approach is effective in reducing illegal drug use among adolescents. There are also significant issues around ethics, civil liberties and confidentiality over test results. There is also a significant imbalance when, as is usually the case, it is only young people who are asked to submit to random testing and not the whole school community, including the adults.

Information and dealing with social pressure

Reviews of the different approaches to smoking and young people, like that of Faiza Baksh (2006), show that knowledge of health risks is not enough to stop young people smoking when the social pressures are strong. The more effective programmes with young people, for any of the risks described in this section, cover reliable information about dangers, but they are also part of initiatives to support older children and young people with decision-making, resisting peer pressure and with boosting a sense of self-worth.

The first half of adolescence can be a high-risk time for starting smoking cigarettes and younger adolescents can often access alcohol and drugs.

Over this period, young people are especially vulnerable to what their peers think of them. Young males and females want to feel they belong, so they are very sensitive to messages that their choices make them stand out as odd. When social pressures are strongly towards smoking, drinking or trying drugs, a bald message from adults of 'just say "no"' is close to useless.

- Older children and young people often say that they welcome information, so long as it is not delivered with adult finger-wagging. The problems as they see them are not all about illegal drugs. They genuinely want to know about the effects of alcohol, how to tell when you are being badly affected and what to do then.

- This younger generation is likely to encounter illegal drugs in ordinary social situations. Advice has to cover strategies for opting out of something that may be regarded as normal by acquaintances, if not friends. Cost is often not a hurdle; the street price of many drugs has fallen dramatically in some parts of the UK.

- Information about health consequences is important and many adolescents feel immortal. They take a blasé approach to what they regard as health problems for 'old people' and are ignorant about the chances of serious illness, even death, from alcohol poisoning in early adulthood.

- Some young people feel sure they will have changed their behaviour by that distant future. Young adults may be confident that they will have stopped smoking cigarettes, yet have no real idea how difficult it is to stop, once a serious, addictive habit is established. Young people are also sometimes unaware that long-term use of cannabis shares many health risks of smoking nicotine, including higher risk for several types of cancer.

- Advice about a balanced diet for adolescents really needs to include that generous amounts of alcohol will block the body's absorption of some vitamins – now, not in the distant future. Additionally, alcohol significantly reduces the body's ability to metabolise fats from what is eaten. Young heavy drinkers (or any age) deliver a double problem to their system through the alcohol and through the snacks or fast food that often accompany this pattern.

Taking care

The use of ecstasy (or E) developed from the 1980s and young people are very likely to encounter the drug in clubs or as part of other social activities. Practical drug education usually recognises that at least some adolescents are going to try this drug, whatever they are told and so advice aims to tell them how to keep safe. The chemical in ecstasy acts on serotonin, which occurs naturally within the human brain and helps to

> ### MAKE THE CONNECTION WITH . . .
> ### WHAT CONCERNS YOUNG PEOPLE
>
> Some young women seem to be attracted to smoking nicotine on the grounds that it will depress their appetite. The risks of respiratory problems, emphysema and a higher risk of lung and other cancers seem to be so far ahead as to not matter. Dr Thomas Stuttaford (writing in *The Times*, 28 September 2006) pointed out that smoking also weakens the connective tissue in the face, breasts and buttocks. Young people might be more responsive to the dangers of smoking their way to serious wrinkles and droopiness well before old age.

regulate memory, sleep, libido and body temperature. Ecstasy does not exactly create the sense of happiness that users feel; it lets the feelings out. Since the drug lifts the barriers to emotions, users sometimes feel sadness.

Ecstasy interferes with pain regulation. So users often carry on with energetic dancing when, under normal circumstances, their body would make them slow down. Users can put themselves at risk from respiratory or heart failure, especially if their friends are not in a fit state to persuade them to stop. Immediate health risks are linked with the way that ecstasy disturbs the body rhythms, especially inducing a rise in temperature, so that users can dangerously overheat: hypothermia, the opposite to hyperthermia when the risk arises from extreme cold. The most practical counter-action is to take regular drinks of water. Young people need to know not to drink an excessive amount of water over a short period because it floods their body, disturbing the chemical balance in ways that can be life threatening.

Children and adolescents need to be fully informed about the short- and long-term health risks of all illegal drugs and inhalation of glue and other materials, called volatile substance abuse. However, any drug education has to acknowledge the pleasant effects, which explain partly why young people, or adults, continue in the pattern. Camila Batmanghelidjh (2006) has a practical section, along with street names for drugs applicable when she wrote her book. You can find more information from resources listed at the end of this chapter on page 326. Look at page 256 for use of steroids.

A final issue about drug and alcohol abuse arises from the health risk of timing. Adolescents have not yet completed all their brain development. During mid-adolescence there is another burst of brain development as human bodies try to bring together emotions, complex intellectual functions, information processing and judgement. Adolescence and very early adulthood are the worst times to experiment with substances that turn the mind upside down. There is increasing concern about drug use, including cannabis, triggering a mental health crisis in young people, with long-term damage to their well-being. It is possible that some young people were emotionally vulnerable and a non-drug experience could have triggered their crisis. However, the developmental vulnerability of young people creates that further risk factor.

If you want to find out more

❖ **Advisory Council on the Misuse of Drugs** (2003) *Hidden harm: responding to the needs of children of problem drug users.* See www.homeoffice.gov.uk.

❖ **Bailey, Shaun** (2005) *No man's land: how Britain's inner city youth are being failed.* London: Centre for Young Policy Studies. See www.cps.org.uk.

❖ **Baksh, Faiza** (2006) *Smoking and young people.* Highlight no. 224. London: National Children's Bureau.

❖ **Barnard, Marina** (2005) *Drugs in the family: the impact on parents and siblings.* York: Joseph Rowntree Foundation. Summary and report on www.jrf.org.uk/knowledge/findings/socialpolicy/0215.asp.

❖ **Barrett, Helen** (2003) *Parenting programmes for families at risk: a source book.* London: National Family and Parenting Institute.

❖ **Batmanghelidjh, Camila** (2006) *Shattered lives: children who live with courage and dignity.* London: Jessica Kingsley.

❖ **Blake, Simon** and **Navidi, Ute** (2005) *Dangerous highs: children and young people calling ChildLine about volatile substance abuse.* London: Childline and National Children's Bureau.

❖ **British Medical Association** (2006) *Child and adolescent mental health – a guide for healthcare professionals.* Summary at www.bma.org.uk.

❖ **Brooks, Robert** and **Goldstein, Sam** (2001) *Raising resilient children.* New York: McGraw Hill.

❖ **Brooks, Robert** and **Goldstein, Sam** (2003) *Nurturing resilience in our children.* New York: McGraw Hill.

✢ **Bywaters, Paul** and **Rolfe, Alison** (undated, published approx 2002) *Look beyond the scars: understanding and responding to self-injury and self-harm.* See www.nch.org.uk/information/index.php?i=136.

✢ **Clough, Roger** (2006) *What works in residential care?* Highlight no. 227, the first in a series of six about residential care. London: National Children's Bureau.

✢ **Clough, Roger; Bullock, Roger** and **Ward, Adrian** (2006) *What works in residential childcare: a review of research evidence and the practical considerations.* See www.ncb.org.uk/ncercc. Go in through 'Practice Documents'.

✢ **Coleman, Lester** and **Cater, Suzanne** (2005) *Underage 'risky' drinking: motivations and outcomes.* York: Joseph Rowntree Foundation. Summary and report on www.jrf.org.uk/knowledge/findings/socialpolicy/0045.asp.

✢ **Gorin, Sarah** (2004) *Understanding what children say about living with domestic violence, parental substance abuse or parental health problems.* London: National Children's Bureau. Summary at www.jrf.org.uk/Knowledge/findings/socialpolicy/514.asp.

✢ **Hart, Di** (2006) *Tell them not to forget about us: a guide to practice with looked-after children in custody.* London: National Children's Bureau.

✢ **Hales, Gavin; Lewis, Chris** and **Silverstone, Daniel** (2006) *Gun crime: the market in and use of illegal firearms.* Home Office Research Study No. 298. London: Home Office. Access summary as Findings 279; www.homeoffice.gov.uk/rds/pdfs06/r279.pdf.

✢ **Kay, Susan** (2000) *Volatile substance abuse.* Highlight no. 178. London: National Children's Bureau.

✢ **Katz, Adrienne** (1999) *Leading lads: 1400 lads reveal what they really think about life in Britain today.* East Molesey: Young Voice. See www.young-voice.org.

✢ **Lynch, Jeanie** and **Blake, Simon** (2004) *Sex, alcohol and other drugs: exploring the links in young people's lives.* London: National Children's Bureau.

✢ **McConville, Brigid** (2001) *Saving young lives: calls to ChildLine about suicide.* London: ChildLine.

❖   **McGinnis, Susan** and **Jenkins, Peter** (2006) *Good practice guidance for counselling in schools.* Rugby: British Association for Counselling and Psychotherapy. See www.bacp.co.uk.

❖   **McKeganey, Neil** (2005) *Random drug-testing of schoolchildren: A shot in the arm or a shot in the foot for drug prevention?* York: Joseph Rowntree Foundation. Summary and report on www.jrf.org.uk/knowledge/findings/socialpolicy/0095.asp.

❖   **McNamara, Sarah** (2005) *Helping young people to beat stress: a practical guide.* London: Continuum.

❖   **Mental Health Foundation** (1999) *Bright Futures: promoting children's and young people's mental health.* London: Mental Health Foundation.

❖   **Mental Health Foundation** (2002) *The mental health of looked-after children – bright futures: working with vulnerable young people.* Available for download from www.mentalhealth.org.uk.

❖   **Mental Health Foundation** and **Camelot Foundation** (2006) *The truth about self harm: for young people and their friends and families.* See www.mentalhealth.org.uk.

❖   **Morgan, Roger** (2006) *Running away: a children's views report.* See www.rights4me.org.uk. (Reports are under 'Be Heard' on the website.)

❖   **O'Kane, Claire** (2002) *Cannabis: its effects on children and young people.* Highlight no. 189. London: National Children's Bureau.

❖   **Scott, Sarah** and **Skidmore, Paula** (2006) *Reducing the risk: Barnardo's support for sexually exploited young people.* Summary and full report on www.barnardos.org.uk/. Search with the first three words of the title.

❖   **Scott, Stephen**; **O'Connor, Thomas** and **Futh, Annabel** (2006) *What makes parenting programmes work in disadvantaged areas? The PALS trial.* York: Joseph Rowntree Foundation. Summary and report on www.jrf.org.uk/knowledge/findings/socialpolicy/0386.asp.

❖   **Webster, Colin**; **Simpson, Donald**; **MacDonald, Robert**; **Abbas, Andreas**; **Cieslik, Mark**; **Shildrick, Tracy** and **Simpson, Mark** (2004) *Poor transitions: social exclusion and young adults.* Bristol: The Policy Press. Summary and full report on http://www.jrf.org.uk/knowledge/findings/socialpolicy/d54.asp

❖ **Young Minds** (2004) *Minority voices: don't fret, get on the net* – a resource listing online support groups. Other useful materials on www.youngminds.org.uk.

❖ **www.selfharm.org.uk** – a website with a range of useful resources and reports, suitable for practitioners and some directed at young people themselves.

Useful organisations and websites

All addresses for organisations are in the UK. Guidance for good practice on any of the sites is always of general interest, but you need to be alert for information that is linked more closely with the legal or educational framework for only part of the UK.

- *4 Nations Child Policy Network* www.childpolicy.org.uk. Online resource about law and politics that directs you to sites relevant to England, Wales, Scotland and Northern Ireland.

- *Child Accident Prevention Trust.* 4th Floor, Cloister Court, 22–26 Farringdon Lane, London, EC1R 3AT. Tel: 020 7608 3828. National charity committed to reducing accidental injury and death for children and young people.

- *ChildLine* www.ChildLine.org.uk. Support service for children and young people who wish to talk in confidence about any problem. The website has papers and summary reports.

- *Children in Wales (Plant yng Nghymru)* www.childreninwales.org.uk. 25 Windsor Place, Cardiff, CF1 3BZ. Tel: 02920 342434. Works with services involved with children and their families in Wales.

- *Children in Scotland (Clann An Alba)* www.childreninscotland.org.uk. Princes House, 5 Shandwick Place, Edinburgh, EH2 4RG. Tel: 0131 228 8484. Brings together professionals working with children and families in Scotland.

- *Children Now* www.childrennow.co.uk/news/index.cfm. Tel: 020 8606 7500. Weekly magazine, with news, updates and features relevant across all services. Online archive of previous issues.

- *Children's Play Council* www.ncb.org.uk/cpc. Wakley Street, London, EC1V 7QE. Tel: 020 7843 6094. An alliance of organisations to promote children's play.

- *Children's Legal Centre* www.childrenslegalcentre.com. University of Essex, Wivenhoe Park, Colchester, Essex, CO4 3SQ. Tel 01206 872466. Advice for information about the law in England and Wales.

- *Children's Play Information Service* www.ncb.org.uk/library/cpis. Wakley Street, London, EC1V 7QE. Tel: 020 7843 6303. Information about children's play, factsheets and issues of *Play Today*.

- *Citizens Advice Bureau* www.adviceguide.org.uk. Summaries of the legal position on many social issues, as the law works in different parts of the UK. This is the only website I have found that covers the law in general for Northern Ireland.

✛ *Commission for Social Care Inspection* www.rights4me.org.uk. CSCI has a legal responsibility for listening to the views of children and young people living away from home – reports under 'Be Heard' on the website.

✛ *Coram Family* www.coram.org.uk. 49 Mecklenburgh Square, London, WC1N 2QA. Tel: 020 7520 0330. Services and projects for children, adolescents and families under stress, see for instance their boys2MEN project.

✛ *Council for Disabled Children* www.ncb.org.uk/cdc. Wakley Street, London, EC1V 7QE. Tel: 020 7843 6082. National forum for policy and practice relating to disabled children, young people and their families.

✛ *Department for Education Lifelong Learning and Skills* http://new.wales.gov.uk. Cathays Park, Cardiff, CF10 3NQ. Tel: 0845 010 3300. Information about services including the school curriculum in Wales.

✛ *Department of Education Northern Ireland* www.deni.gov.uk. Rathgael House, Balloo Road, Bangor, BT19 7PR. Tel: 028 9127 9279. Information about the school curriculum in Northern Ireland.

✛ *Family and Parenting Institute* www.familyandparenting.org. 430 Highgate Studios, 53–79 Highgate Road, London, NW5 1TL. Tel: 020 7424 3460. Aims to make the views of families heard by policy-makers and commissions research.

✛ *Fathers Direct* www.fathersdirect.com. Herald House, Lamb's Passage, Bunhill Row, London, EC1Y 8TQ. Tel: 0845 634 1328. National information centre on fatherhood, with briefing papers and guides.

✛ *Freeplay Network* www.freeplaynetwork.org.uk. An online photo exhibition of images of play, briefing papers and links to other useful sites.

✛ *I CAN* www.ican.org.uk. 4 Dyer's Building, London, EC1N 2QP. Tel: 0845 225 4071. Aims to foster the development of communication for all children, with special focus on children with a communication disability.

✛ *Informal Education Homepage* www.infed.org.uk. A source of information, views and some articles as part of their *encyclopedia of informal education*. Some articles are a good start for discussion.

*A happy childhood? A fair request
from children and adolescents*

❖ *Joseph Rowntree Foundation* www.jrf.org.uk. The Homestead, 14
Water End, York, North Yorkshire, YO30 6WP. Tel: 01904 629241.
Involved in social policy research and development – studies and
research reviews that can be downloaded in full or summary on
www.jrf.org.uk/knowledge/findings.

❖ *Kids* National Development Division www.kids.org.uk. 6 Aztec Row,
Berners Road, London, N1 0PW. Tel: 020 7359 3073. Supports
disabled children and their families, also the Playwork Inclusion
Project (PIP) to promote and ensure inclusion in mainstream play
and leisure services.

❖ *Learning Through Landscapes* www.ltl.org.uk. 3rd Floor, Southside
Offices, The Law Courts, Winchester, SO 23 9DL. Tel: 01962
845811. Consultation and development work about school grounds,
information and examples on the website.

❖ *Learning and Teaching Scotland* www.ltscotland.org.uk. The Optima, 58 Robertson Street, Glasgow, G2 8DU. Tel: 08700 100 297. Information about the school curriculum in Scotland. Resources and advice for any professionals involved with children and young people.

❖ *Mental Health Foundation* www.mentalhealth.org.uk. 1100 Sea Containers House, 20 Upper Ground, London, SE1 9QB. Tel: 020 7803. Aims to help people recover from and prevent mental health problems. Reports and papers on the website.

❖ *National Centre for Excellence in Residential Childcare* www.ncb.org.uk/ncercc. 8 Wakley Street, London, EC1V 7QE. Tel: 020 7843 1168. A collaborative initiative to improve practice and outcomes for children and young people in residential care.

❖ *National Children's Bureau* www.ncb.org.uk. Wakley Street, London, EC1V 7QE. Tel: 020 7843 6000. Works in partnership to share knowledge, resources and services to improve the lives of children and young people in England and Northern Ireland. Go in through 'our structure' for the list of semi-independent organisations and networks under the same roof. The website was being redeveloped when this book went to press, so routes and availability of online resources may be changed.

❖ *National Educational Research Forum* www.nerf-uk.org/bulletin. Online bulletin *Evidence for Teaching and Learning*.

❖ *Save the Children* www.savethechildren.org.uk. 17 Grove Lane, London, SE5 8RD. Tel: 020 7703 5400. Supports a wide range of research projects and other units, such as on supporting children's rights.

❖ *Scottish Centre for Research in Education* www.scre.ac.uk. Information and summaries of research undertaken in Scotland. The Spotlight section has downloadable research papers.

❖ *Scottish Child Law Centre* www.sclc.org.uk. 54 East Crosscauseway, Edinburgh, EH8 9HD. Tel: 0131 667 6333. Freephone for under-18s: 0800 328 8970 Advice and information about the law in Scotland.

❖ *Standards Site* www.standards.dfes.gov.uk/research. Includes The Research Informed Practice Site (TRIPS), an online database to help access to academic research.

❖ *Teachernet* www.teachernet.gov.uk/research. Information about projects, guidance for practice in schools, direct links with TRIPS and other online research information. Information about the school curriculum in England.

❖ *The Psychologist* www.bps.org.uk/publications/thepsychologist/search-the-psychologist-online.cfm. Monthly journal from the British Psychological Society. Articles can be accessed online, except the most recent six issues.

❖ *Trust for the Study of Adolescence* www.tsa.uk.com. 23 New Road, Brighton, East Sussex, BN1 1WZ. Tel: 01273 693311. Aims to address lack of knowledge and understanding about adolescents and young people through research, publications and training.

❖ www.scotland.gov.uk. Information about services in Scotland. Reports and research reviews can be downloaded.

❖ *Young Minds* www.youngminds.org.uk. 48–50 St John Street, London, EC1M 4DG. Tel: 0800 018 2138. Committed to improving the mental health of children and young people. Downloads available on the website and a helpline for anyone concerned about a child or young person.

❖ *Young People Now* www.ypnmagazine.com.home.index.cfm. Tel: 020 8606 7500. Weekly magazine with news and articles for professionals involved with young people across the range of services. Online archive of previous issues.

❖ *Young Voice* www.young-voice.org. 25a Creek Road, East Molesey, Surrey, KT8 9HE. Tel: 020 8979 4991. Aims to make the views of young people count by inviting and publishing their views on important issues.

INDEX

INDEX

INDEX